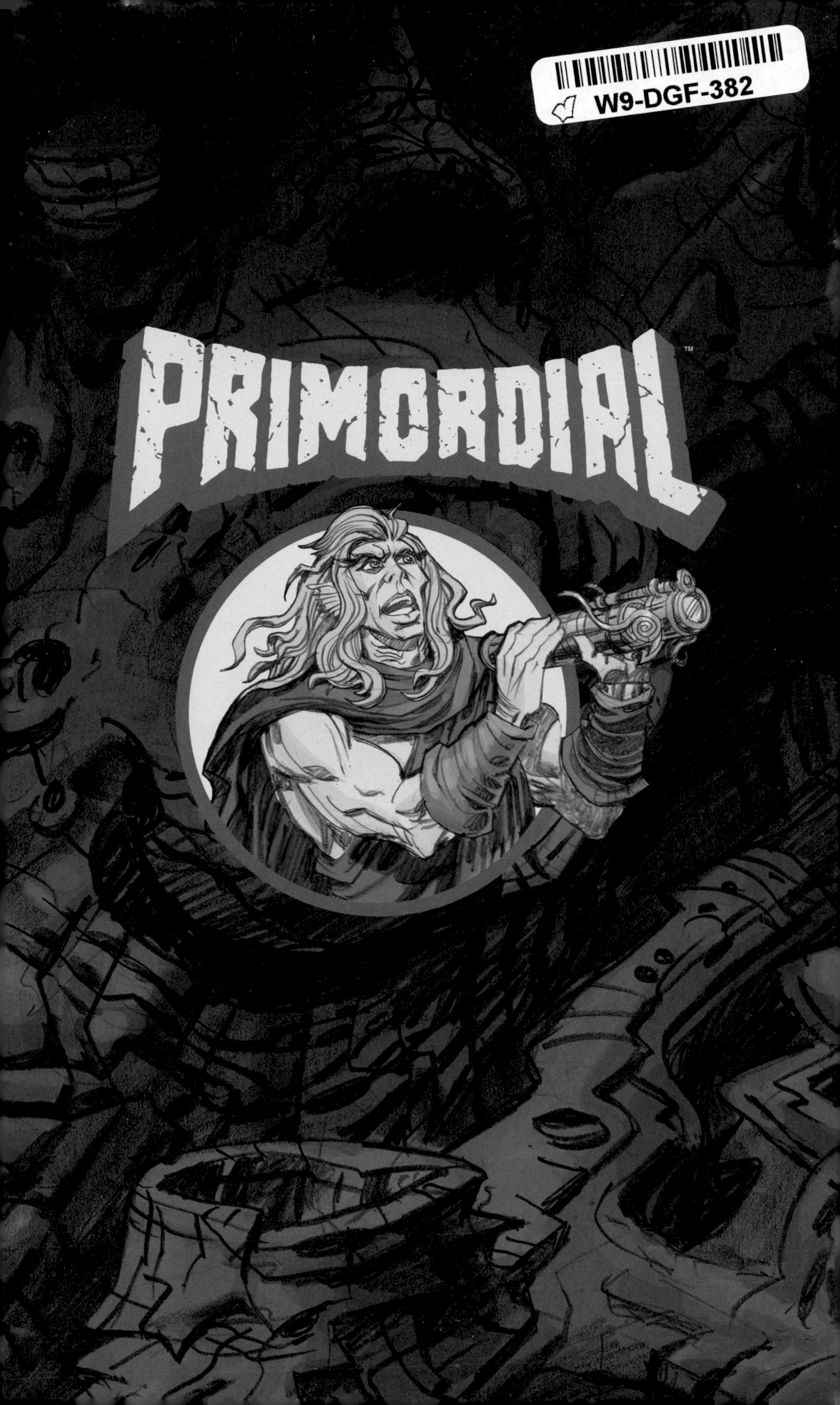
PRIMORDIAL™

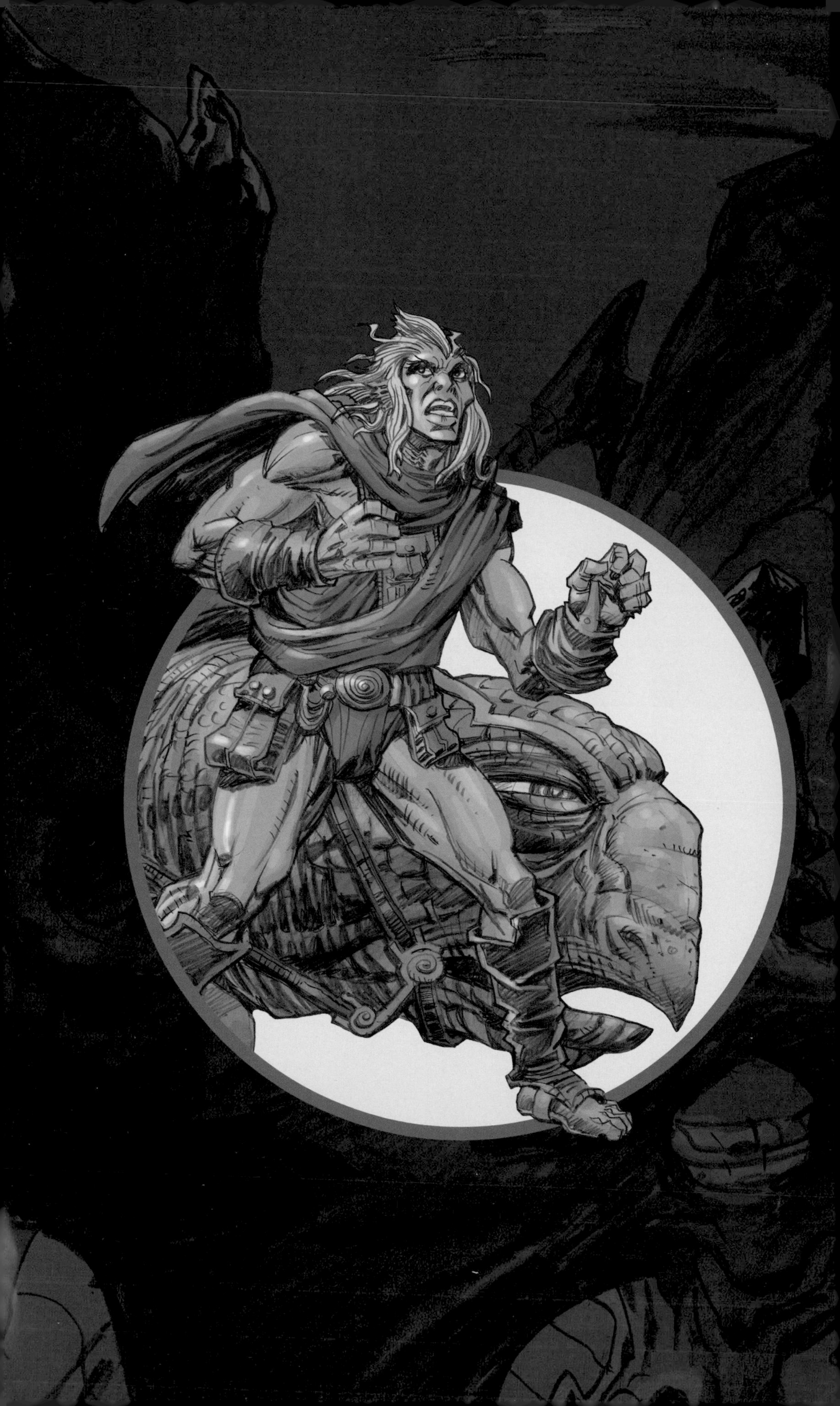

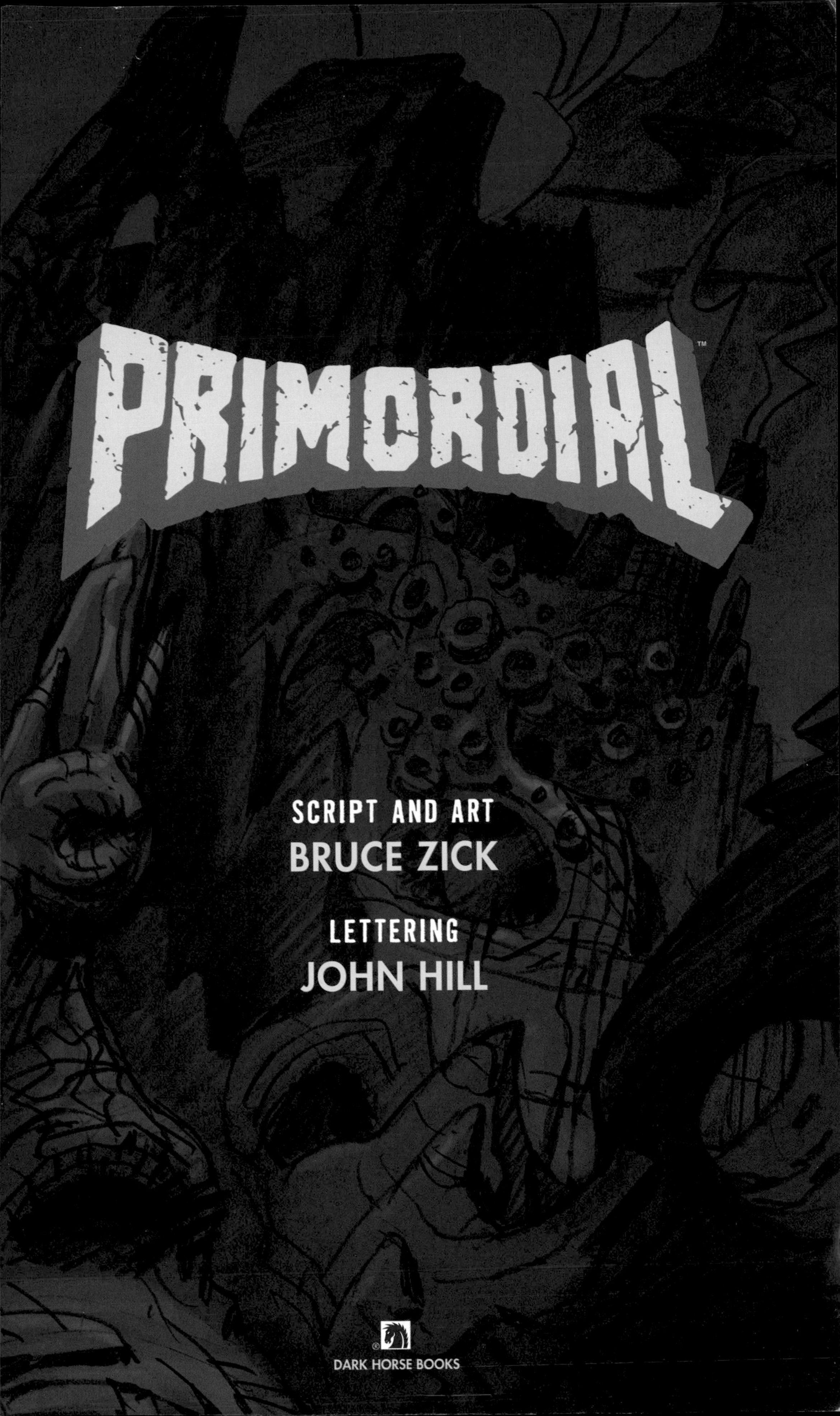

PRIMORDIAL™

SCRIPT AND ART
BRUCE ZICK

LETTERING
JOHN HILL

DARK HORSE BOOKS

PRESIDENT AND PUBLISHER
MIKE RICHARDSON

EDITOR
RANDY STRADLEY

ASSISTANT EDITOR
JUDY KHUU

DESIGNER
KATHLEEN BARNETT

DIGITAL ART TECHNICIAN
CHRIS HORN

NEIL HANKERSON Executive Vice President • TOM WEDDLE Chief Financial Officer • RANDY STRADLEY Vice President of Publishing • NICK McWHORTER Chief Business Development Officer • DALE LaFOUNTAIN Chief Information Officer • MATT PARKINSON Vice President of Marketing • VANESSA TODD-HOLMES Vice President of Production and Scheduling • MARK BERNARDI Vice President of Book Trade and Digital Sales • KEN LIZZI General Counsel • DAVE MARSHALL Editor in Chief • DAVEY ESTRADA Editorial Director • CHRIS WARNER Senior Books Editor • CARY GRAZZINI Director of Specialty Projects • Lia Ribacchi Art Director • MATT DRYER Director of Digital Art and Prepress • MICHAEL GOMBOS Senior Director of Licensed Publications • KARI YADRO Director of Custom Programs • KARI TORSON Director of International Licensing • SEAN BRICE Director of Trade Sales

PRIMORDIAL

Published by Dark Horse Books
A division of Dark Horse Comics LLC
10956 SE Main Street
Milwaukie, OR 97222

DarkHorse.com

To find a comics shop in your area, visit comicshoplocator.com

Library of Congress Cataloging-in-Publication Data

Names: Zick, Bruce, author, artist.
Title: Primordial / script, Bruce Zick ; art, Bruce Zick.
Description: Milwaukie, OR : Dark Horse Books, 2020. | Summary: "A wanderer roams through a barbarian world of savage men and beasts on a quest to find home"-- Provided by publisher.
Identifiers: LCCN 2020010180 | ISBN 9781506721361 (paperback)
Subjects: LCSH: Graphic novels.
Classification: LCC PN6727.Z555 P75 2020 | DDC 741.5/973--dc23
LC record available at https://lccn.loc.gov/2020010180

First edition: September 2021
Ebook ISBN 978-1-50672-536-9
Trade Paperback ISBN 978-1-50672-136-1

10 9 8 7 6 5 4 3 2 1

Printed in China

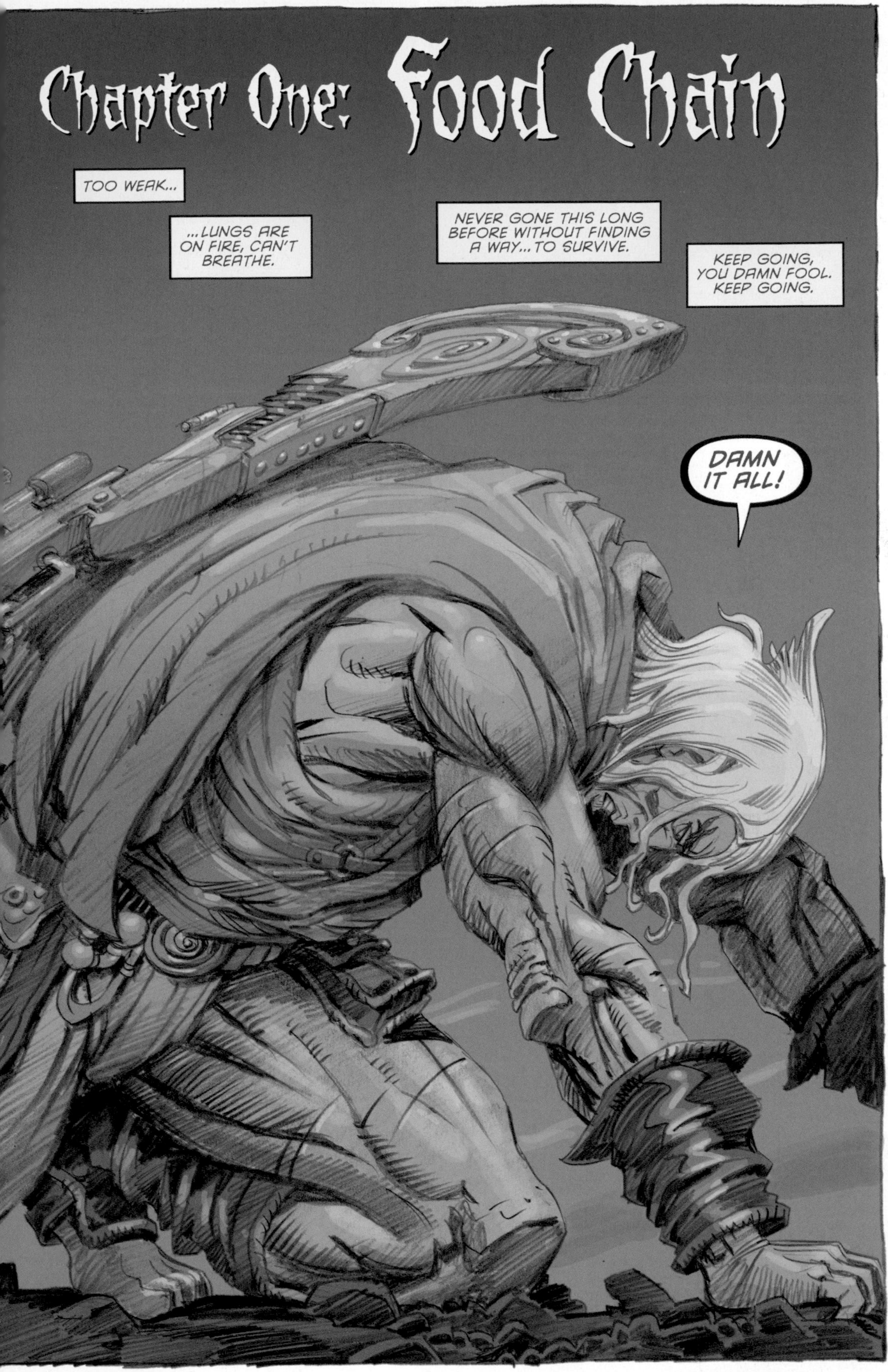
Chapter One: Food Chain
TOO WEAK...
...LUNGS ARE ON FIRE, CAN'T BREATHE.
NEVER GONE THIS LONG BEFORE WITHOUT FINDING A WAY... TO SURVIVE.
KEEP GOING, YOU DAMN FOOL. KEEP GOING.
DAMN IT ALL!

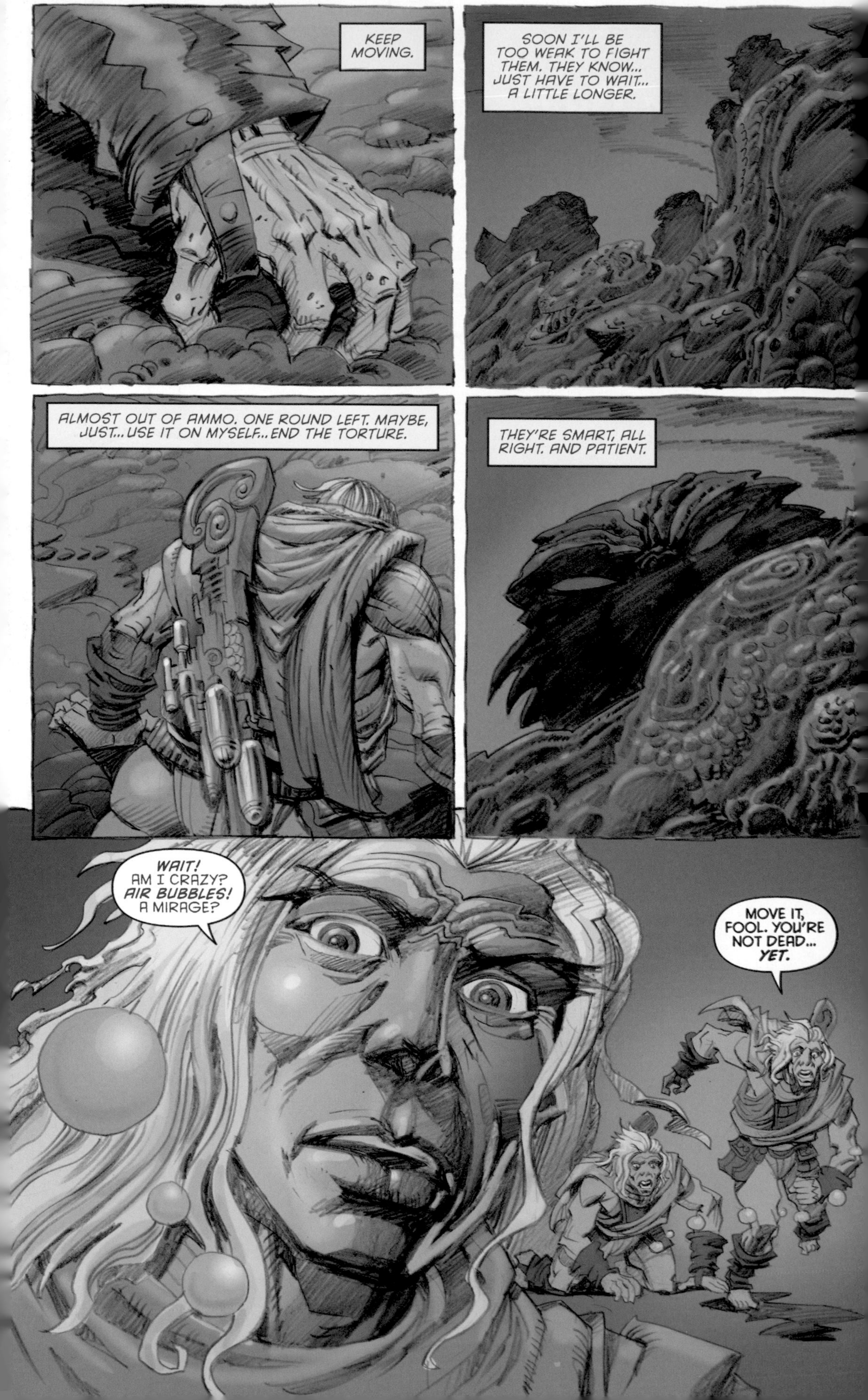
KEEP MOVING.
SOON I'LL BE TOO WEAK TO FIGHT THEM. THEY KNOW... JUST HAVE TO WAIT... A LITTLE LONGER.
ALMOST OUT OF AMMO. ONE ROUND LEFT. MAYBE, JUST...USE IT ON MYSELF...END THE TORTURE.
THEY'RE SMART, ALL RIGHT. AND PATIENT.
WAIT! AM I CRAZY? AIR BUBBLES! A MIRAGE?
MOVE IT, FOOL. YOU'RE NOT DEAD... YET.

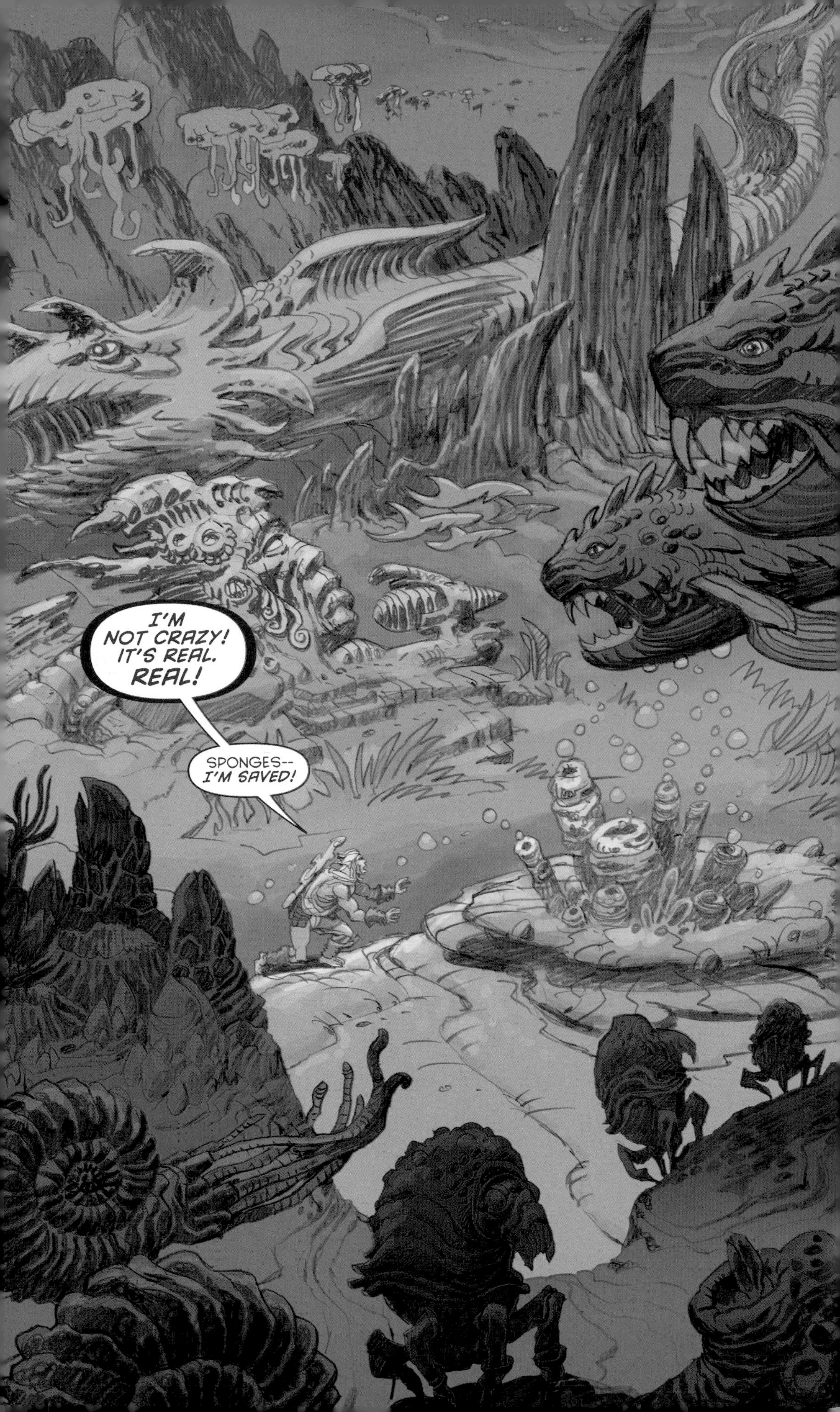
I'M NOT CRAZY! IT'S REAL. REAL!
SPONGES-- I'M SAVED!

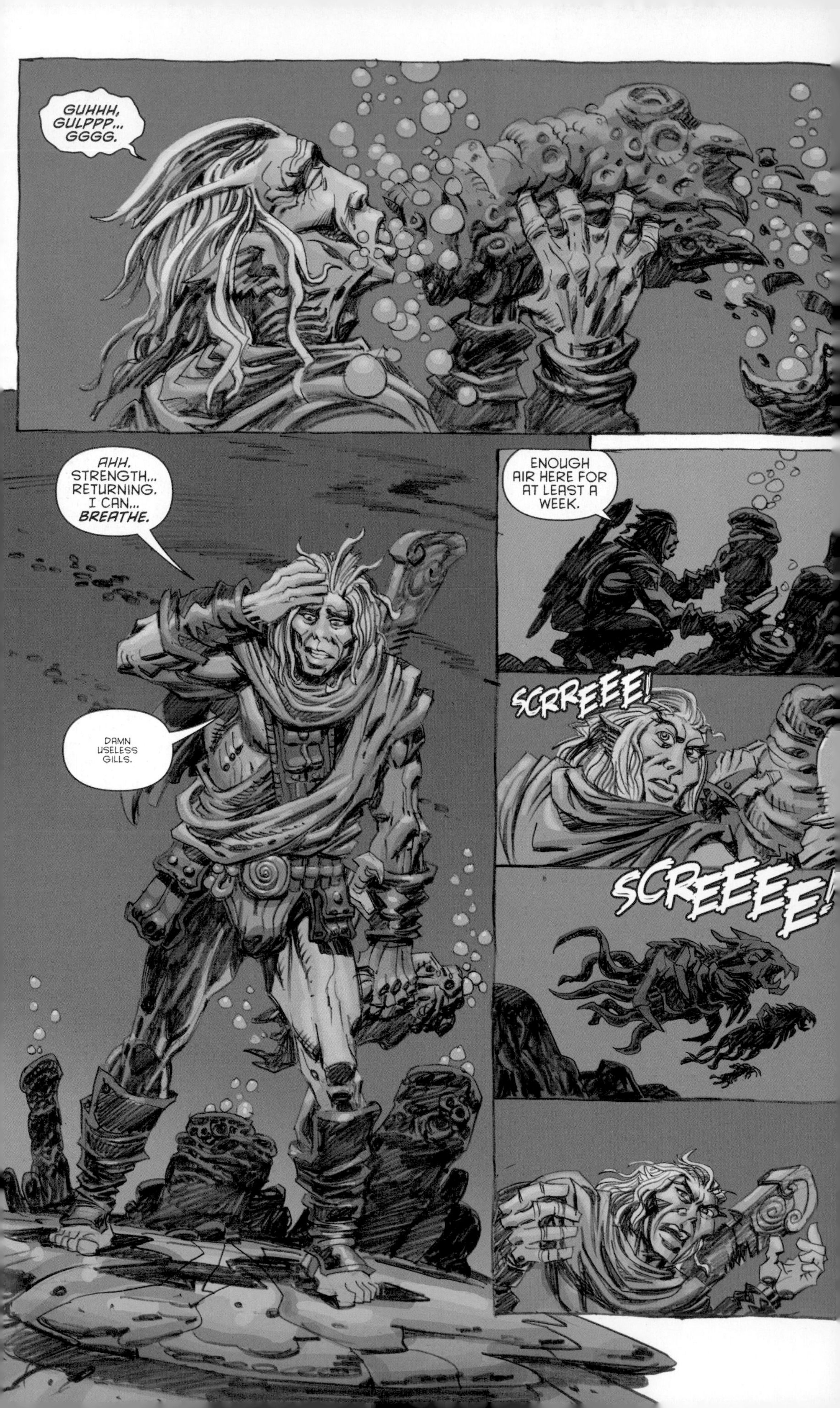
GUHHH, GULPPP... GGGG.
AHH. STRENGTH... RETURNING. I CAN... BREATHE.
DAMN USELESS GILLS.
ENOUGH AIR HERE FOR AT LEAST A WEEK.
SCRREEE!
SCREEEEE!

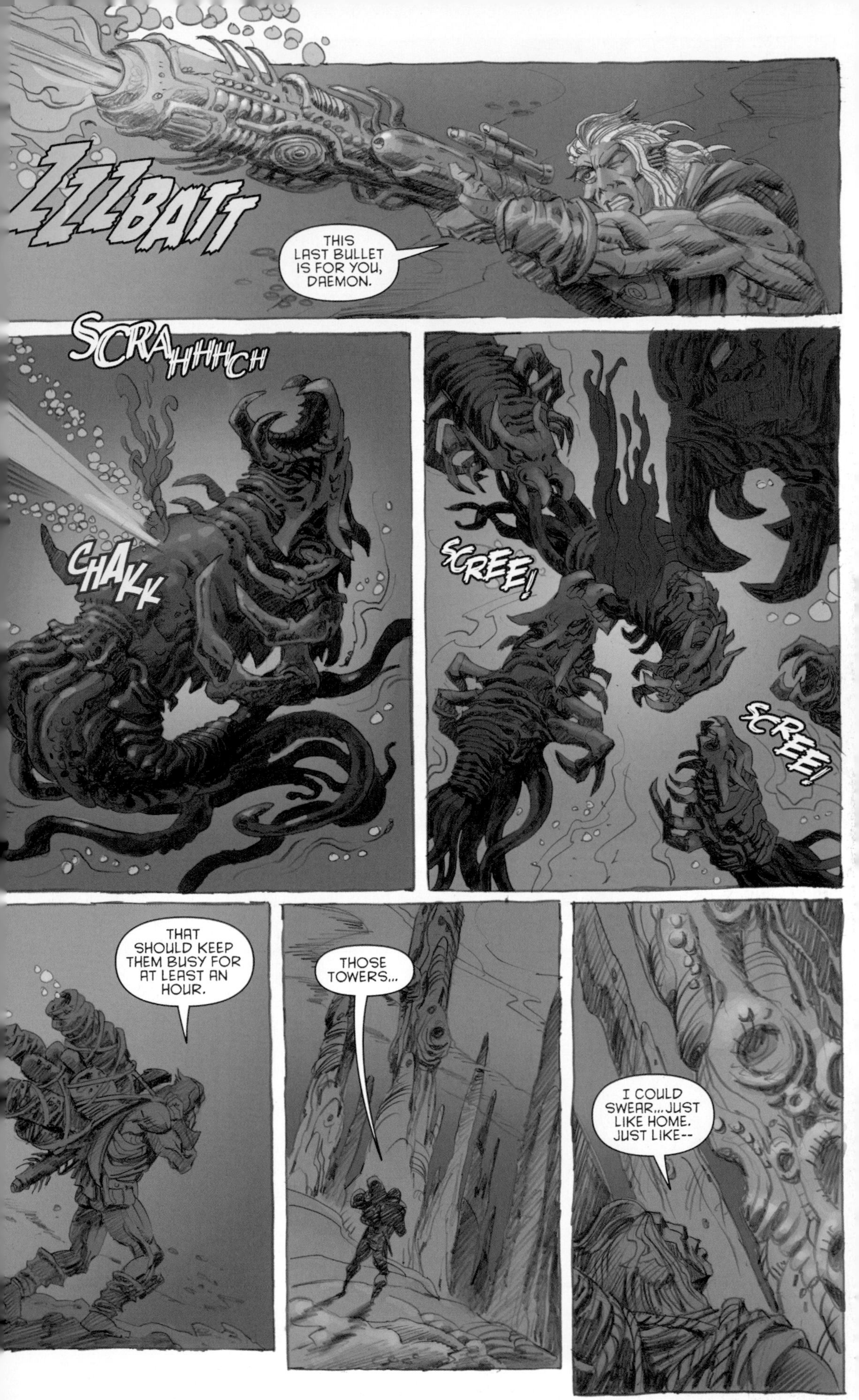

ZZZBATT
THIS LAST BULLET IS FOR YOU, DAEMON.
SCRAHHHCH
CHAKK
SCREE!
SCREE!
THAT SHOULD KEEP THEM BUSY FOR AT LEAST AN HOUR.
THOSE TOWERS...
I COULD SWEAR... JUST LIKE HOME. JUST LIKE--

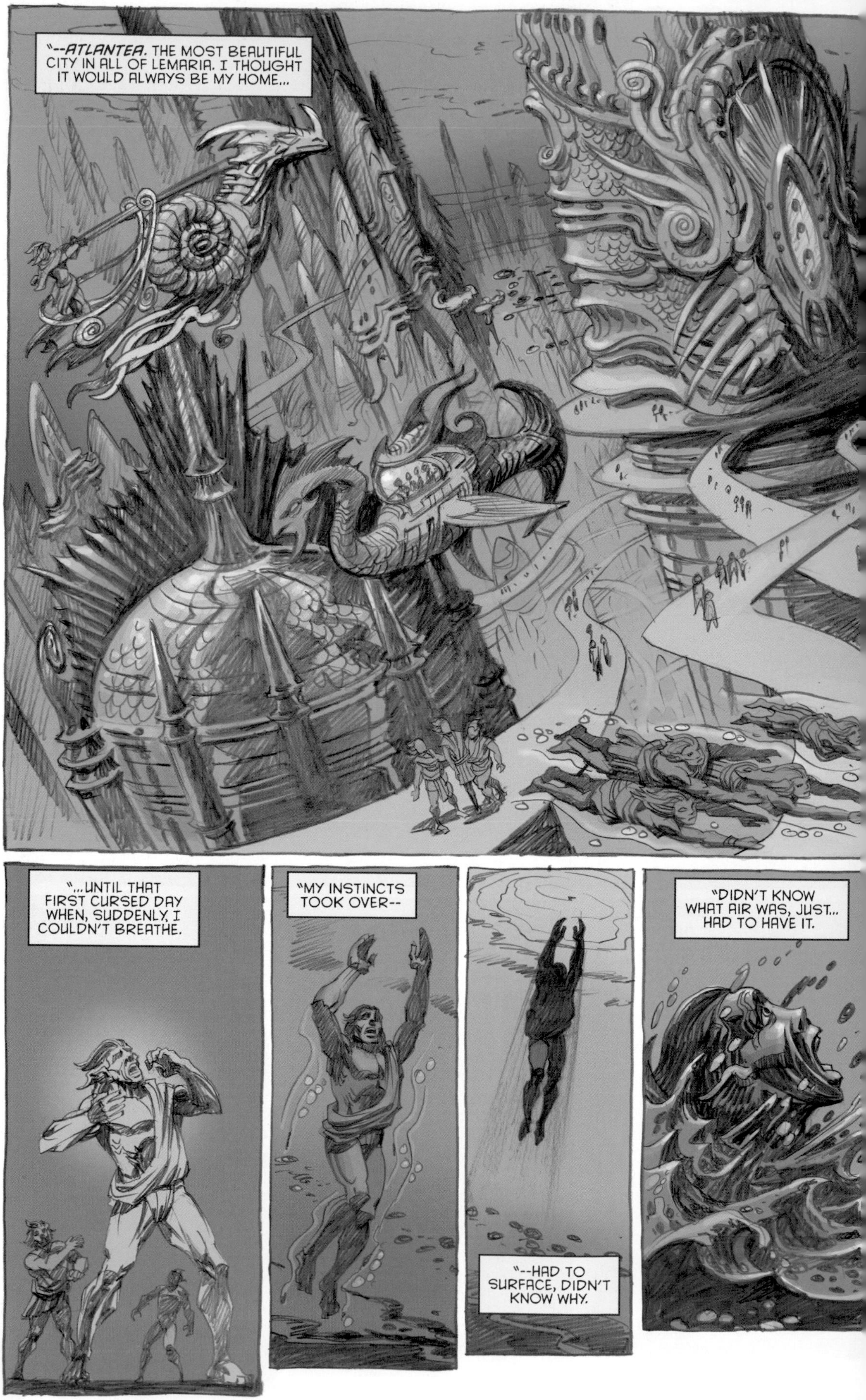

"--ATLANTEA. THE MOST BEAUTIFUL CITY IN ALL OF LEMARIA. I THOUGHT IT WOULD ALWAYS BE MY HOME...
"...UNTIL THAT FIRST CURSED DAY WHEN, SUDDENLY, I COULDN'T BREATHE.
"MY INSTINCTS TOOK OVER--
"--HAD TO SURFACE, DIDN'T KNOW WHY.
"DIDN'T KNOW WHAT AIR WAS, JUST... HAD TO HAVE IT.

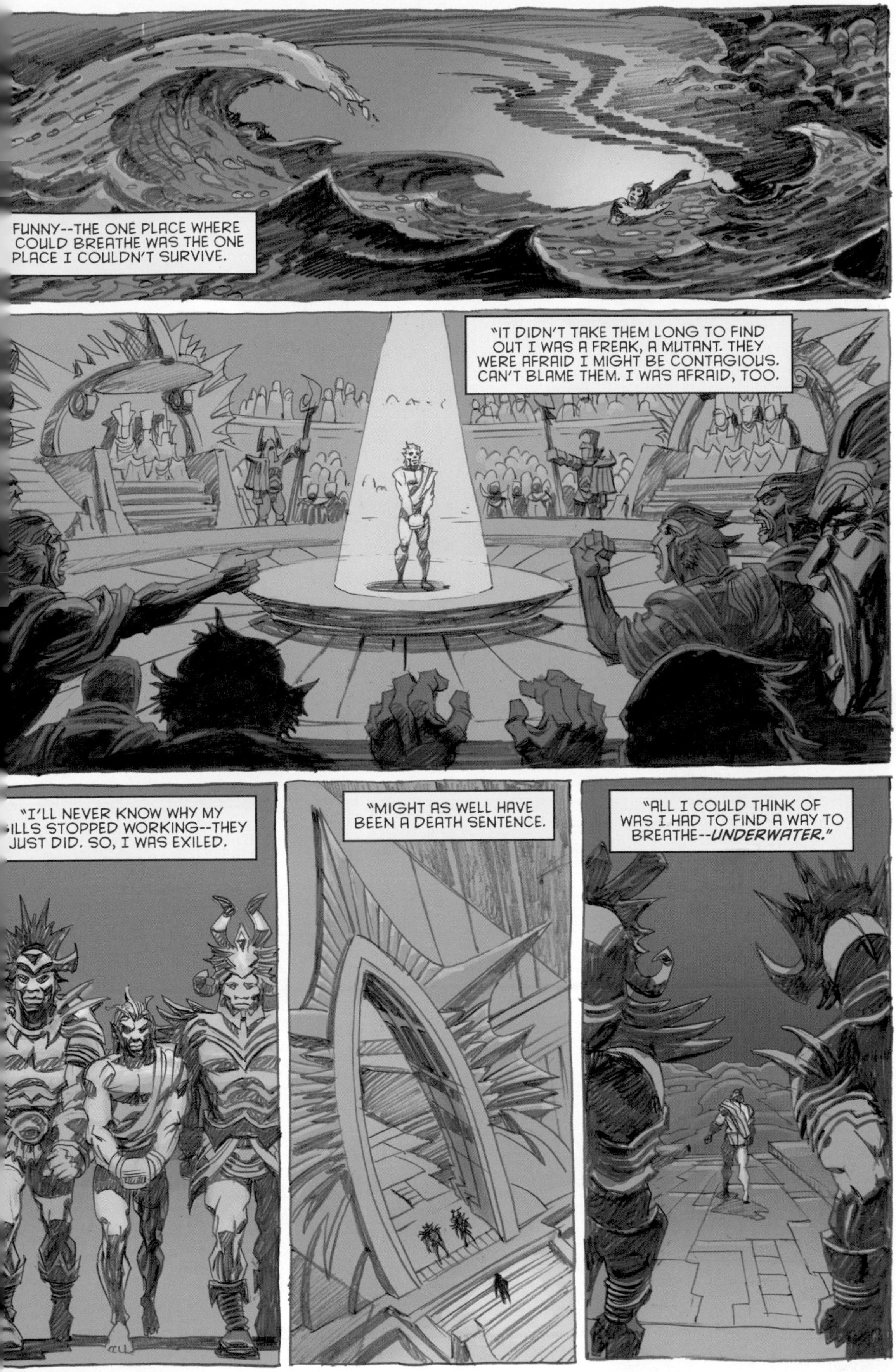
FUNNY--THE ONE PLACE WHERE
COULD BREATHE WAS THE ONE
PLACE I COULDN'T SURVIVE.
"IT DIDN'T TAKE THEM LONG TO FIND OUT I WAS A FREAK, A MUTANT. THEY WERE AFRAID I MIGHT BE CONTAGIOUS. CAN'T BLAME THEM. I WAS AFRAID, TOO.
"I'LL NEVER KNOW WHY MY
ILLS STOPPED WORKING--THEY
JUST DID. SO, I WAS EXILED.
"MIGHT AS WELL HAVE BEEN A DEATH SENTENCE.
"ALL I COULD THINK OF WAS I HAD TO FIND A WAY TO BREATHE--*UNDERWATER.*"

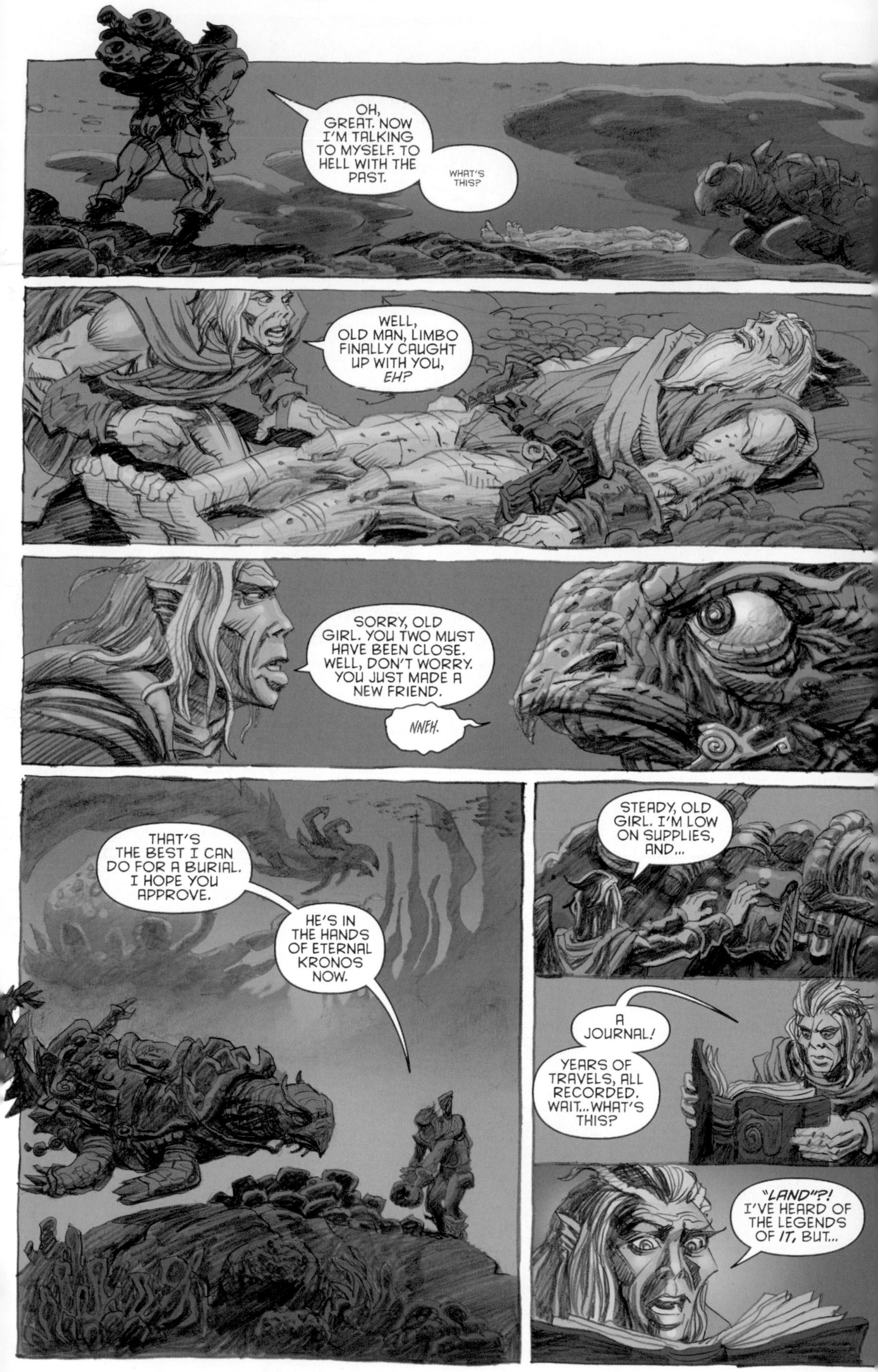
OH, GREAT. NOW I'M TALKING TO MYSELF. TO HELL WITH THE PAST.
WHAT'S THIS?
WELL, OLD MAN, LIMBO FINALLY CAUGHT UP WITH YOU, *EH?*
SORRY, OLD GIRL. YOU TWO MUST HAVE BEEN CLOSE. WELL, DON'T WORRY. YOU JUST MADE A NEW FRIEND.
NNEH.
THAT'S THE BEST I CAN DO FOR A BURIAL. I HOPE YOU APPROVE.
HE'S IN THE HANDS OF ETERNAL KRONOS NOW.
STEADY, OLD GIRL. I'M LOW ON SUPPLIES, AND...
A JOURNAL!
YEARS OF TRAVELS, ALL RECORDED. WAIT... WHAT'S THIS?
"LAND"?! I'VE HEARD OF THE LEGENDS OF *IT*, BUT...

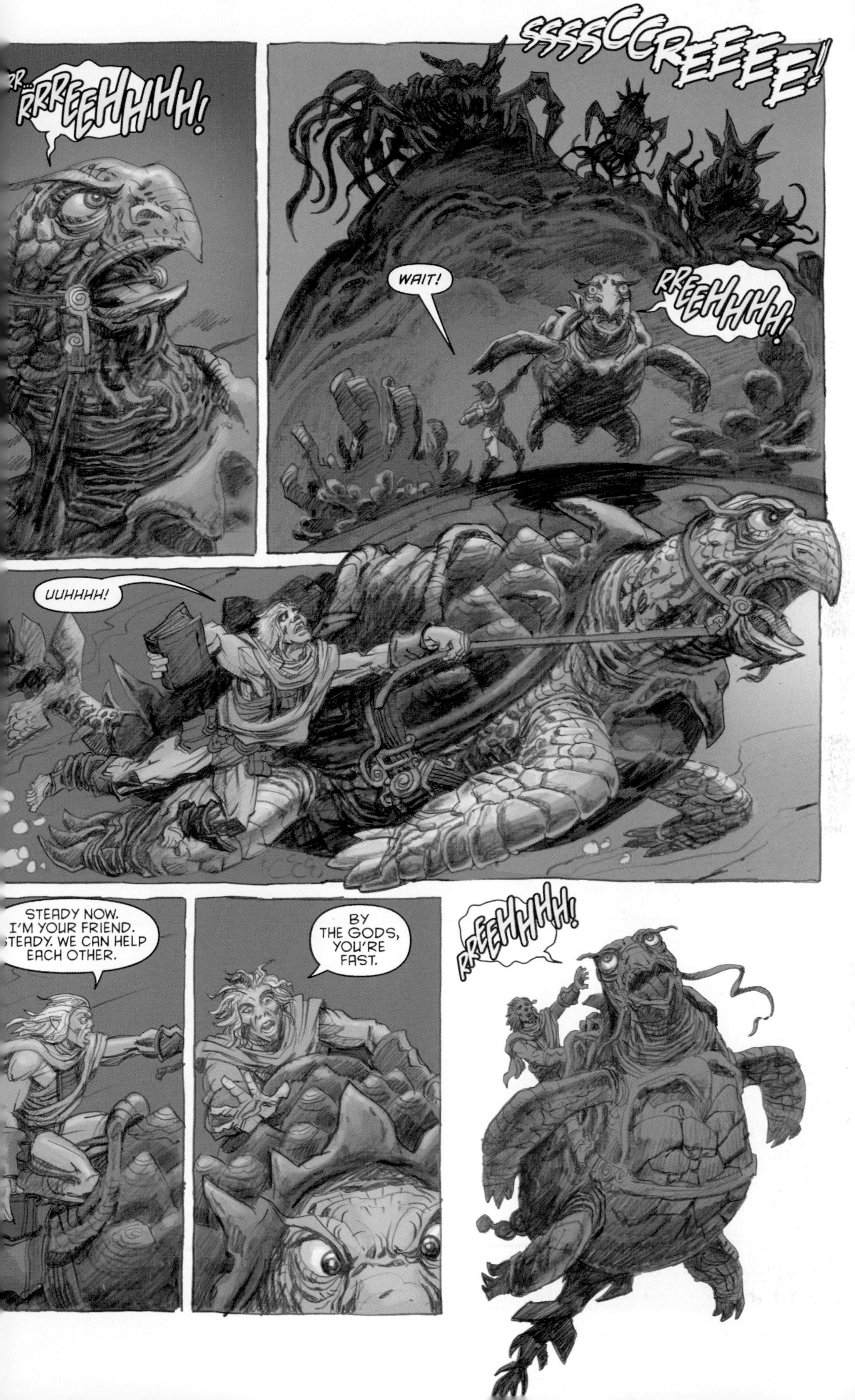
RR... RRREEHHHHH!
SSSSCCREEEEE!
WAIT!
RREEHHHHH!
UUHHHH!
STEADY NOW. I'M YOUR FRIEND. STEADY. WE CAN HELP EACH OTHER.
BY THE GODS, YOU'RE FAST.
RREEHHHHH!

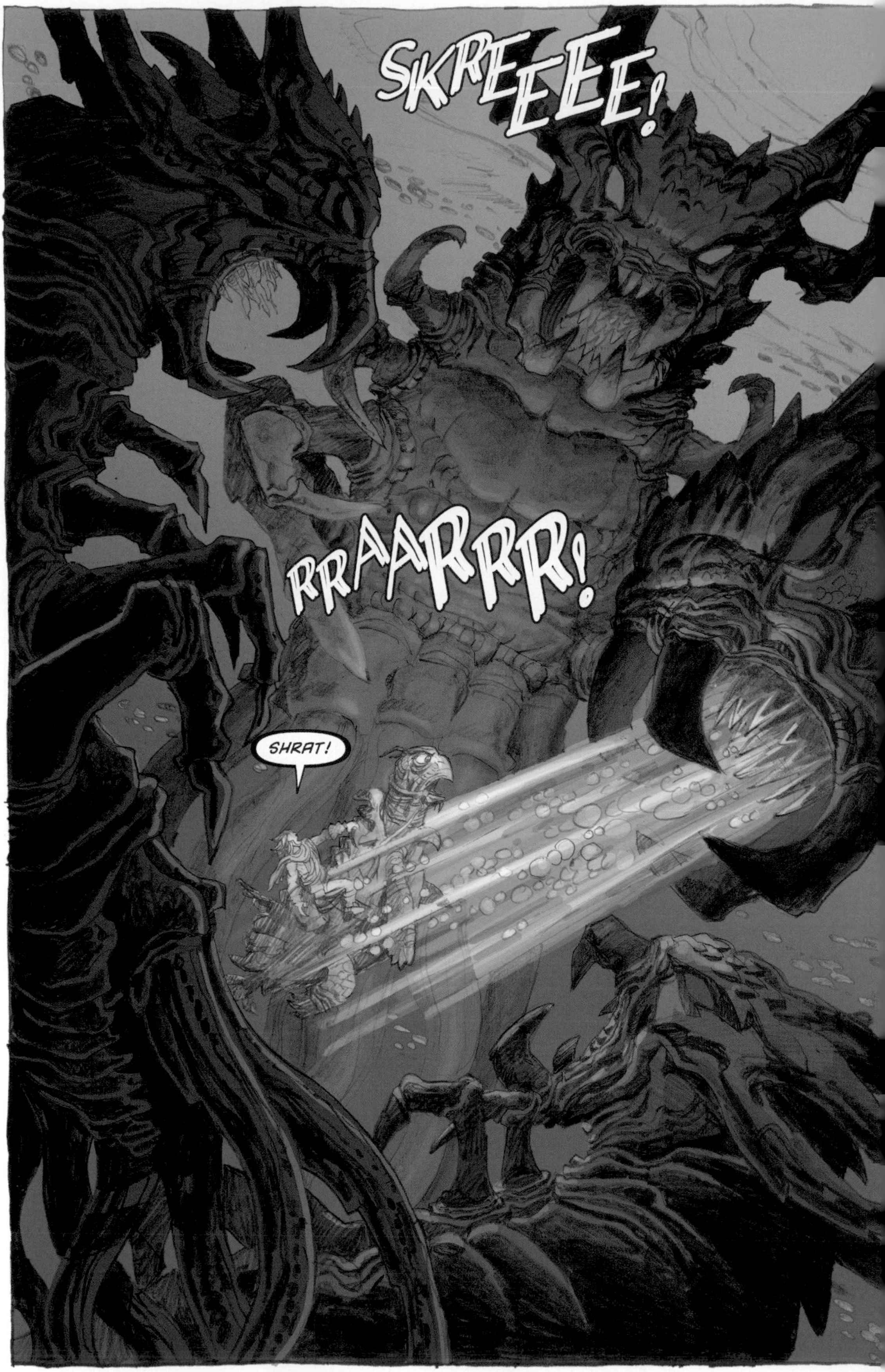
SKREEEEE!
RRAARRR!
SHRAT!

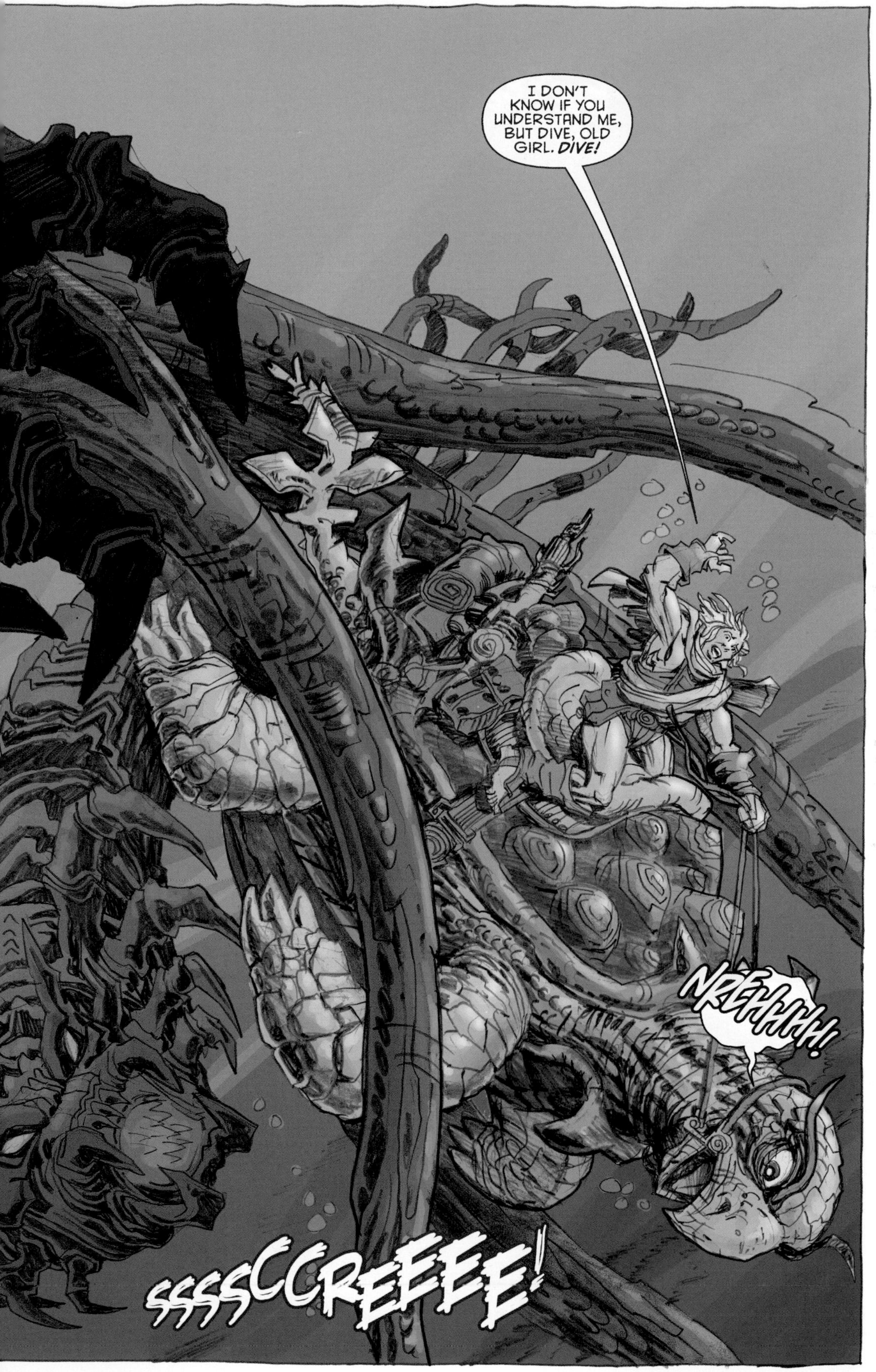
I DON'T KNOW IF YOU UNDERSTAND ME, BUT DIVE, OLD GIRL. *DIVE!*
NREHHHH!
SSSSSCCREEEEE!

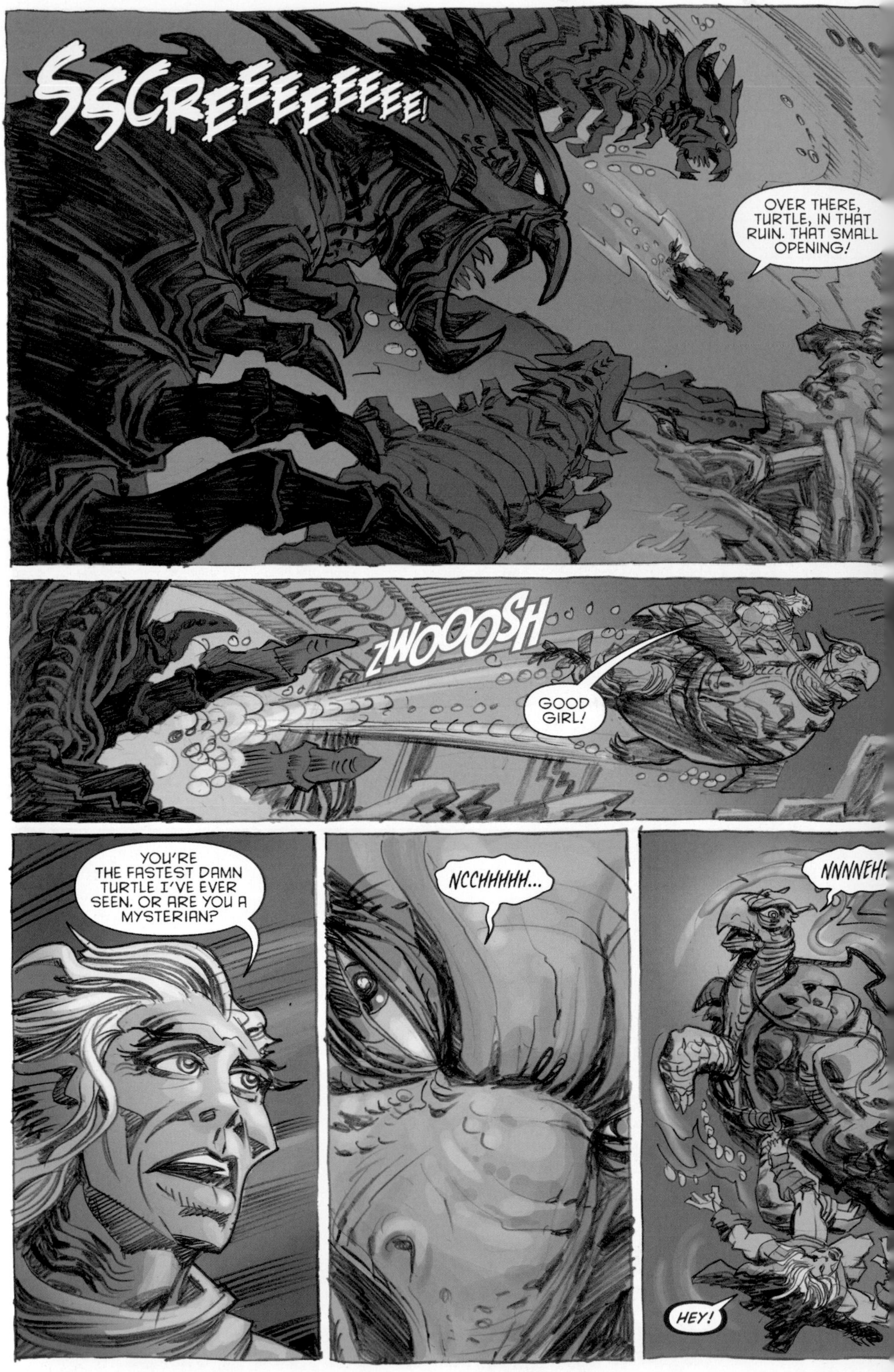
SSCREEEEEEEE!
OVER THERE, TURTLE, IN THAT RUIN. THAT SMALL OPENING!
ZWOOOSH
GOOD GIRL!
YOU'RE THE FASTEST DAMN TURTLE I'VE EVER SEEN. OR ARE YOU A MYSTERIAN?
NCCHHHHH...
HEY!

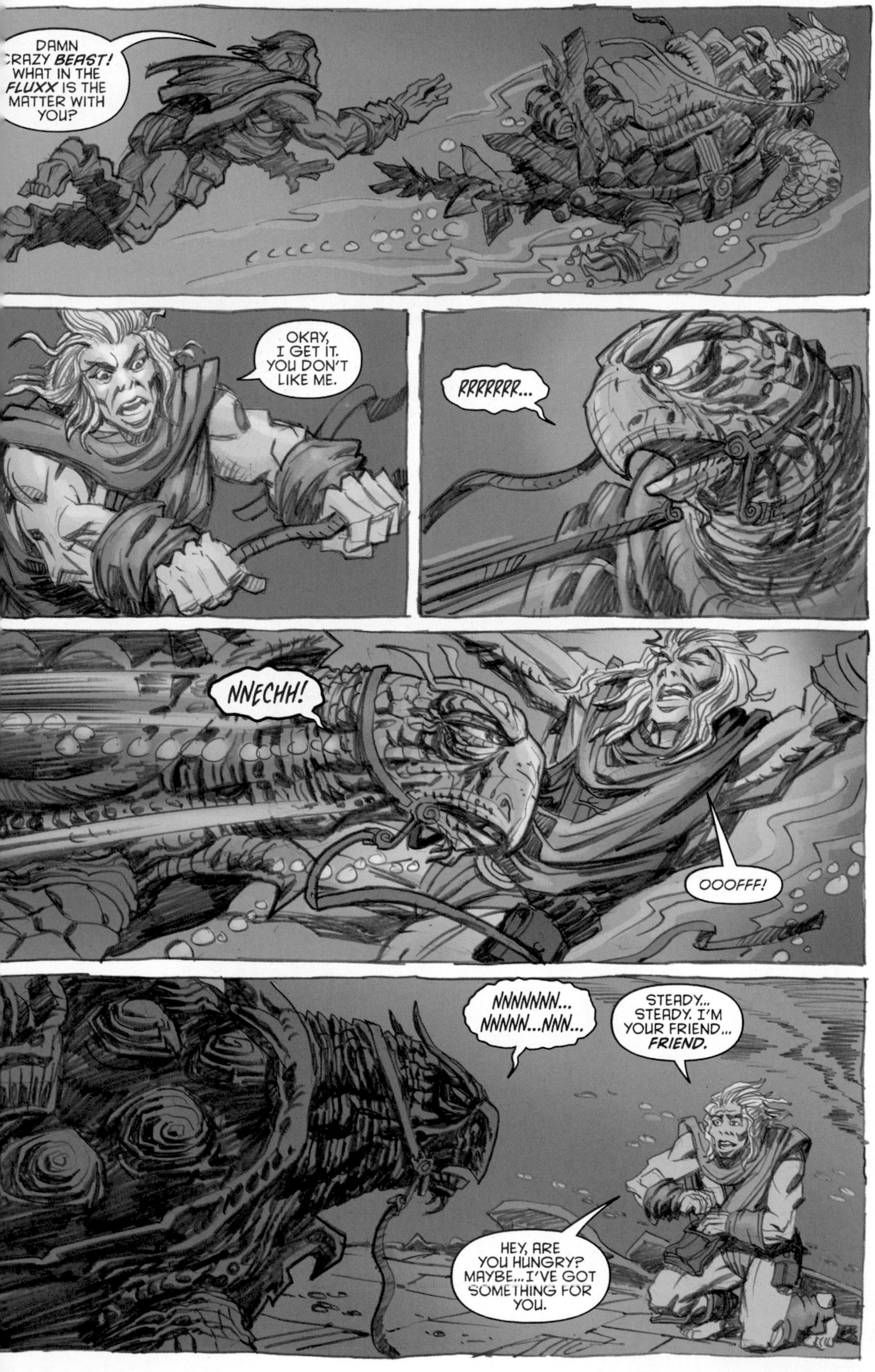
DAMN CRAZY *BEAST!* WHAT IN THE *FLUXX* IS THE MATTER WITH YOU?
OKAY, I GET IT. YOU DON'T LIKE ME.
RRRRRRR...
NNECHH!
OOOFFF!
NNNNNNN... NNNNN...NNN...
STEADY... STEADY. I'M YOUR FRIEND... *FRIEND.*
HEY, ARE YOU HUNGRY? MAYBE... I'VE GOT SOMETHING FOR YOU.

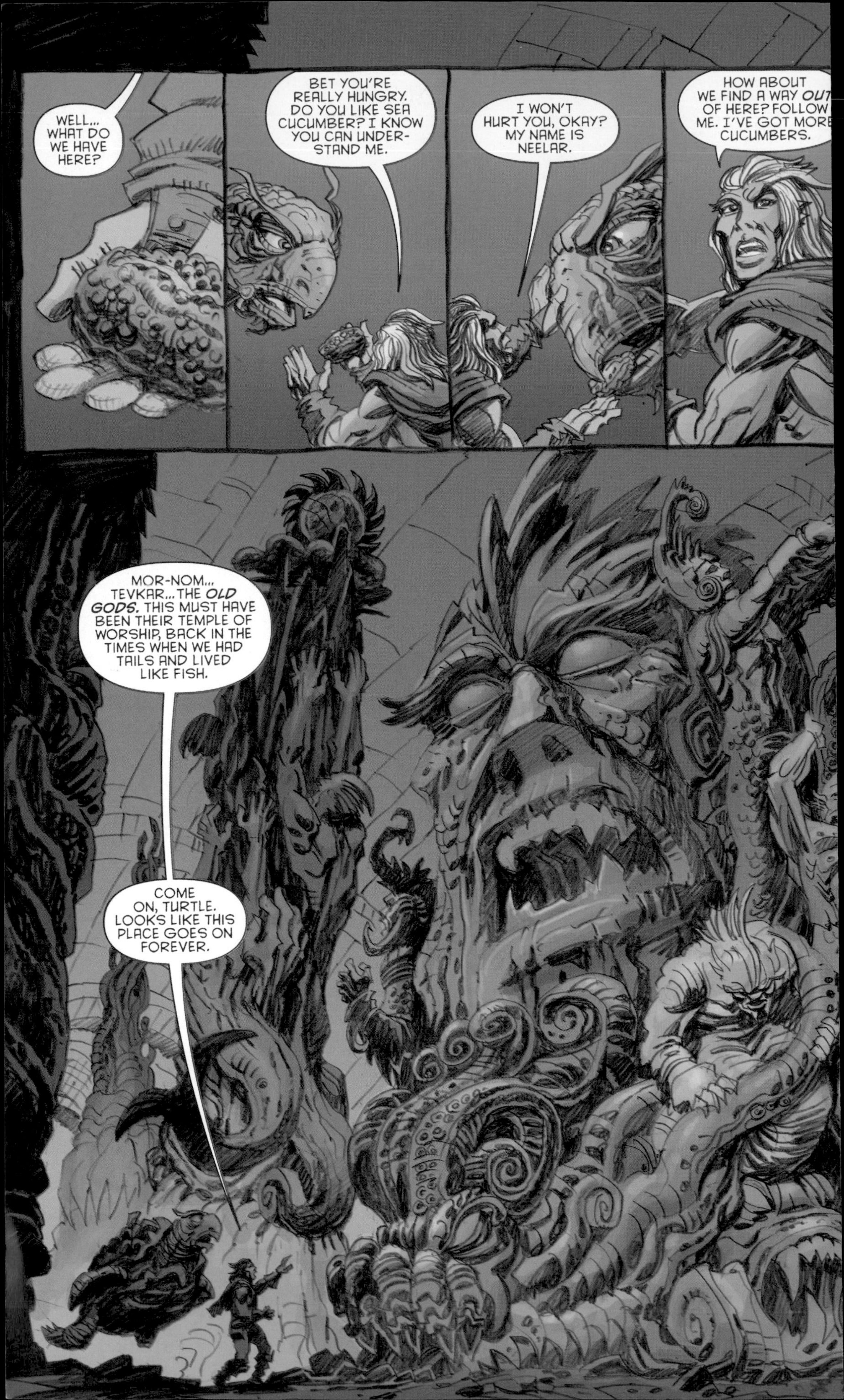
WELL... WHAT DO WE HAVE HERE?
BET YOU'RE REALLY HUNGRY. DO YOU LIKE SEA CUCUMBER? I KNOW YOU CAN UNDER-STAND ME.
I WON'T HURT YOU, OKAY? MY NAME IS NEELAR.
HOW ABOUT WE FIND A WAY OUT OF HERE? FOLLOW ME. I'VE GOT MORE CUCUMBERS.
MOR-NOM... TEVKAR... THE OLD GODS. THIS MUST HAVE BEEN THEIR TEMPLE OF WORSHIP, BACK IN THE TIMES WHEN WE HAD TAILS AND LIVED LIKE FISH.
COME ON, TURTLE. LOOKS LIKE THIS PLACE GOES ON FOREVER.

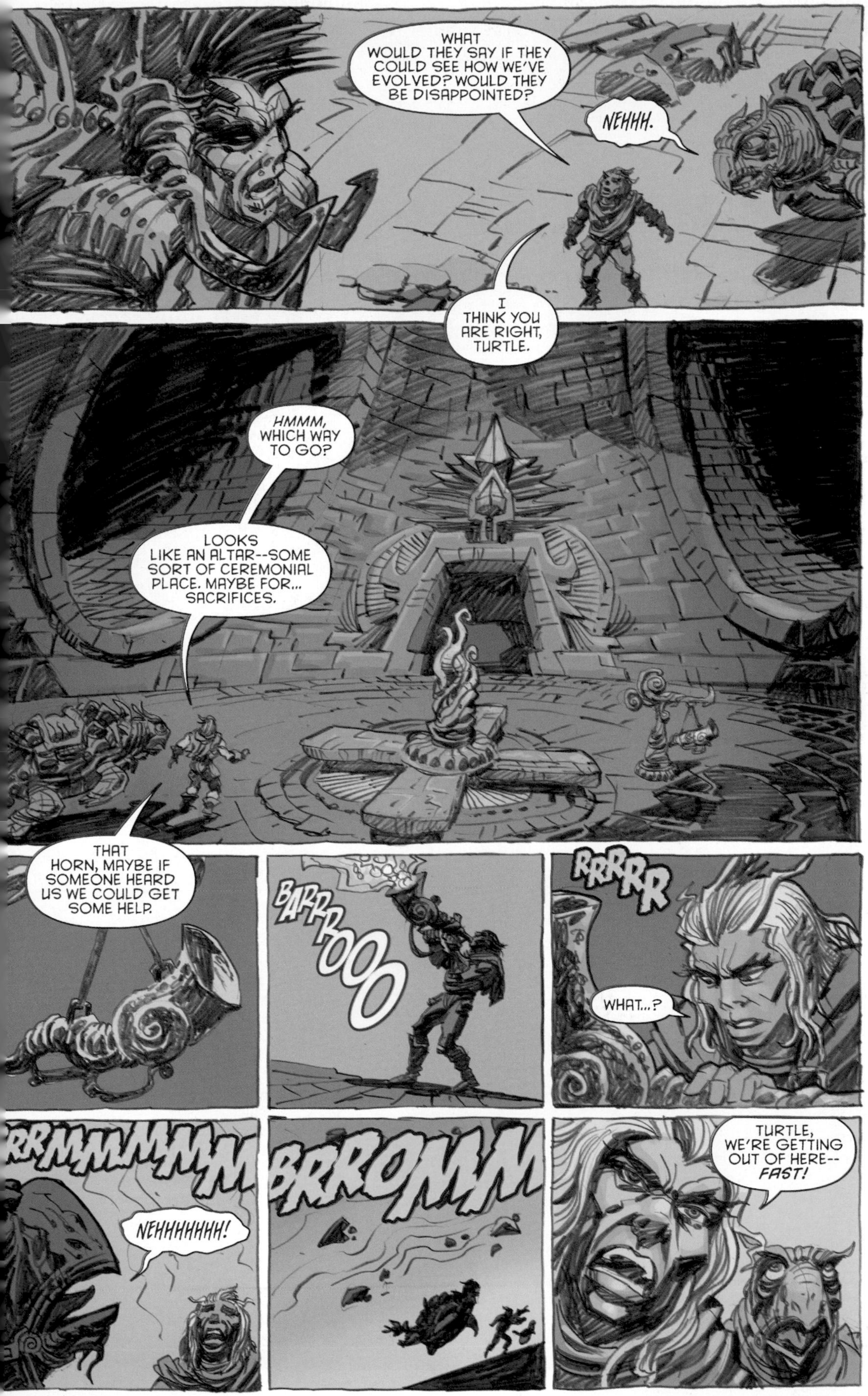
WHAT WOULD THEY SAY IF THEY COULD SEE HOW WE'VE EVOLVED? WOULD THEY BE DISAPPOINTED?
NEHHH.
I THINK YOU ARE RIGHT, TURTLE.
HMMM, WHICH WAY TO GO?
LOOKS LIKE AN ALTAR--SOME SORT OF CEREMONIAL PLACE. MAYBE FOR... SACRIFICES.
THAT HORN, MAYBE IF SOMEONE HEARD US WE COULD GET SOME HELP.
BARRROOO
RRRRR
WHAT...?
RRMMMMMM
BRROMM
NEHHHHHHH!
TURTLE, WE'RE GETTING OUT OF HERE-- FAST!

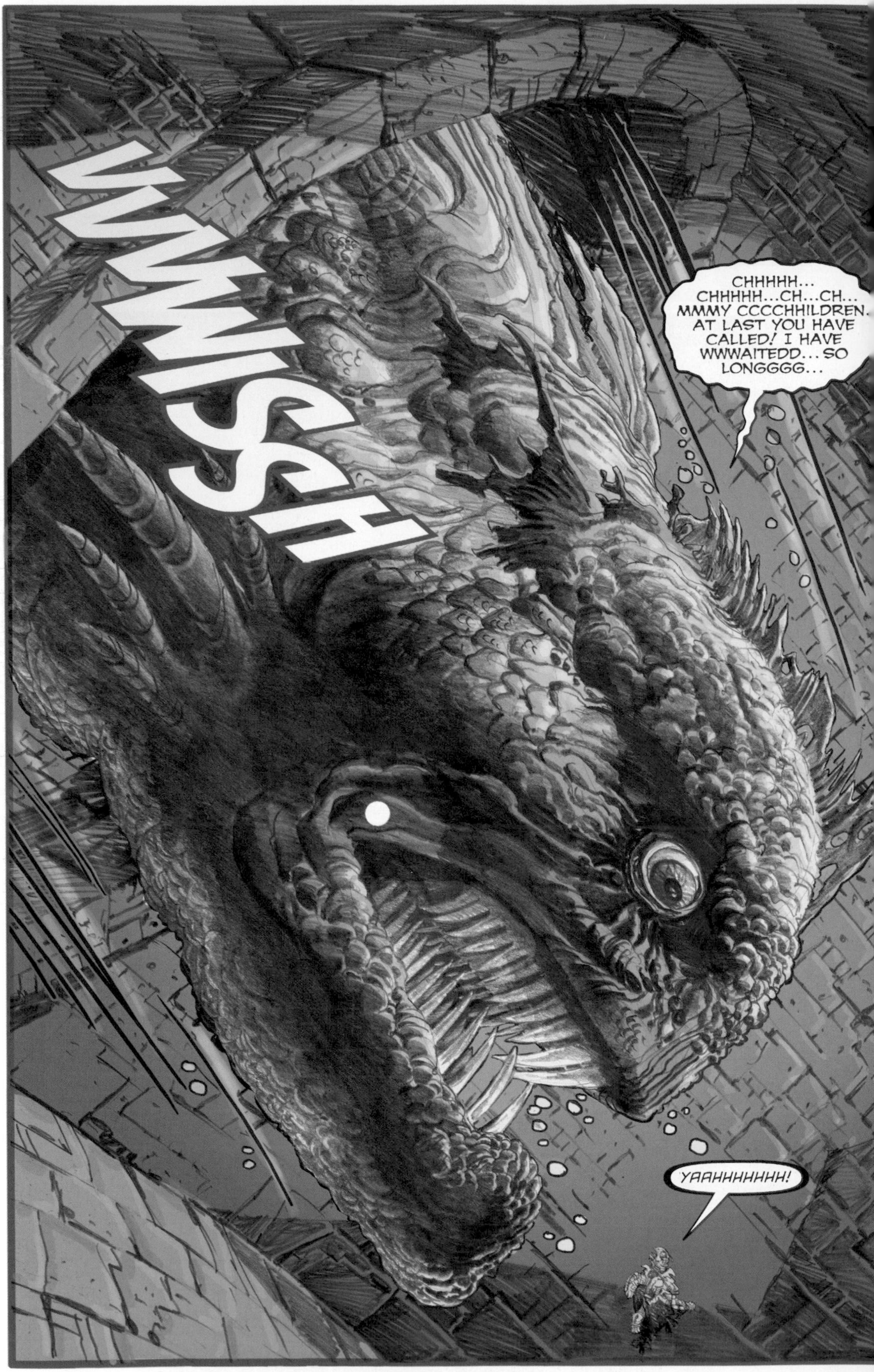
VWWISH
CHHHHH... CHHHHH...CH...CH... MMMY CCCCHHILDREN. AT LAST YOU HAVE CALLED! I HAVE WWWAITEDD... SO LONGGGG...
YAAHHHHHHH!

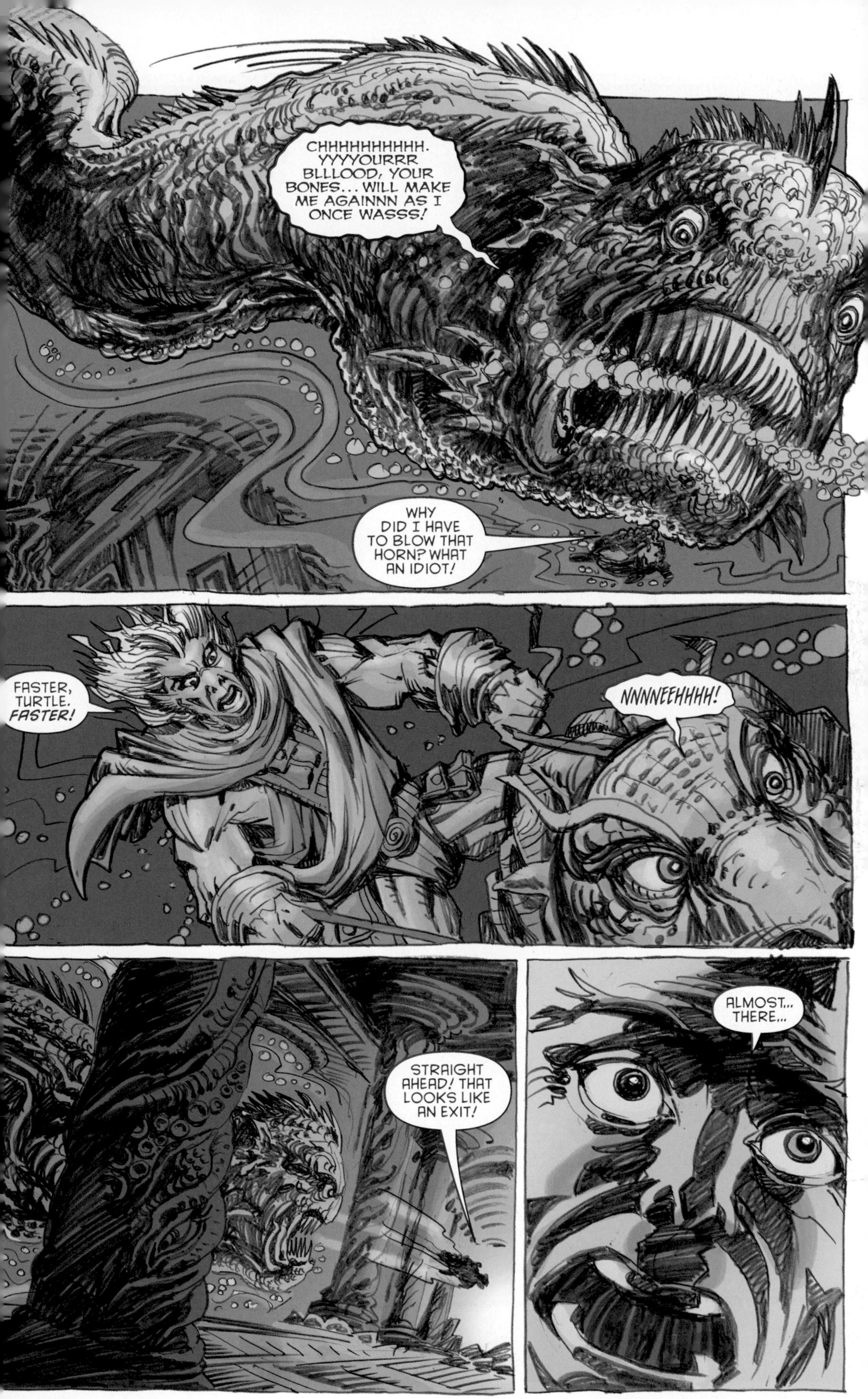
CHHHHHHHHHH. YYYYOURRR BLLLOOD, YOUR BONES... WILL MAKE ME AGAINNN AS I ONCE WASSS!
WHY DID I HAVE TO BLOW THAT HORN? WHAT AN IDIOT!
FASTER, TURTLE. FASTER!
NNNNEEHHHH!
STRAIGHT AHEAD! THAT LOOKS LIKE AN EXIT!
ALMOST... THERE...

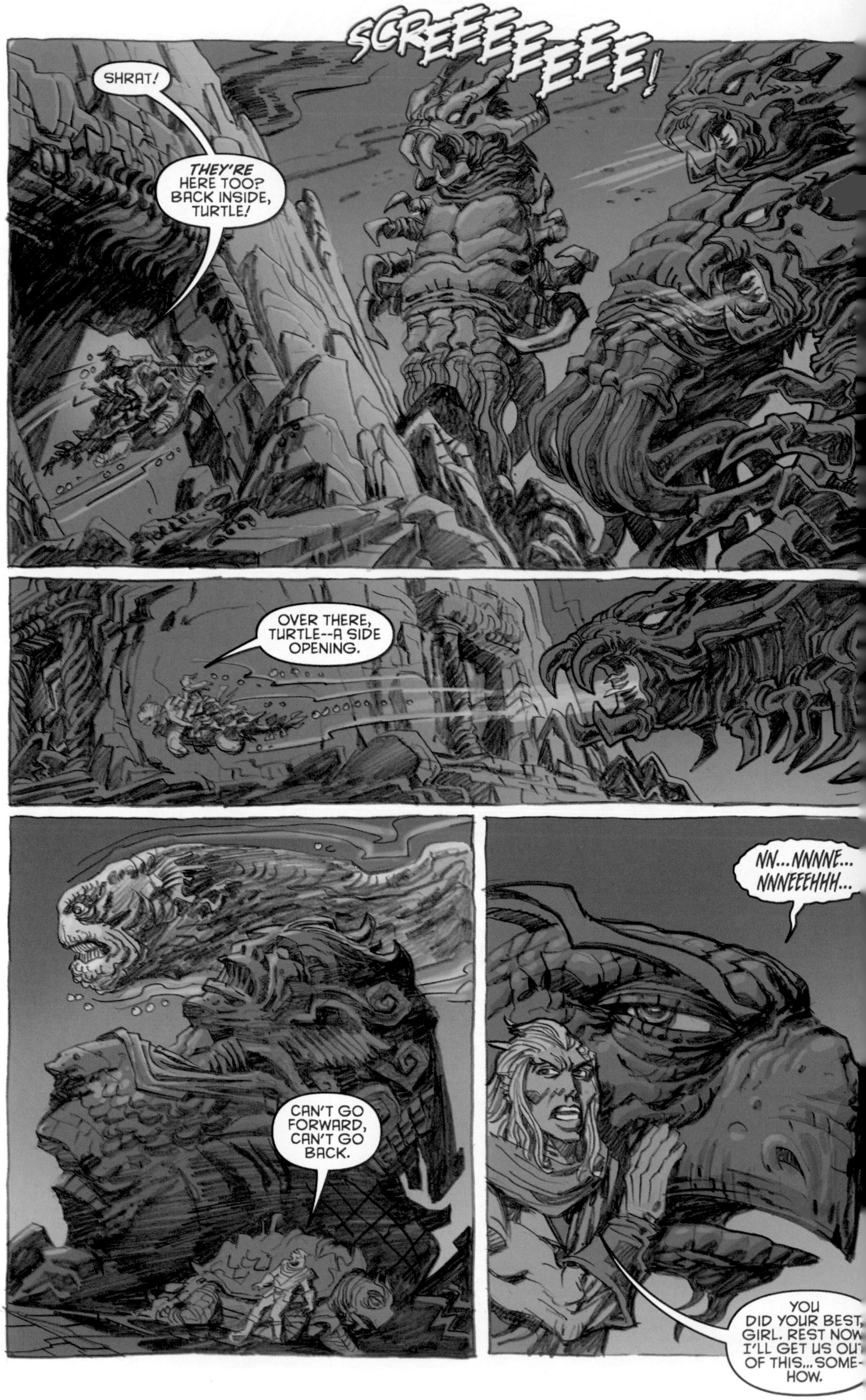
SCREEEEEEEEE!
SHRAT!
THEY'RE HERE TOO? BACK INSIDE, TURTLE!
OVER THERE, TURTLE--A SIDE OPENING.
CAN'T GO FORWARD, CAN'T GO BACK.
NN...NNNNE... NNNEEEHHH...
YOU DID YOUR BEST, GIRL. REST NOW. I'LL GET US OUT OF THIS...SOME-HOW.

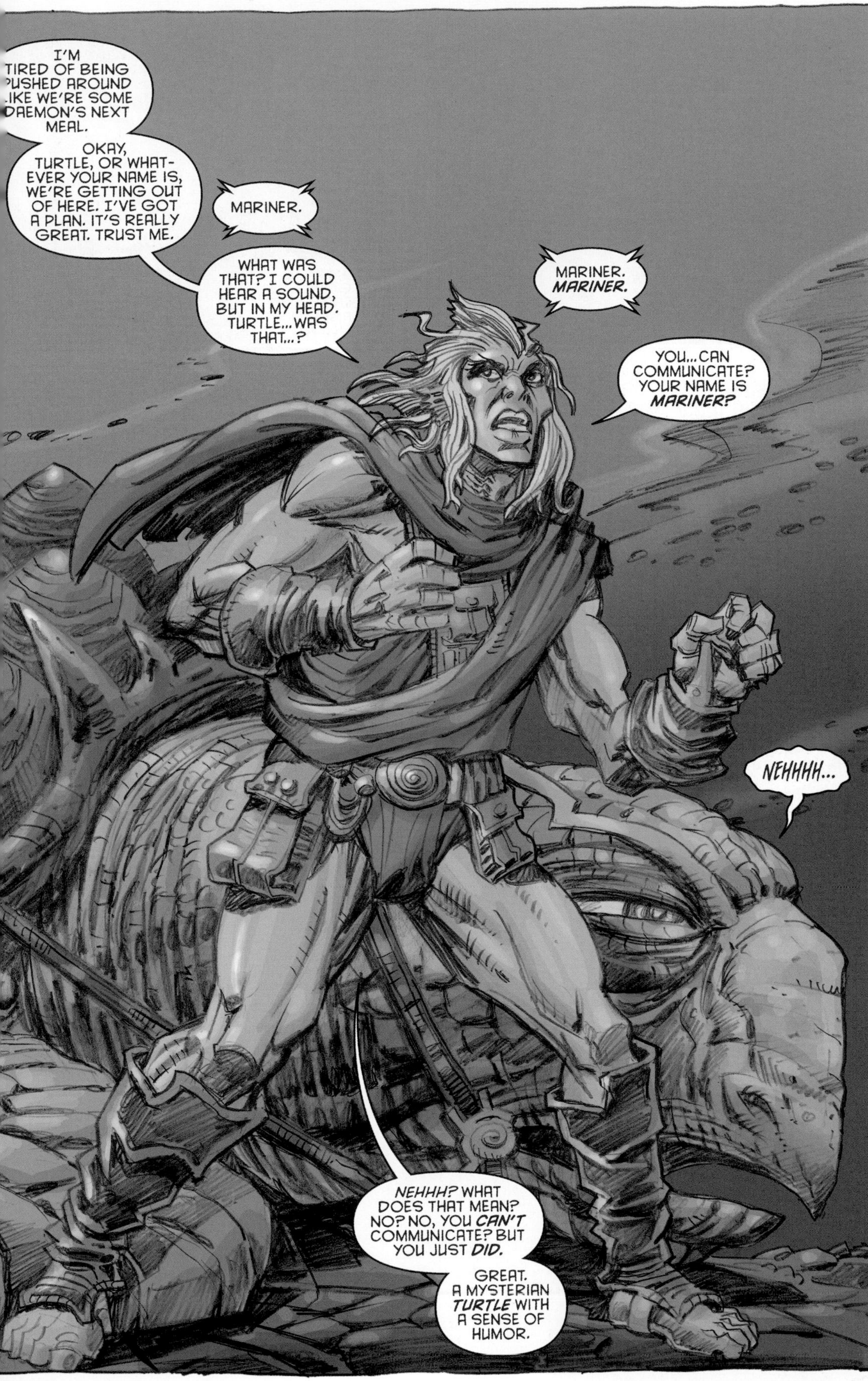
I'M TIRED OF BEING PUSHED AROUND LIKE WE'RE SOME DAEMON'S NEXT MEAL.
OKAY, TURTLE, OR WHATEVER YOUR NAME IS, WE'RE GETTING OUT OF HERE. I'VE GOT A PLAN. IT'S REALLY GREAT. TRUST ME.
MARINER.
WHAT WAS THAT? I COULD HEAR A SOUND, BUT IN MY HEAD. TURTLE...WAS THAT...?
MARINER. *MARINER.*
YOU...CAN COMMUNICATE? YOUR NAME IS *MARINER?*
NEHHHH...
NEHHH? WHAT DOES THAT MEAN? NO? NO, YOU *CAN'T* COMMUNICATE? BUT YOU JUST *DID.*
GREAT. A MYSTERIAN *TURTLE* WITH A SENSE OF HUMOR.

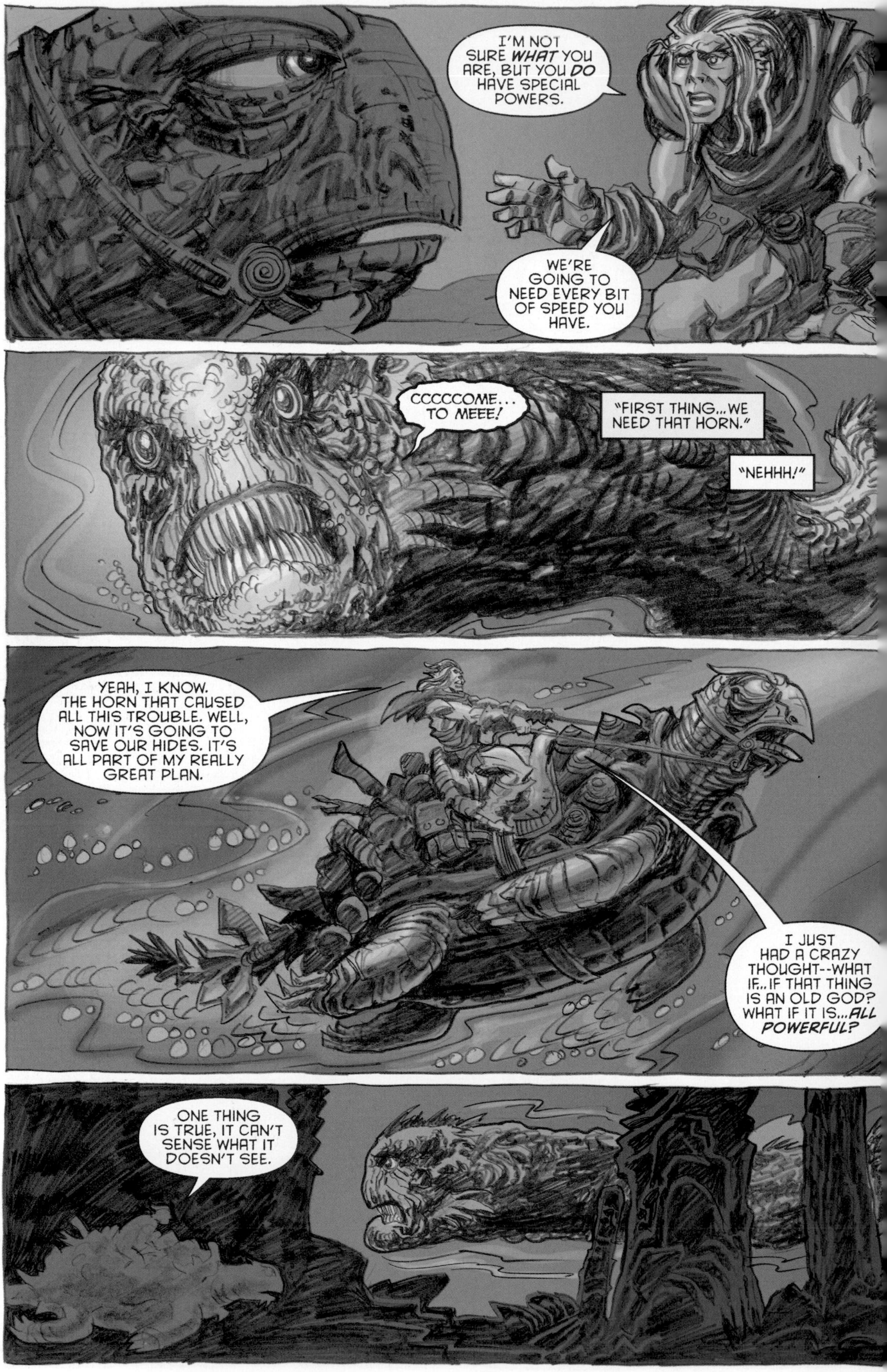

I'M NOT SURE *WHAT* YOU ARE, BUT YOU *DO* HAVE SPECIAL POWERS.
WE'RE GOING TO NEED EVERY BIT OF SPEED YOU HAVE.
CCCCCOME... TO MEEE!
"FIRST THING...WE NEED THAT HORN."
"NEHHH!"
YEAH, I KNOW. THE HORN THAT CAUSED ALL THIS TROUBLE. WELL, NOW IT'S GOING TO SAVE OUR HIDES. IT'S ALL PART OF MY REALLY GREAT PLAN.
I JUST HAD A CRAZY THOUGHT--WHAT IF...IF THAT THING IS AN OLD GOD? WHAT IF IT IS...*ALL POWERFUL?*
ONE THING IS TRUE, IT CAN'T SENSE WHAT IT DOESN'T SEE.

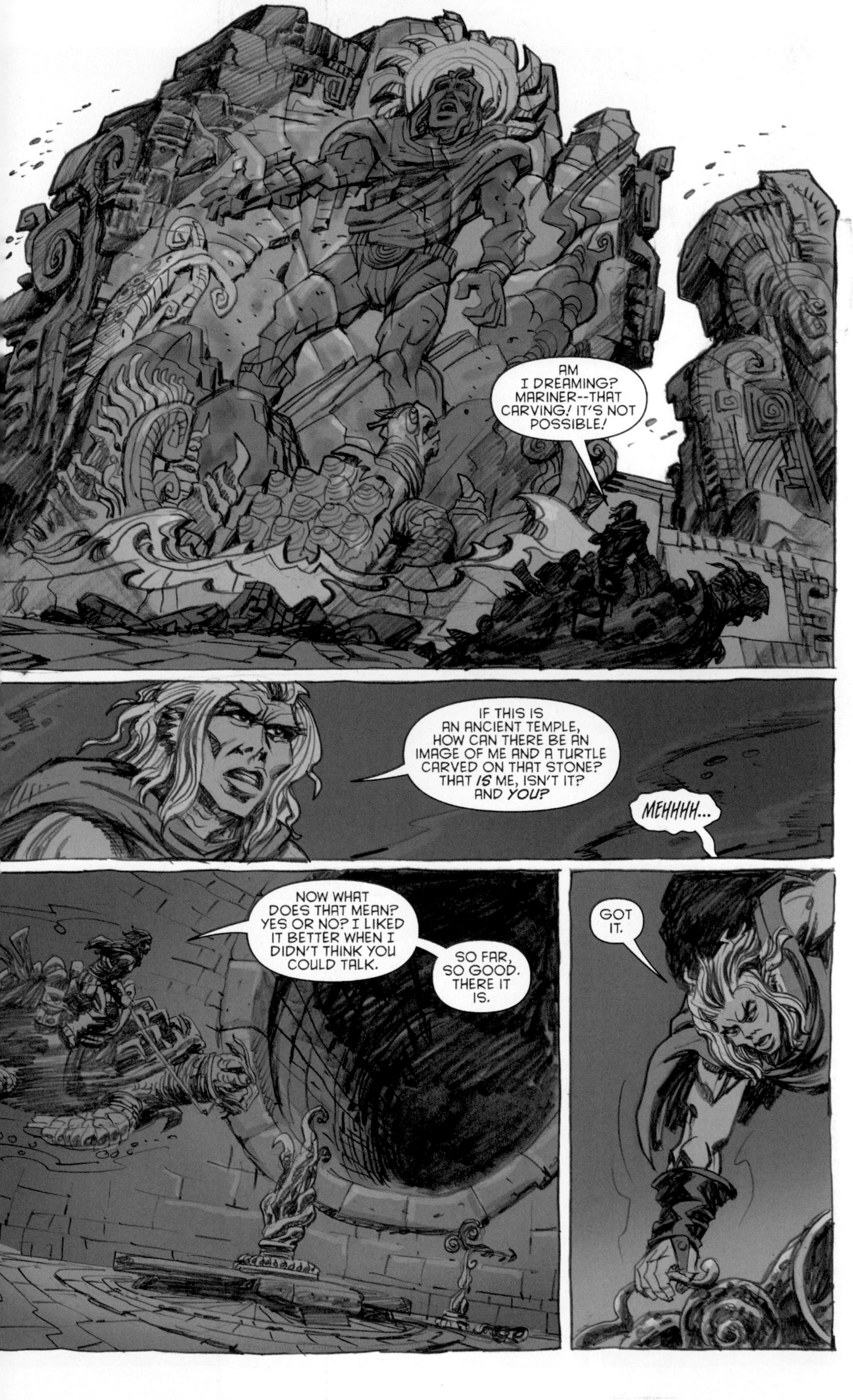
AM I DREAMING? MARINER--THAT CARVING! IT'S NOT POSSIBLE!
IF THIS IS AN ANCIENT TEMPLE, HOW CAN THERE BE AN IMAGE OF ME AND A TURTLE CARVED ON THAT STONE? THAT *IS* ME, ISN'T IT? AND *YOU*?
MEHHHH...
NOW WHAT DOES THAT MEAN? YES OR NO? I LIKED IT BETTER WHEN I DIDN'T THINK YOU COULD TALK.
SO FAR, SO GOOD. THERE IT IS.
GOT IT.

OKAY, HERE GOES...

BBAAROOOOO

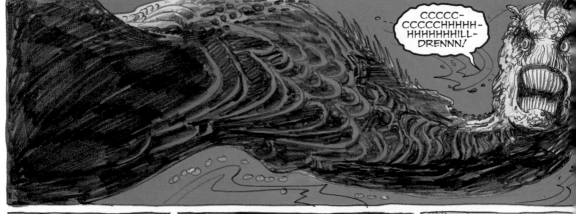

CCCCC-CCCCCHHHHH-HHHHHHHILL-DRENNN!

HERE IT COMES! GO, TURTLE-- GO!

CCCCHHH-CCHHH!

HURRY! BACK OUTSIDE AGAIN!

TRUST ME!

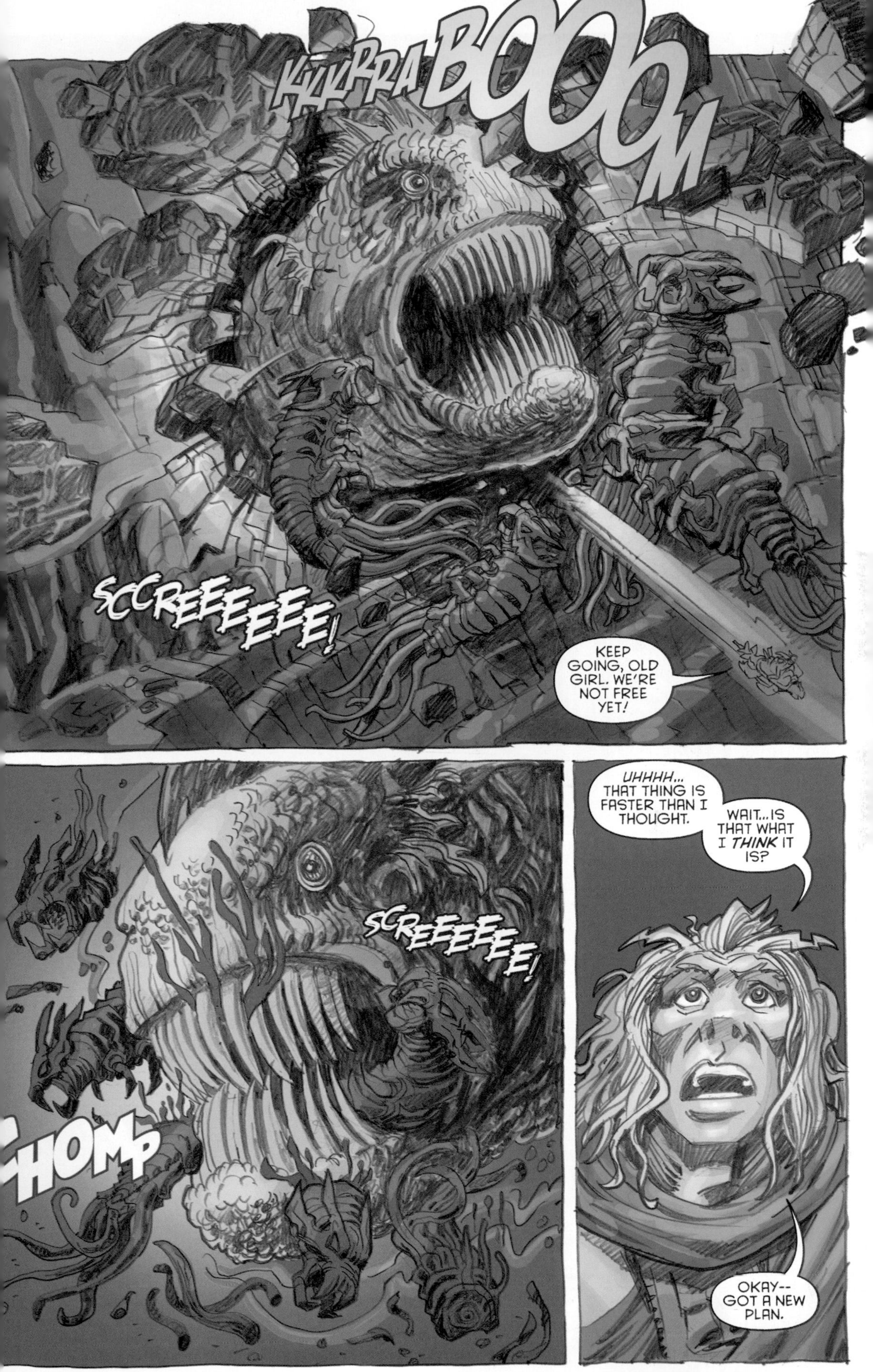
KKKRRRA BOOOOM
SCCREEEEEEE!
KEEP GOING, OLD GIRL. WE'RE NOT FREE YET!
SCREEEEEEE!
CHOMP
UHHHH... THAT THING IS FASTER THAN I THOUGHT.
WAIT... IS THAT WHAT I THINK IT IS?
OKAY-- GOT A NEW PLAN.

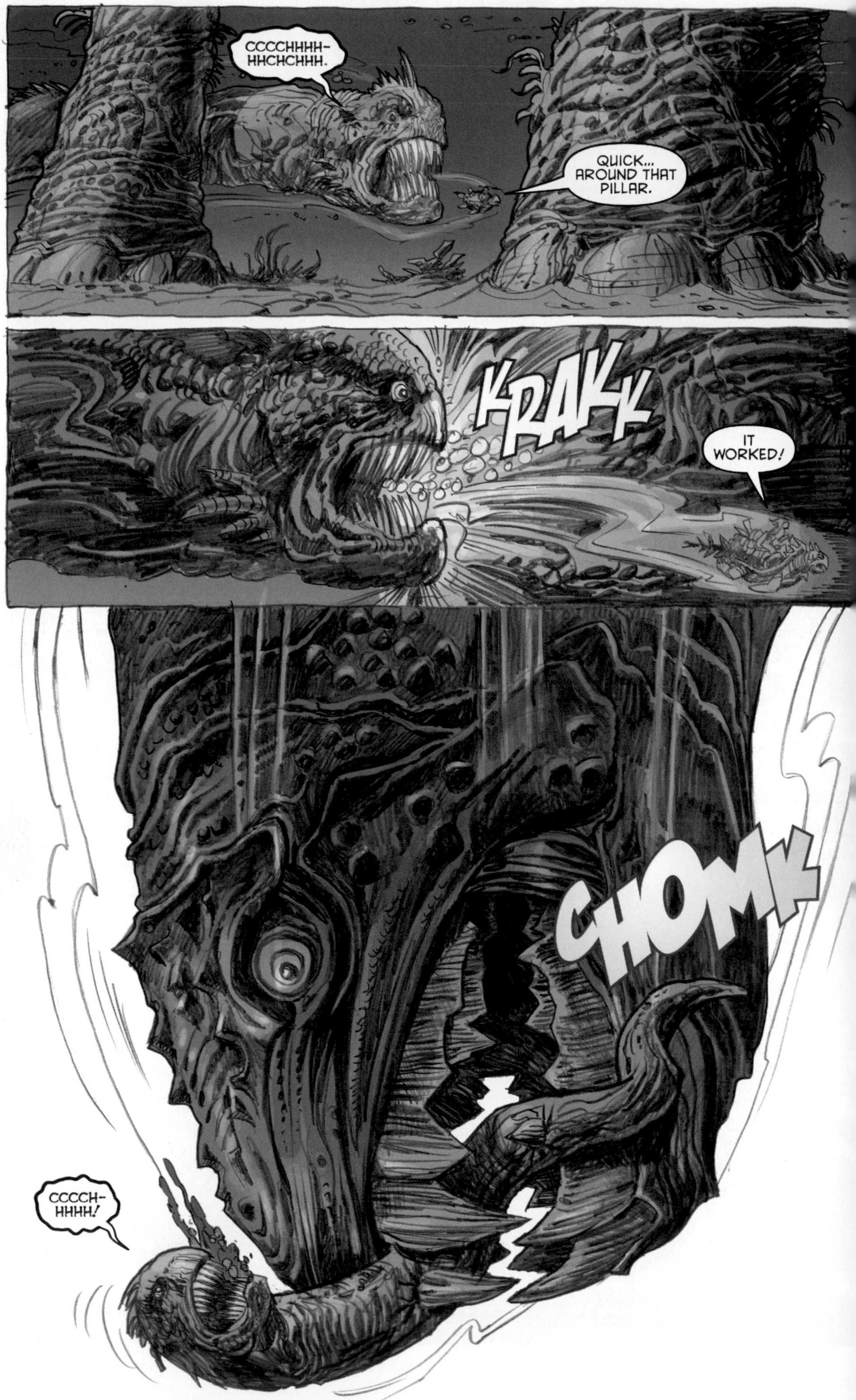

CCCCHHHH-
HHCHCHHH.
QUICK...
AROUND THAT
PILLAR.
KRAKK
IT
WORKED!
CHOMK
CCCCH-
HHHH!

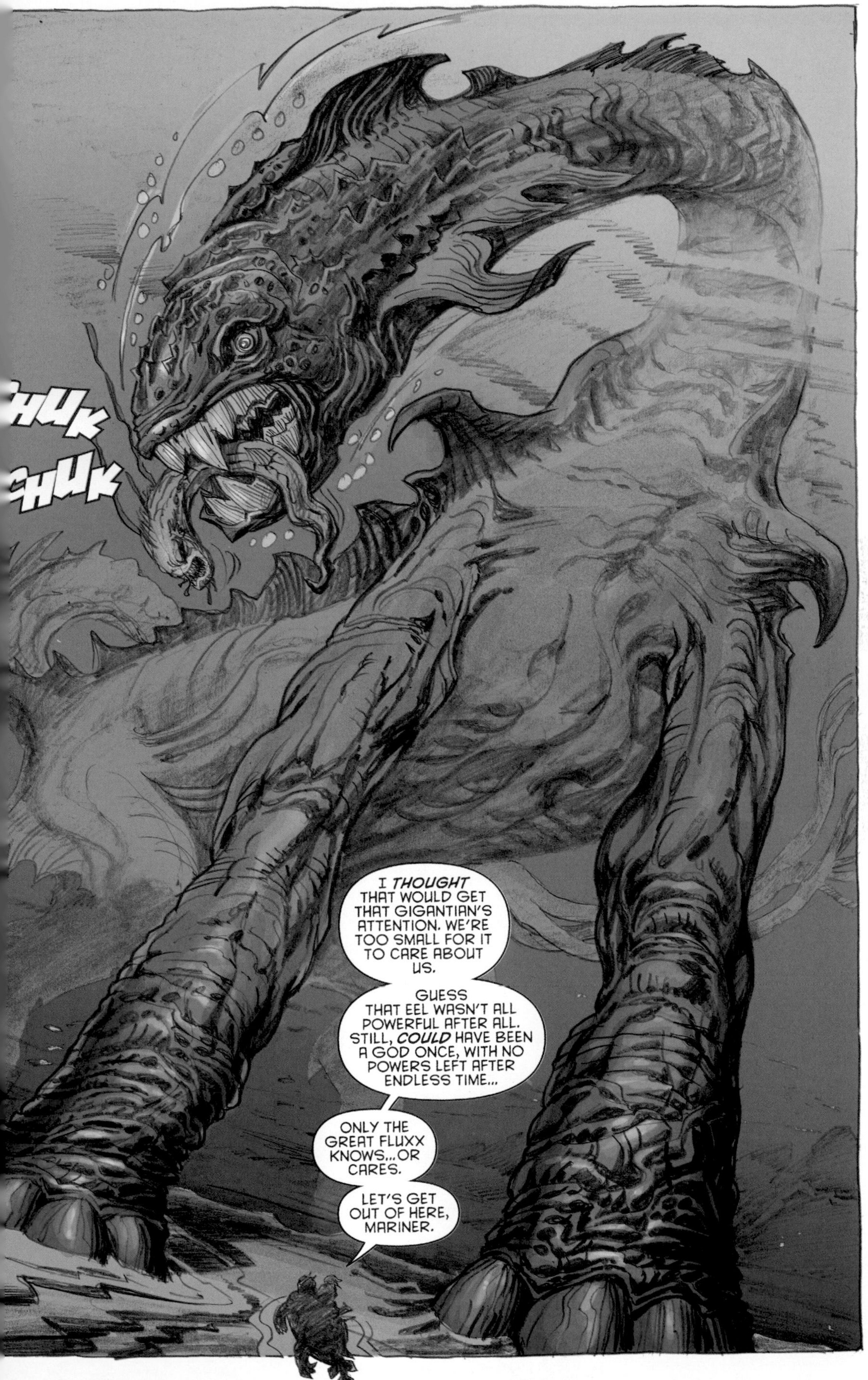

CHUK
CHUK
I *THOUGHT* THAT WOULD GET THAT GIGANTIAN'S ATTENTION. WE'RE TOO SMALL FOR IT TO CARE ABOUT US.
GUESS THAT EEL WASN'T ALL POWERFUL AFTER ALL. STILL, *COULD* HAVE BEEN A GOD ONCE, WITH NO POWERS LEFT AFTER ENDLESS TIME...
ONLY THE GREAT FLUXX KNOWS...OR CARES.
LET'S GET OUT OF HERE, MARINER.

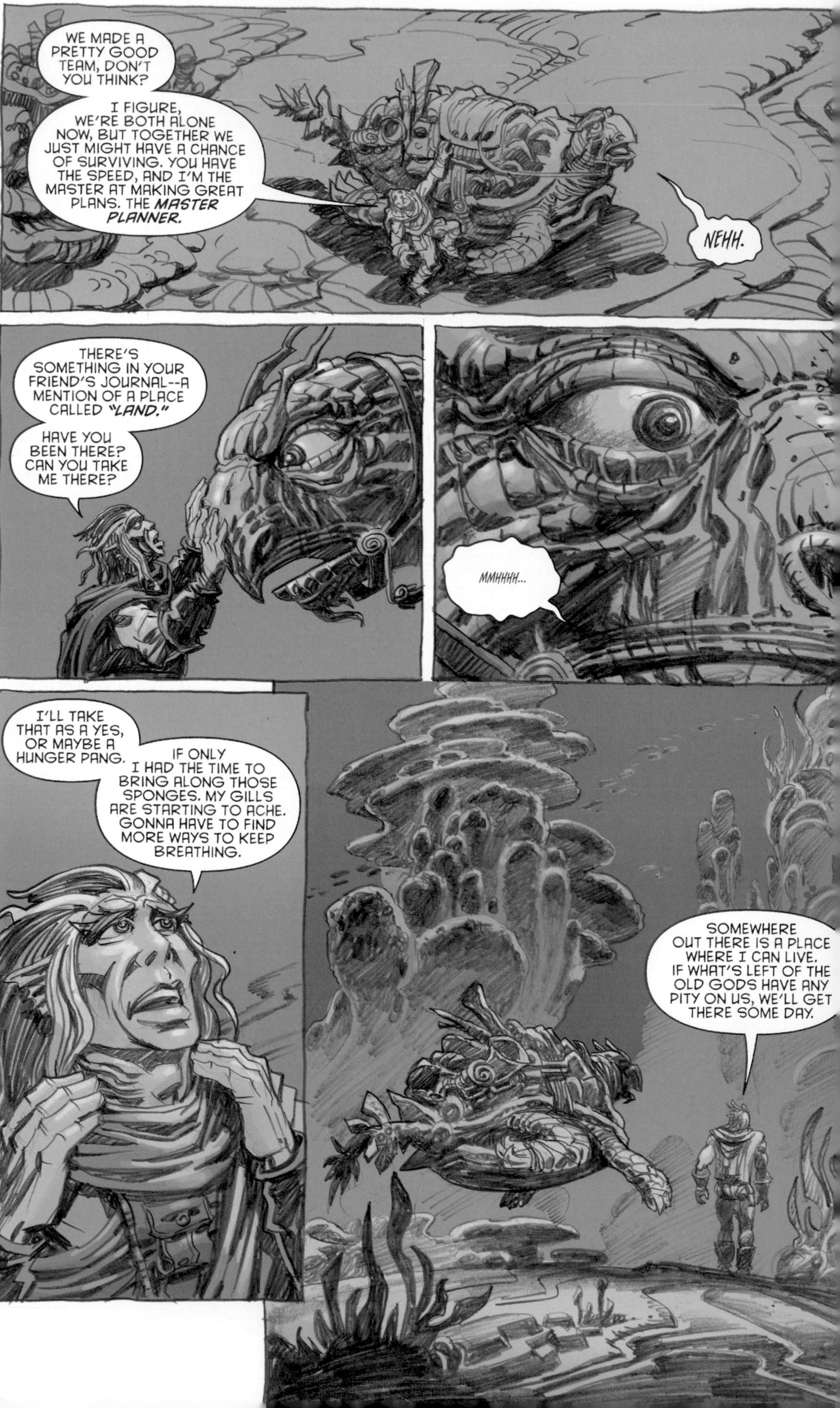
WE MADE A PRETTY GOOD TEAM, DON'T YOU THINK?
I FIGURE, WE'RE BOTH ALONE NOW, BUT TOGETHER WE JUST MIGHT HAVE A CHANCE OF SURVIVING. YOU HAVE THE SPEED, AND I'M THE MASTER AT MAKING GREAT PLANS. THE *MASTER PLANNER.*
NEHH.
THERE'S SOMETHING IN YOUR FRIEND'S JOURNAL--A MENTION OF A PLACE CALLED *"LAND."*
HAVE YOU BEEN THERE? CAN YOU TAKE ME THERE?
MMHHHH...
I'LL TAKE THAT AS A YES, OR MAYBE A HUNGER PANG.
IF ONLY I HAD THE TIME TO BRING ALONG THOSE SPONGES. MY GILLS ARE STARTING TO ACHE. GONNA HAVE TO FIND MORE WAYS TO KEEP BREATHING.
SOMEWHERE OUT THERE IS A PLACE WHERE I CAN LIVE. IF WHAT'S LEFT OF THE OLD GODS HAVE ANY PITY ON US, WE'LL GET THERE SOME DAY.

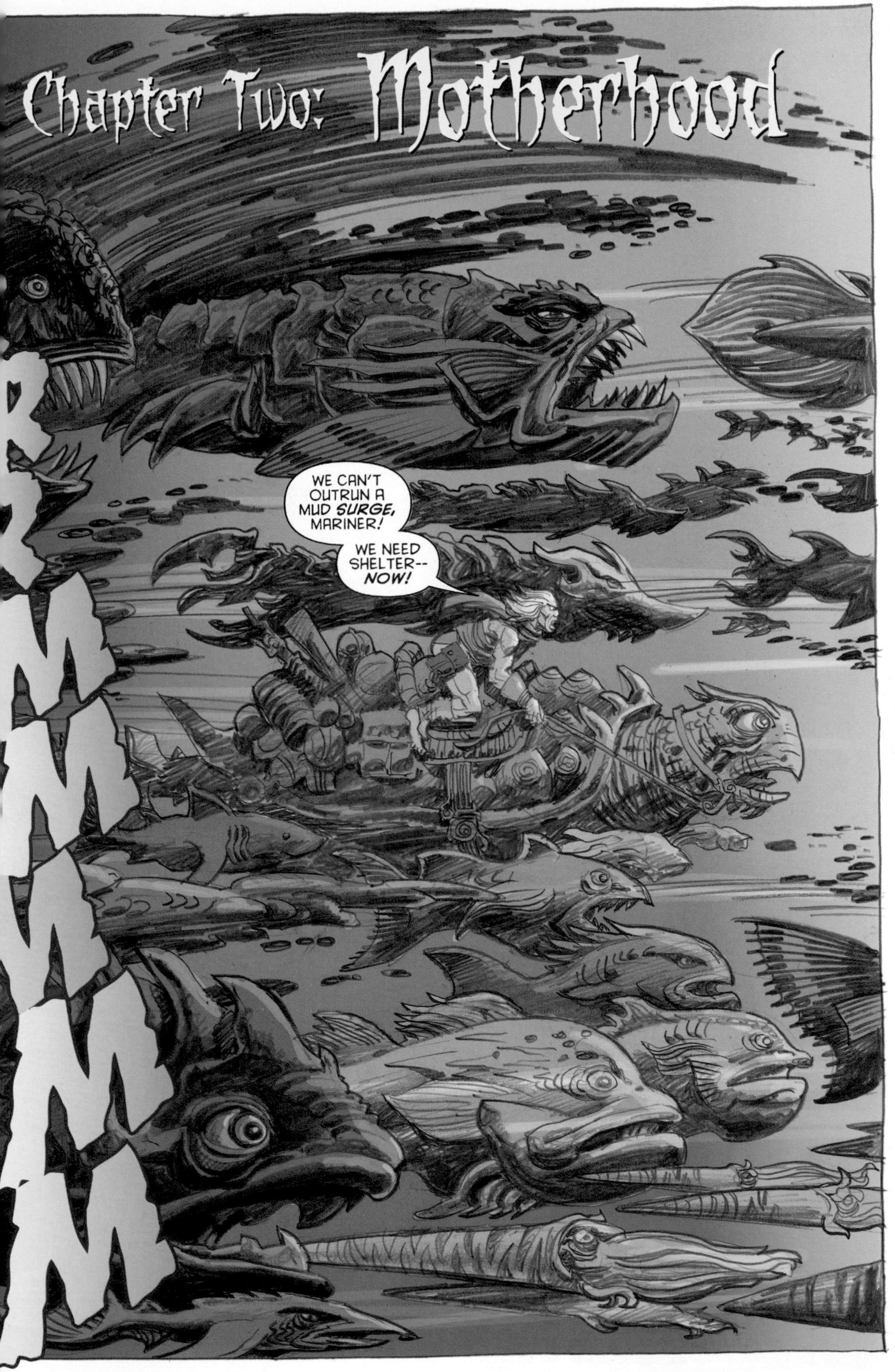
Chapter Two: Motherhood
WE CAN'T OUTRUN A MUD SURGE, MARINER!
WE NEED SHELTER-- NOW!

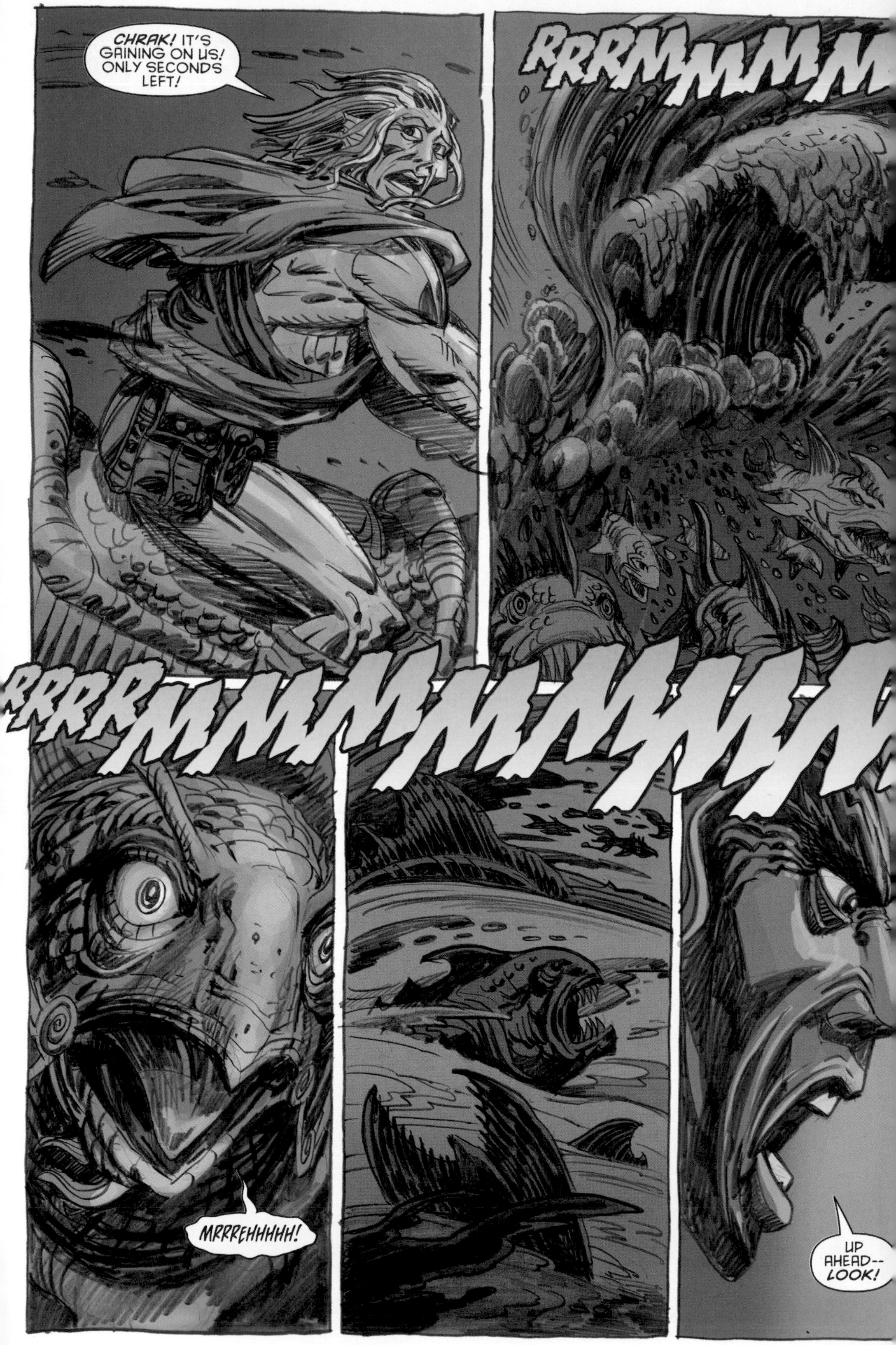
CHRAK! IT'S GAINING ON US! ONLY SECONDS LEFT!
RRRMMMMM
RRRRMMMMMMMMMMMMM
MRRREHHHHH!
UP AHEAD-- LOOK!

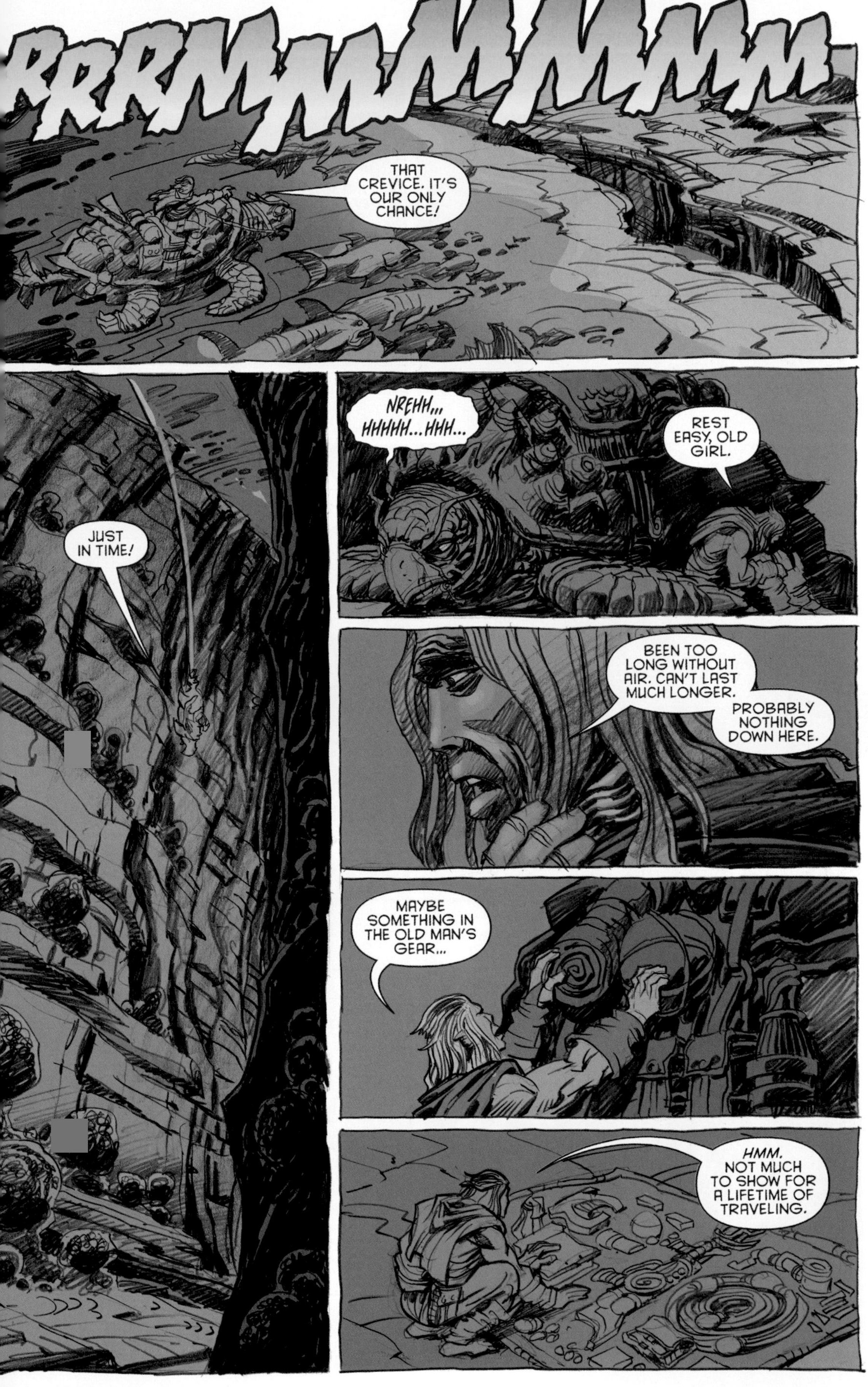
RRRMMMMMMMM
THAT CREVICE. IT'S OUR ONLY CHANCE!
JUST IN TIME!
NREHH,,, HHHHH...HHH...
REST EASY, OLD GIRL.
BEEN TOO LONG WITHOUT AIR. CAN'T LAST MUCH LONGER.
PROBABLY NOTHING DOWN HERE.
MAYBE SOMETHING IN THE OLD MAN'S GEAR...
HMM. NOT MUCH TO SHOW FOR A LIFETIME OF TRAVELING.

RIFLE CARTRIDGES...

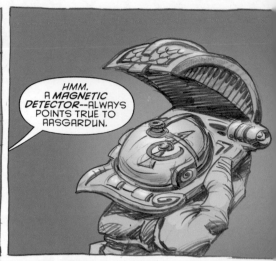

HMM. A *MAGNETIC DETECTOR*--ALWAYS POINTS TRUE TO AASGARDUN.

A RIFLE TO GO WITH THE AMMUNITION...

AHHH... I COULD REALLY USE A MAGNIFIER.

NOTHING TO BREATHE, BUT THE JOURNAL IS ALL THAT MATTERS.

IF THE OLD MAN'S DIRECTIONS CAN LEAD ME TO *"LAND,"* THEY WILL SAVE MY LIFE.

OTHERWISE I'M FISH FOOD.

THE OUTCAST IS A DEAD MAN!

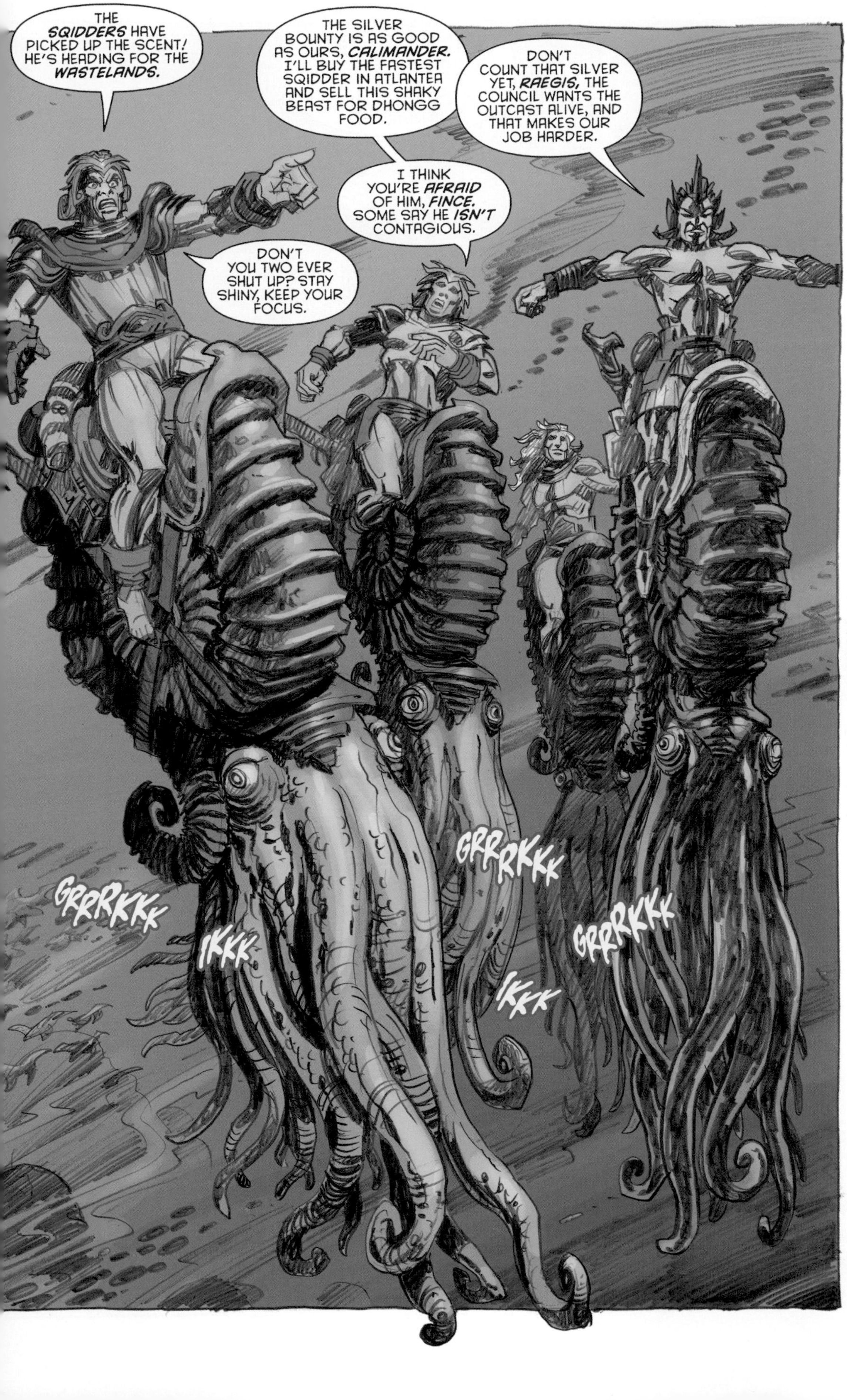
THE SQIDDERS HAVE PICKED UP THE SCENT! HE'S HEADING FOR THE WASTELANDS.
THE SILVER BOUNTY IS AS GOOD AS OURS, CALIMANDER. I'LL BUY THE FASTEST SQIDDER IN ATLANTEA AND SELL THIS SHAKY BEAST FOR DHONGG FOOD.
DON'T COUNT THAT SILVER YET, RAEGIS, THE COUNCIL WANTS THE OUTCAST ALIVE, AND THAT MAKES OUR JOB HARDER.
I THINK YOU'RE AFRAID OF HIM, FINCE. SOME SAY HE ISN'T CONTAGIOUS.
DON'T YOU TWO EVER SHUT UP? STAY SHINY, KEEP YOUR FOCUS.
GRRRKKK
GRRRKKK
IKKK
GRRRKKK
IKKK

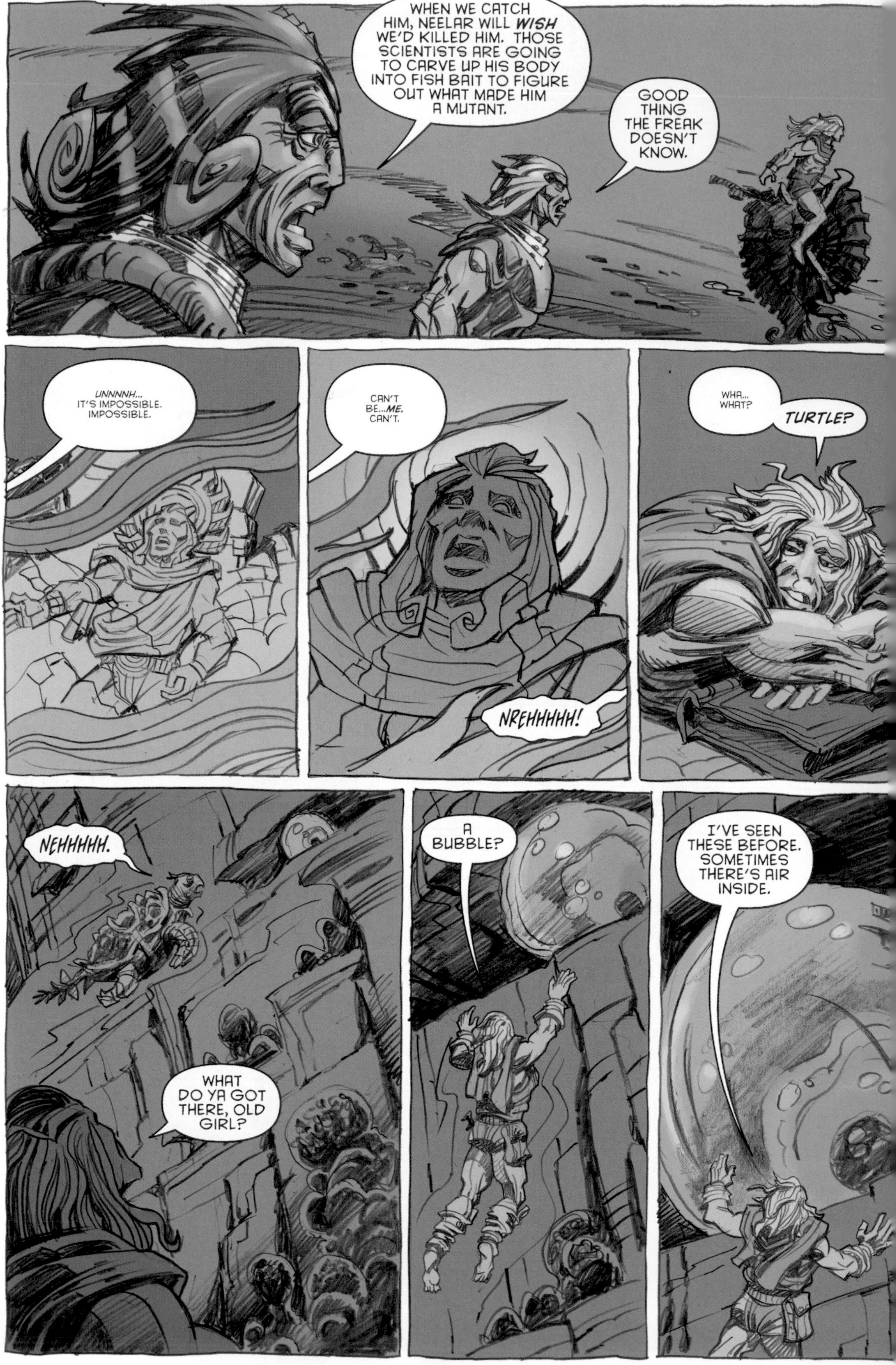
WHEN WE CATCH HIM, NEELAR WILL WISH WE'D KILLED HIM. THOSE SCIENTISTS ARE GOING TO CARVE UP HIS BODY INTO FISH BAIT TO FIGURE OUT WHAT MADE HIM A MUTANT.
GOOD THING THE FREAK DOESN'T KNOW.
UNNNNH... IT'S IMPOSSIBLE. IMPOSSIBLE.
CAN'T BE...ME. CAN'T.
NREHHHHH!
WHA... WHAT?
TURTLE?
NEHHHHH.
WHAT DO YA GOT THERE, OLD GIRL?
A BUBBLE?
I'VE SEEN THESE BEFORE. SOMETIMES THERE'S AIR INSIDE.

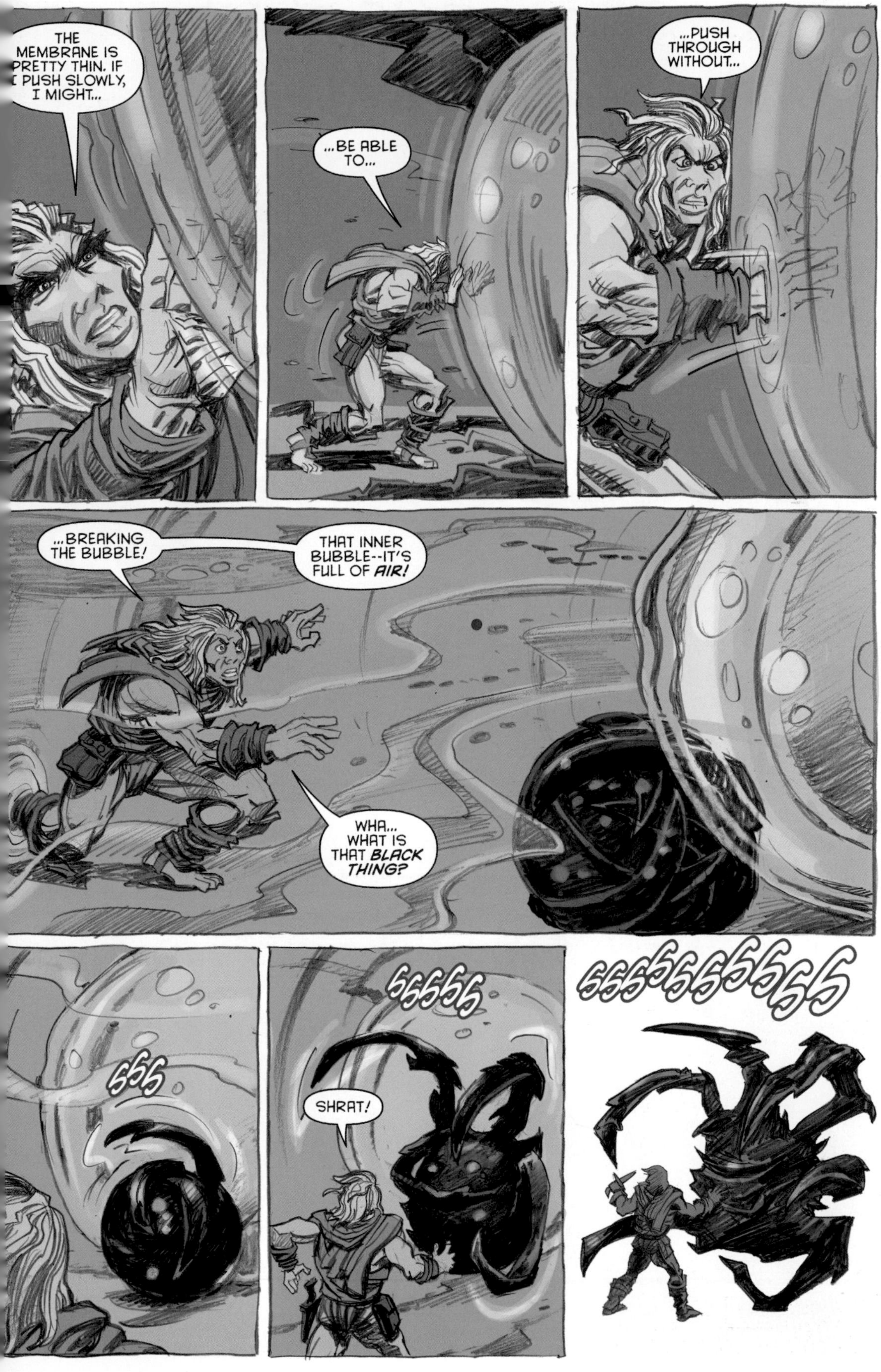
THE MEMBRANE IS PRETTY THIN. IF I PUSH SLOWLY, I MIGHT...
...BE ABLE TO...
...PUSH THROUGH WITHOUT...
...BREAKING THE BUBBLE!
THAT INNER BUBBLE--IT'S FULL OF AIR!
WHA... WHAT IS THAT BLACK THING?
SSS
SSSSS
SHRAT!
SSSSSSSSSSSS

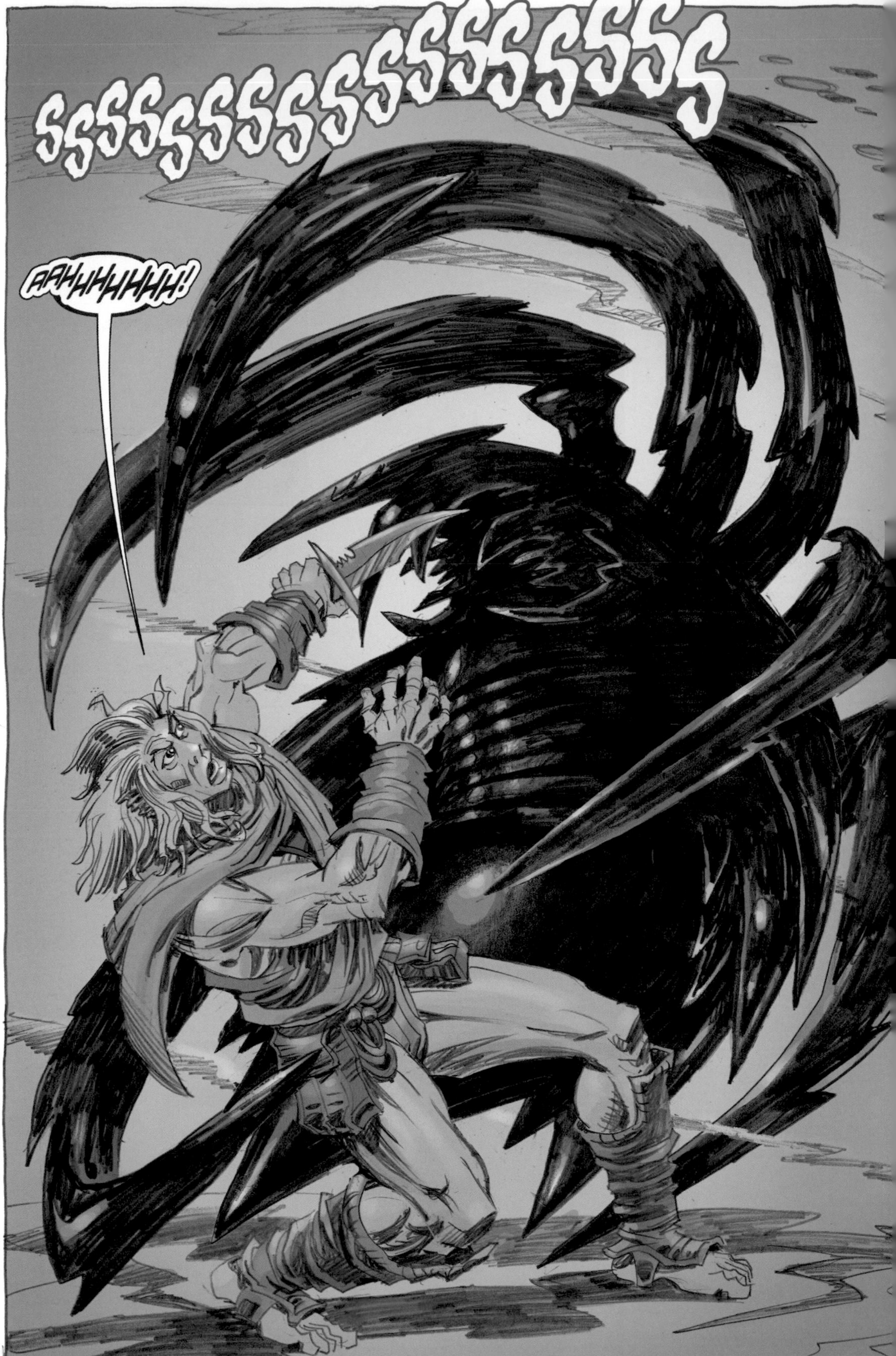

SSSSSSSSSSSSSSSS
AAHHHHHHH!

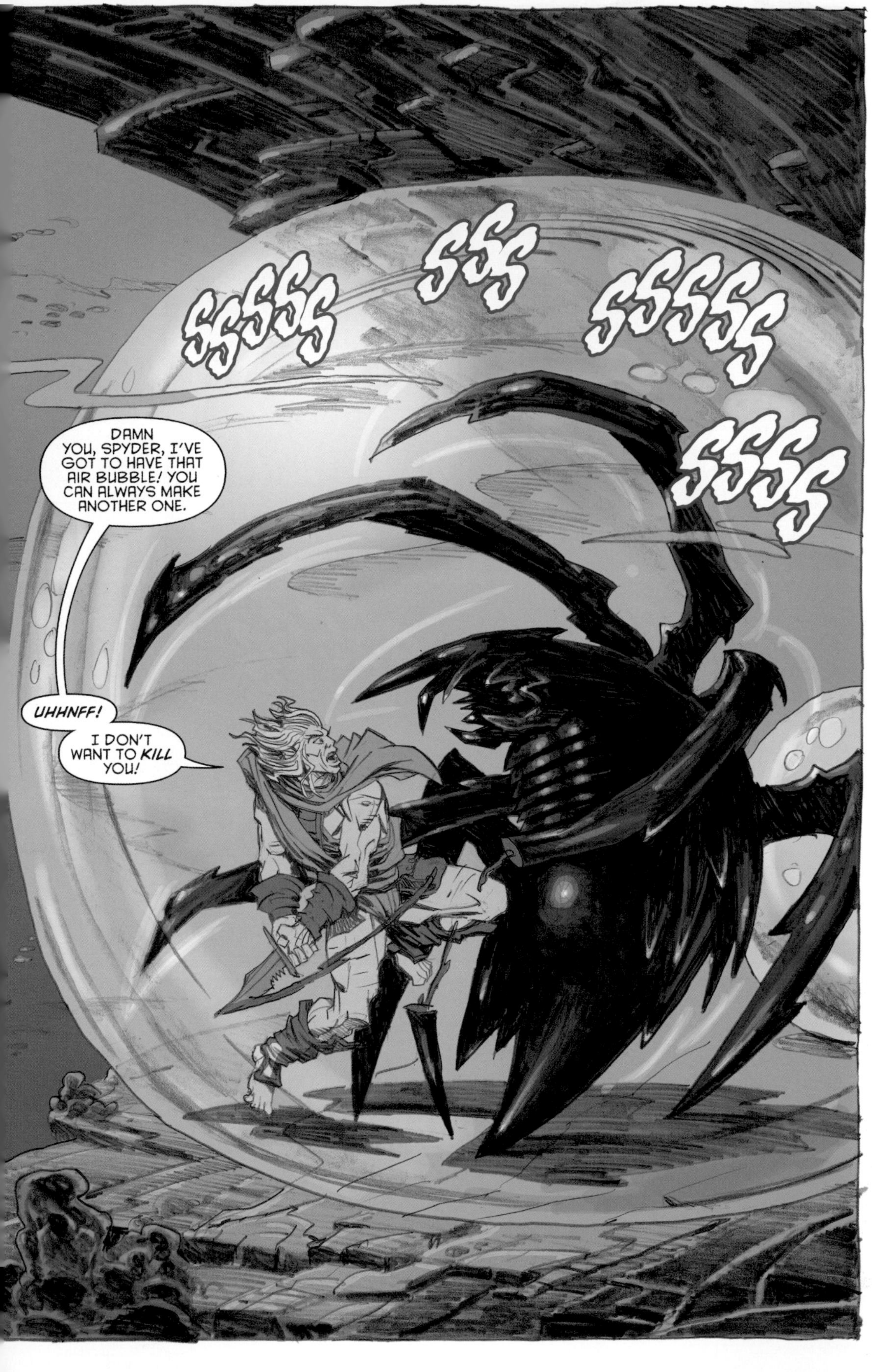
SSSSS
SSS
SSSSS
SSSS
DAMN YOU, SPYDER, I'VE GOT TO HAVE THAT AIR BUBBLE! YOU CAN ALWAYS MAKE ANOTHER ONE.
UHHNFF!
I DON'T WANT TO *KILL* YOU!

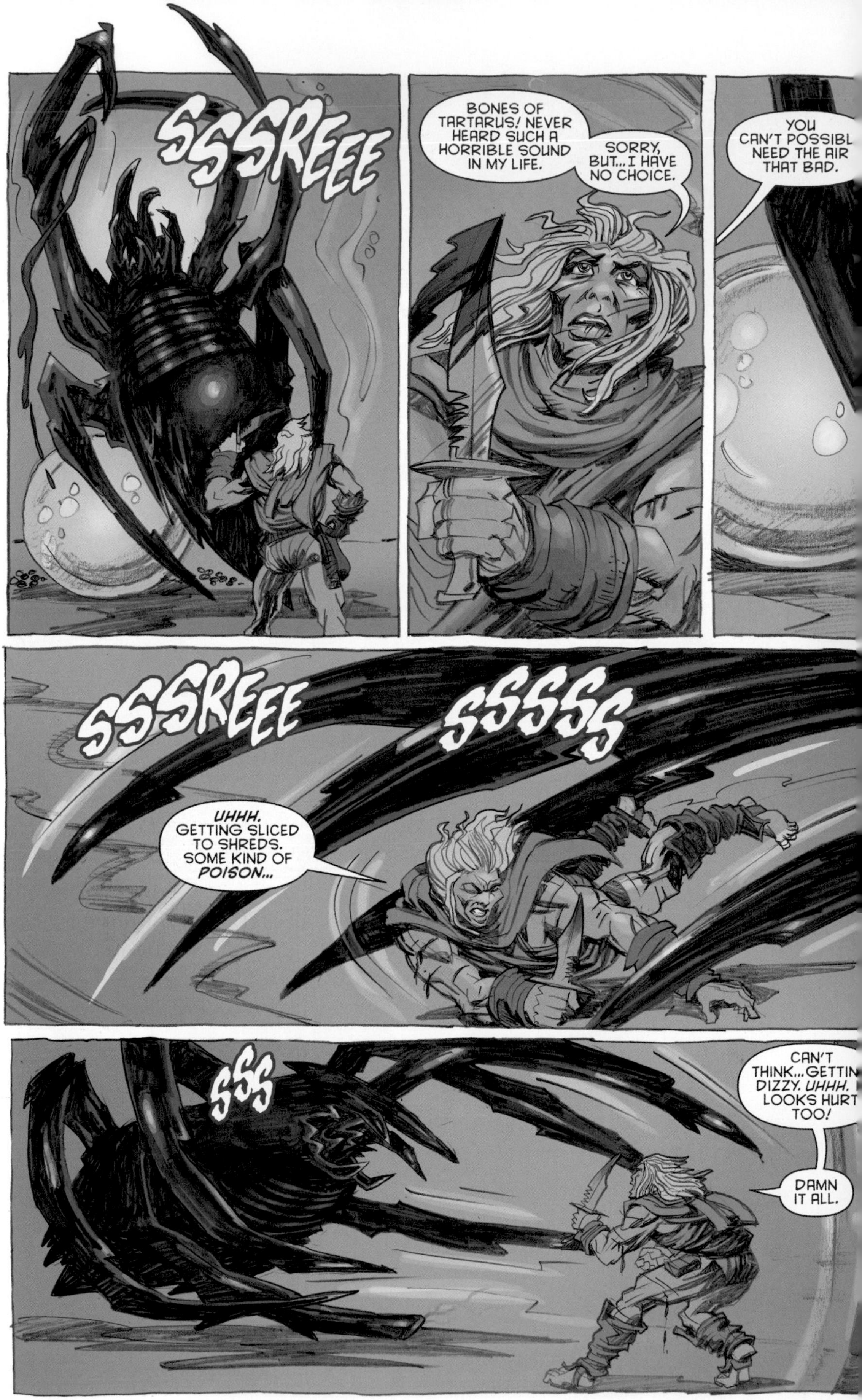
SSSREEE
BONES OF TARTARUS! NEVER HEARD SUCH A HORRIBLE SOUND IN MY LIFE.
SORRY, BUT... I HAVE NO CHOICE.
YOU CAN'T POSSIBL NEED THE AIR THAT BAD.
SSSREEE
SSSSS
UHHH. GETTING SLICED TO SHREDS. SOME KIND OF *POISON...*
SSS
CAN'T THINK... GETTIN DIZZY. *UHHH.* LOOKS HURT TOO!
DAMN IT ALL.

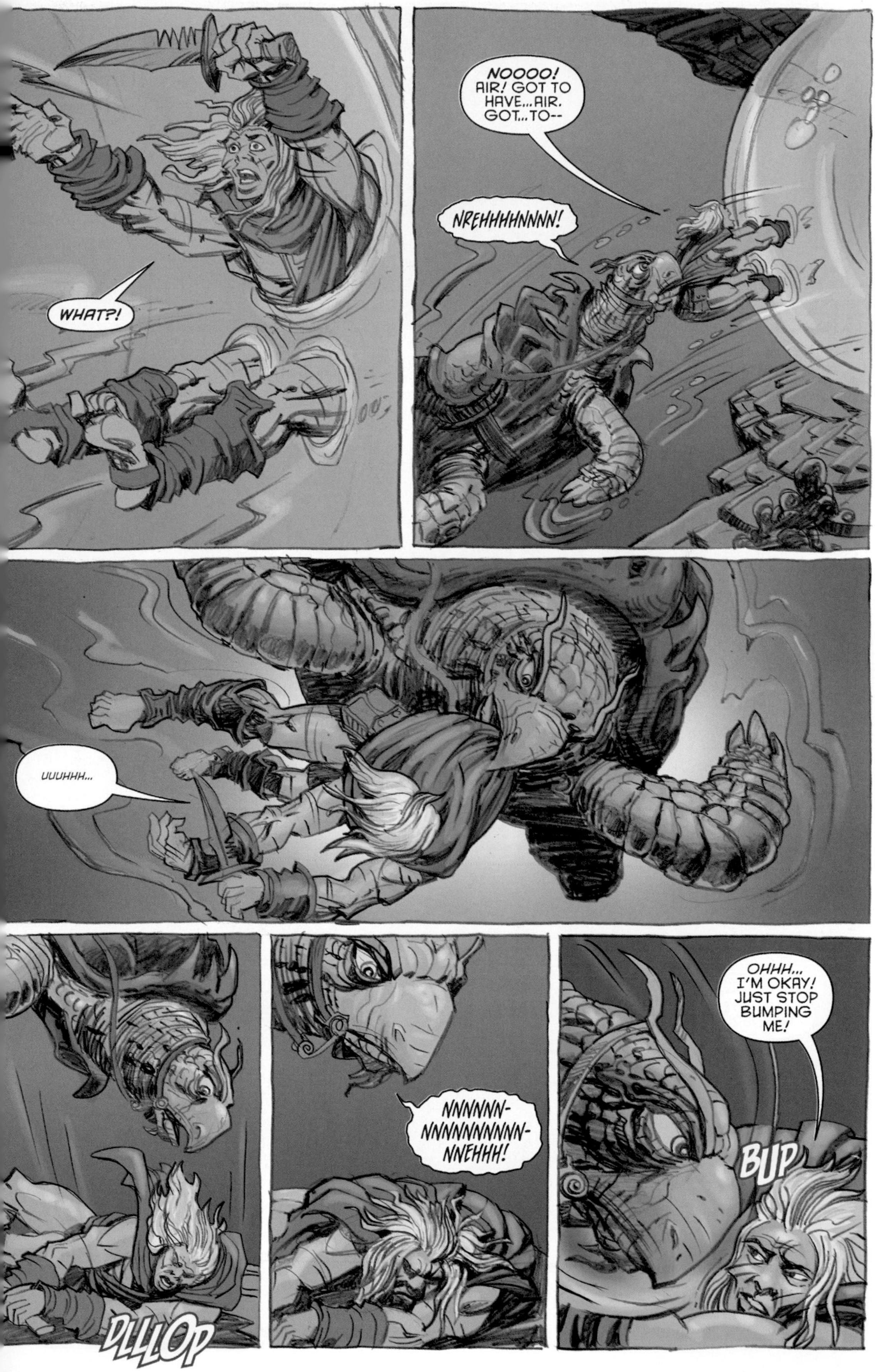
WHAT?!
NOOOO! AIR! GOT TO HAVE...AIR. GOT...TO--
NREHHHHNNNN!
UUUHHH...
DLLLOP
NNNNNN-NNNNNNNNNN-NNEHHH!
OHHH... I'M OKAY! JUST STOP BUMPING ME!
BUP

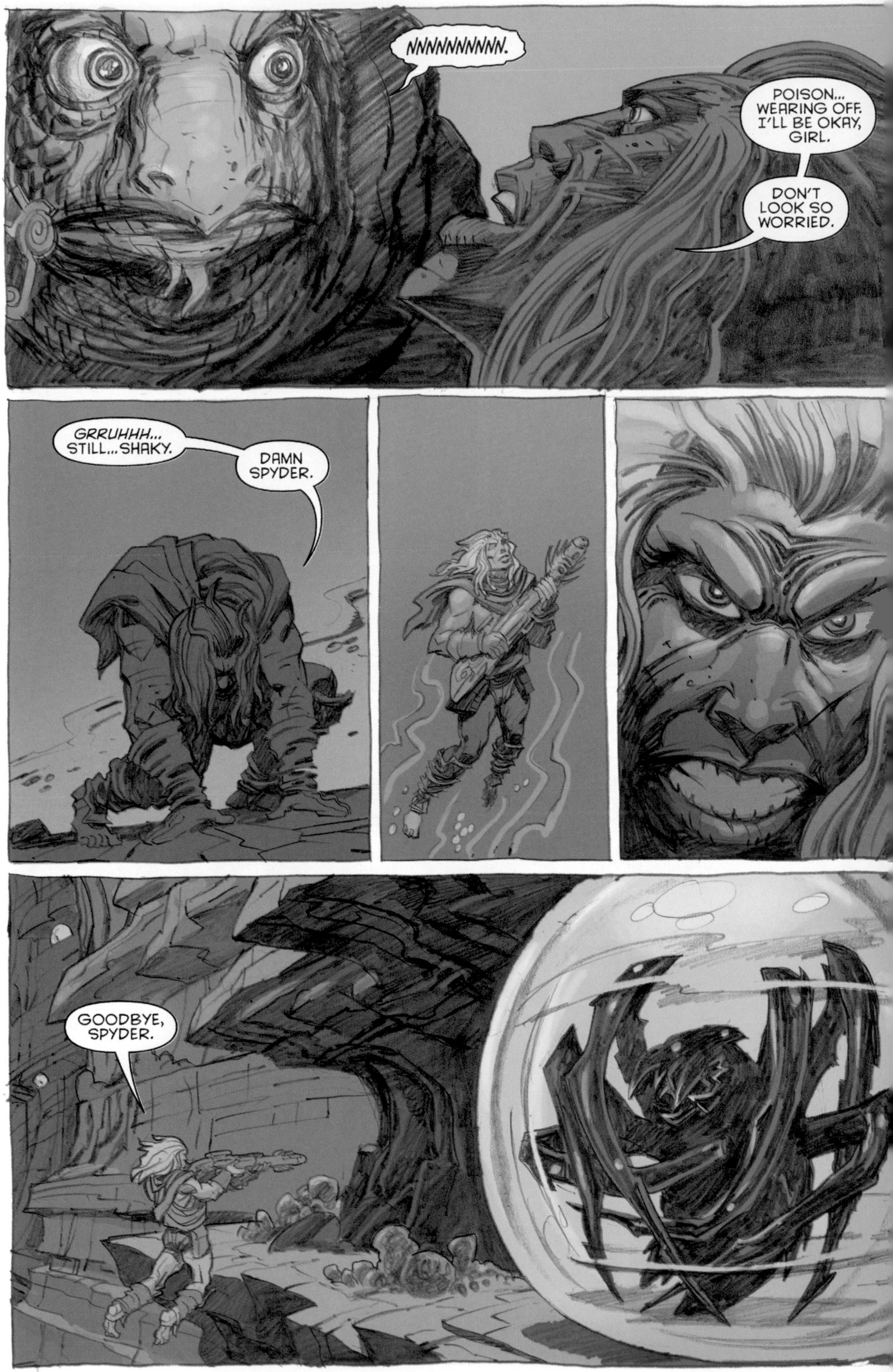
NNNNNNNNNN.
POISON... WEARING OFF. I'LL BE OKAY, GIRL.
DON'T LOOK SO WORRIED.
GRRUHHH... STILL... SHAKY.
DAMN SPYDER.
GOODBYE, SPYDER.

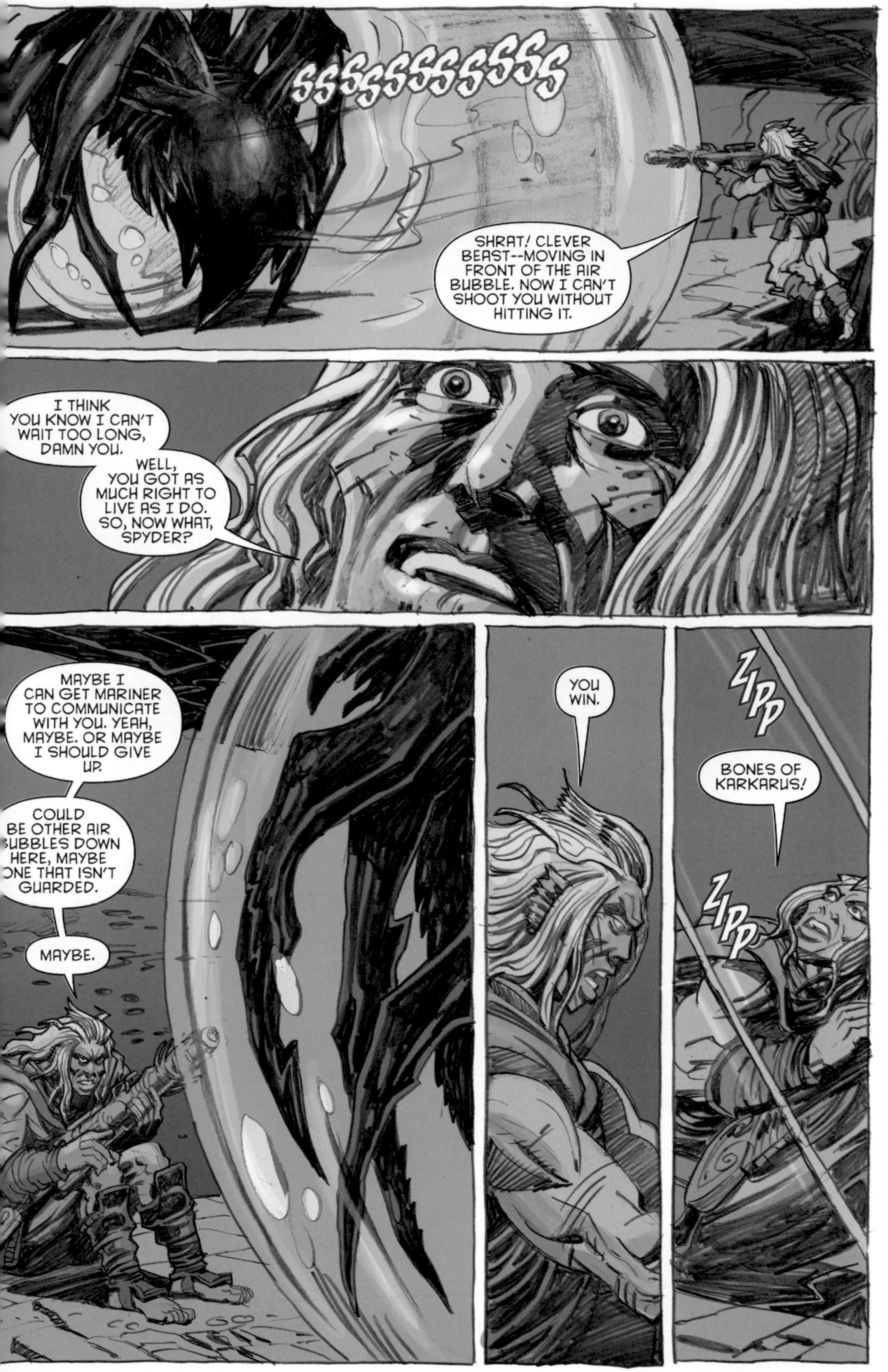
SSSSSSSSSSSS
SHRAT! CLEVER BEAST--MOVING IN FRONT OF THE AIR BUBBLE. NOW I CAN'T SHOOT YOU WITHOUT HITTING IT.
I THINK YOU KNOW I CAN'T WAIT TOO LONG, DAMN YOU.
WELL, YOU GOT AS MUCH RIGHT TO LIVE AS I DO. SO, NOW WHAT, SPYDER?
MAYBE I CAN GET MARINER TO COMMUNICATE WITH YOU. YEAH, MAYBE. OR MAYBE I SHOULD GIVE UP.
COULD BE OTHER AIR BUBBLES DOWN HERE, MAYBE ONE THAT ISN'T GUARDED.
MAYBE.
YOU WIN.
ZIPP
BONES OF KARKARUS!
ZIPP

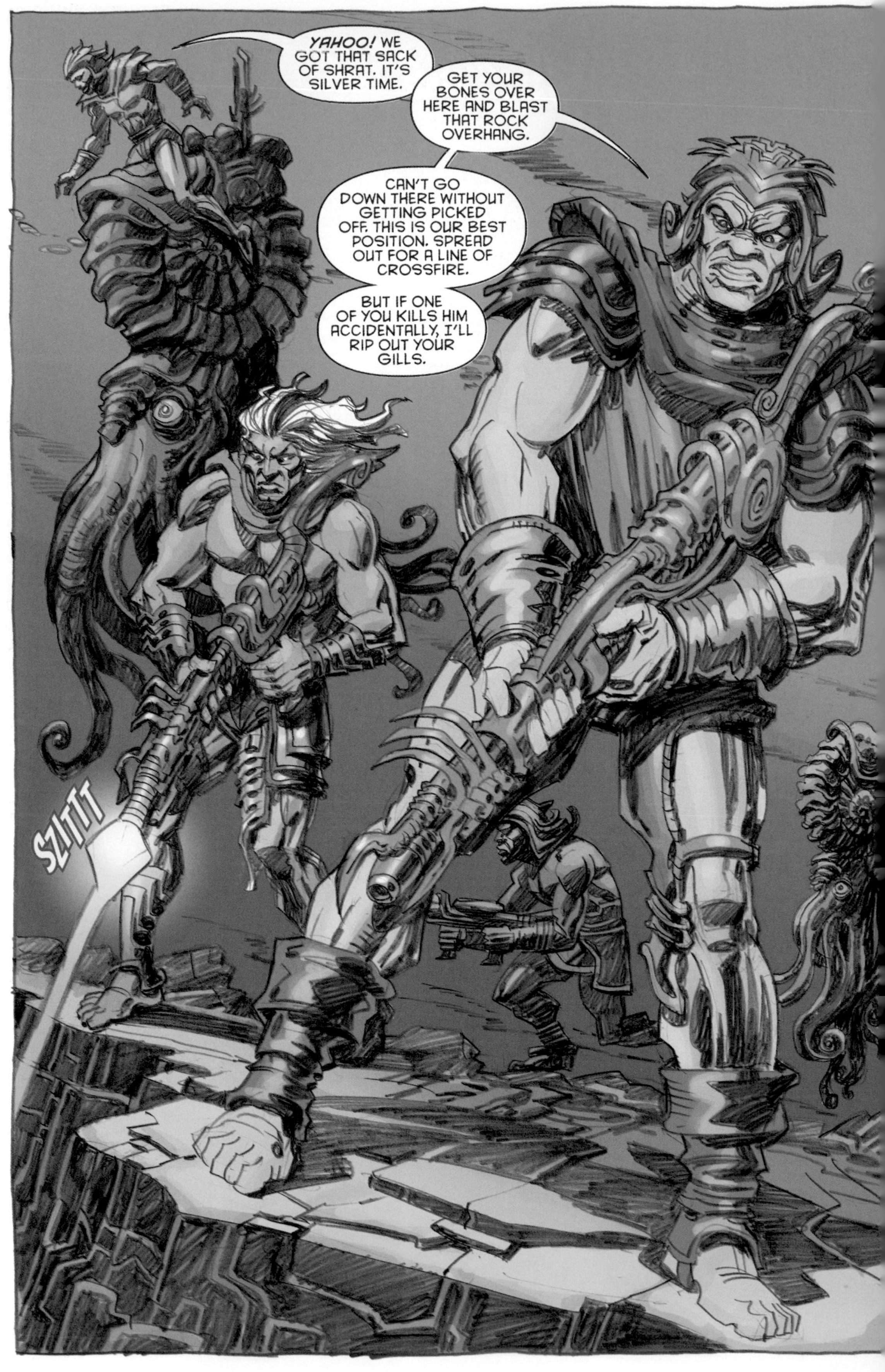

YAHOO! WE GOT THAT SACK OF SHRAT. IT'S SILVER TIME.
GET YOUR BONES OVER HERE AND BLAST THAT ROCK OVERHANG.
CAN'T GO DOWN THERE WITHOUT GETTING PICKED OFF. THIS IS OUR BEST POSITION. SPREAD OUT FOR A LINE OF CROSSFIRE.
BUT IF ONE OF YOU KILLS HIM ACCIDENTALLY, I'LL RIP OUT YOUR GILLS.
SZITTT

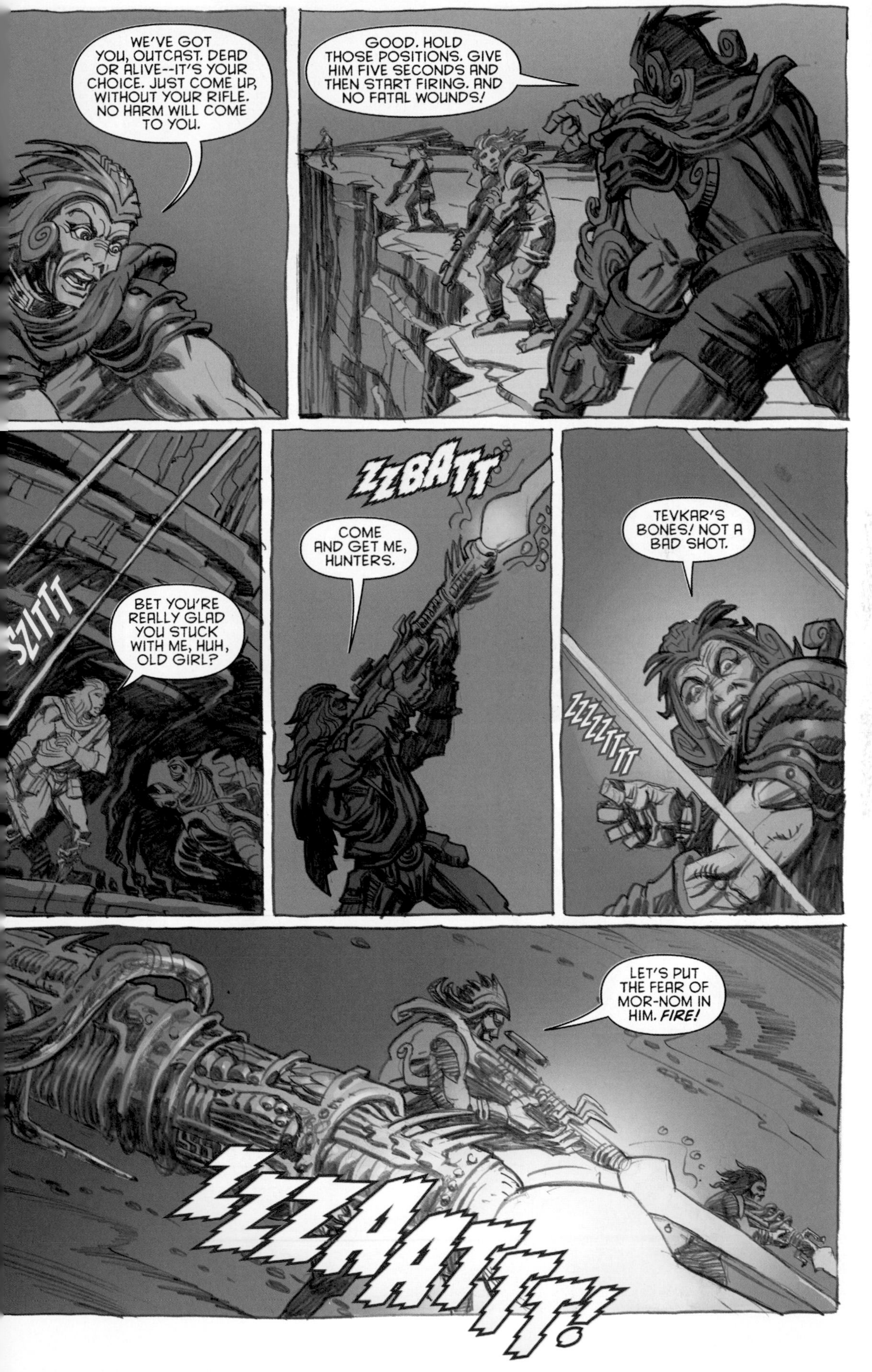
WE'VE GOT YOU, OUTCAST. DEAD OR ALIVE--IT'S YOUR CHOICE. JUST COME UP, WITHOUT YOUR RIFLE. NO HARM WILL COME TO YOU.
GOOD. HOLD THOSE POSITIONS. GIVE HIM FIVE SECONDS AND THEN START FIRING. AND NO FATAL WOUNDS!
SZITTT
BET YOU'RE REALLY GLAD YOU STUCK WITH ME, HUH, OLD GIRL?
ZZBATT
COME AND GET ME, HUNTERS.
TEVKAR'S BONES! NOT A BAD SHOT.
ZZZZZTTTT
LET'S PUT THE FEAR OF MOR-NOM IN HIM. *FIRE!*
ZZZATTTT!

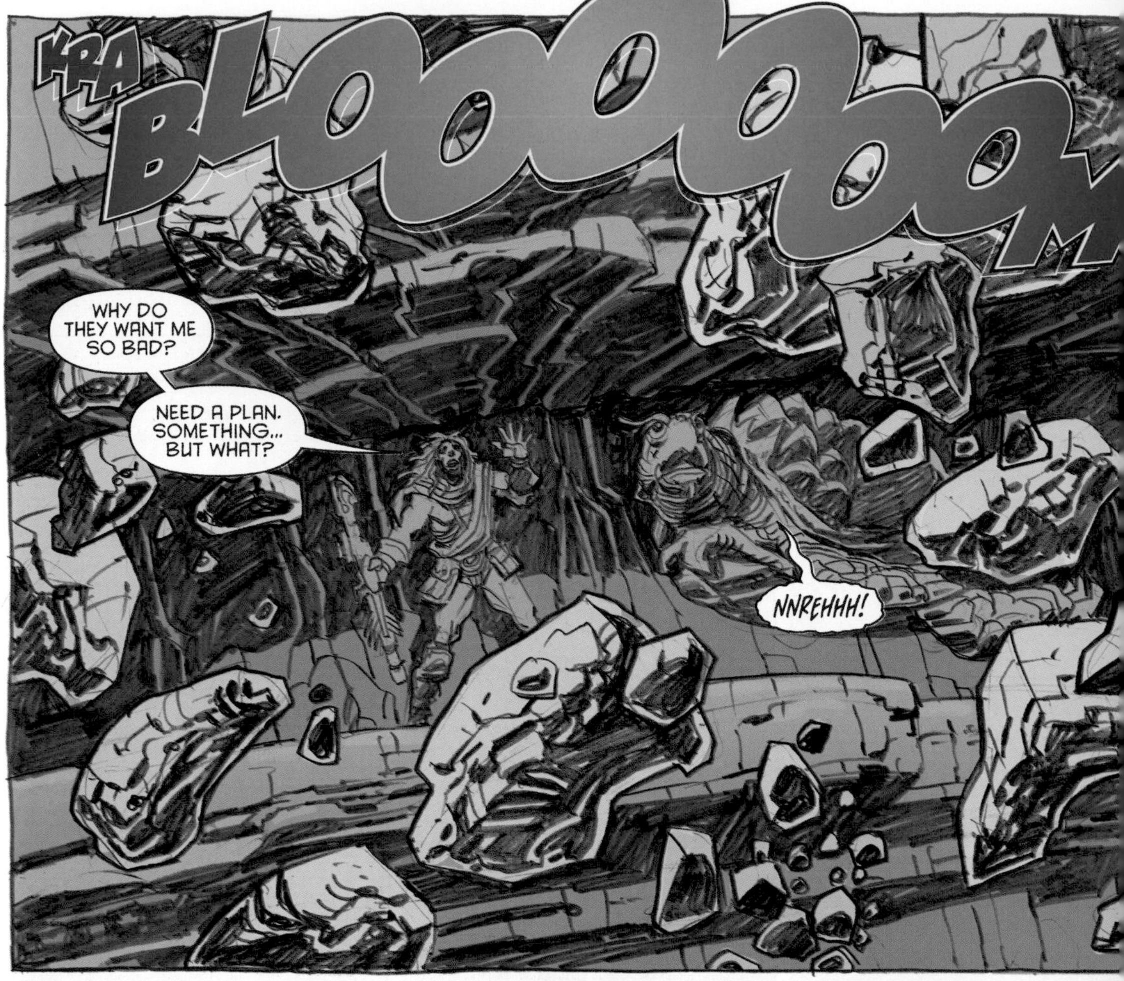
KRA
BLOOOOOM
WHY DO THEY WANT ME SO BAD?
NEED A PLAN. SOMETHING... BUT WHAT?
NNREHHH!
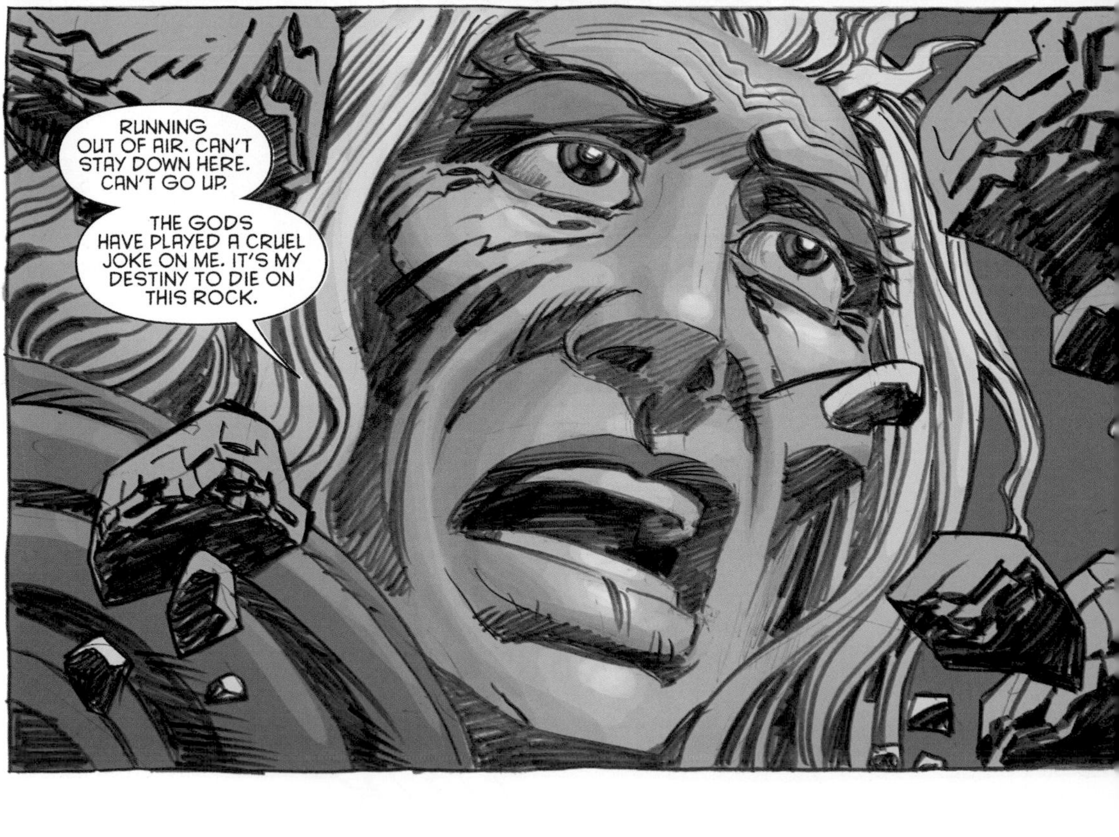
RUNNING OUT OF AIR. CAN'T STAY DOWN HERE. CAN'T GO UP.
THE GODS HAVE PLAYED A CRUEL JOKE ON ME. IT'S MY DESTINY TO DIE ON THIS ROCK.

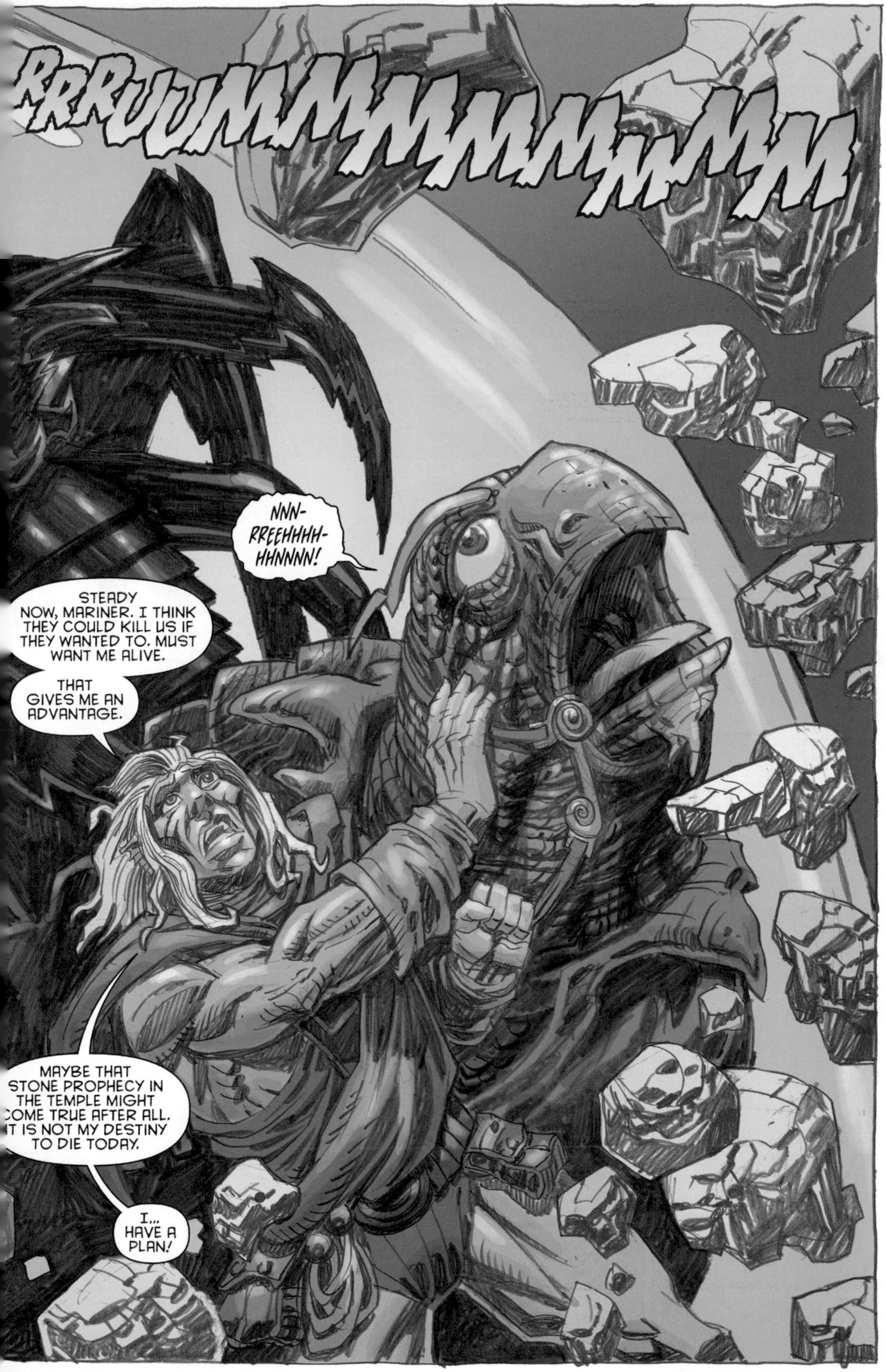
RRRUUMMMMMMMMMMMMMMM
NNN-RREEHHHH-HHNNNN!
STEADY NOW, MARINER. I THINK THEY COULD KILL US IF THEY WANTED TO. MUST WANT ME ALIVE.
THAT GIVES ME AN ADVANTAGE.
MAYBE THAT STONE PROPHECY IN THE TEMPLE MIGHT COME TRUE AFTER ALL. IT IS NOT MY DESTINY TO DIE TODAY.
I... HAVE A PLAN!

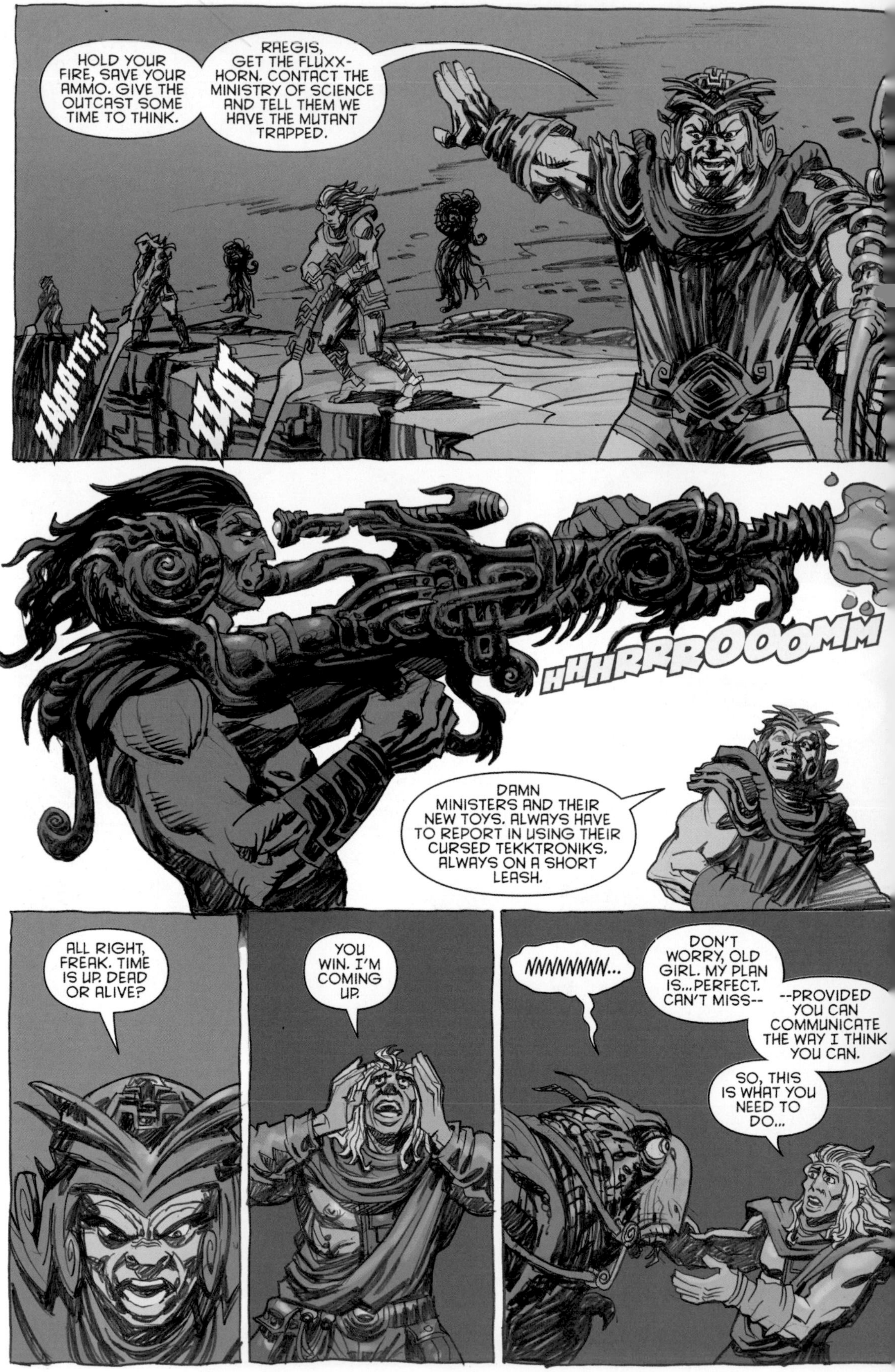
HOLD YOUR FIRE, SAVE YOUR AMMO. GIVE THE OUTCAST SOME TIME TO THINK.
RAEGIS, GET THE FLUXX-HORN. CONTACT THE MINISTRY OF SCIENCE AND TELL THEM WE HAVE THE MUTANT TRAPPED.
ZRATTTT
ZZAT
HHHRRROOOMM
DAMN MINISTERS AND THEIR NEW TOYS. ALWAYS HAVE TO REPORT IN USING THEIR CURSED TEKKTRONIKS. ALWAYS ON A SHORT LEASH.
ALL RIGHT, FREAK. TIME IS UP. DEAD OR ALIVE?
YOU WIN. I'M COMING UP.
NNNNNNNN...
DON'T WORRY, OLD GIRL. MY PLAN IS...PERFECT. CAN'T MISS--
--PROVIDED YOU CAN COMMUNICATE THE WAY I THINK YOU CAN.
SO, THIS IS WHAT YOU NEED TO DO...

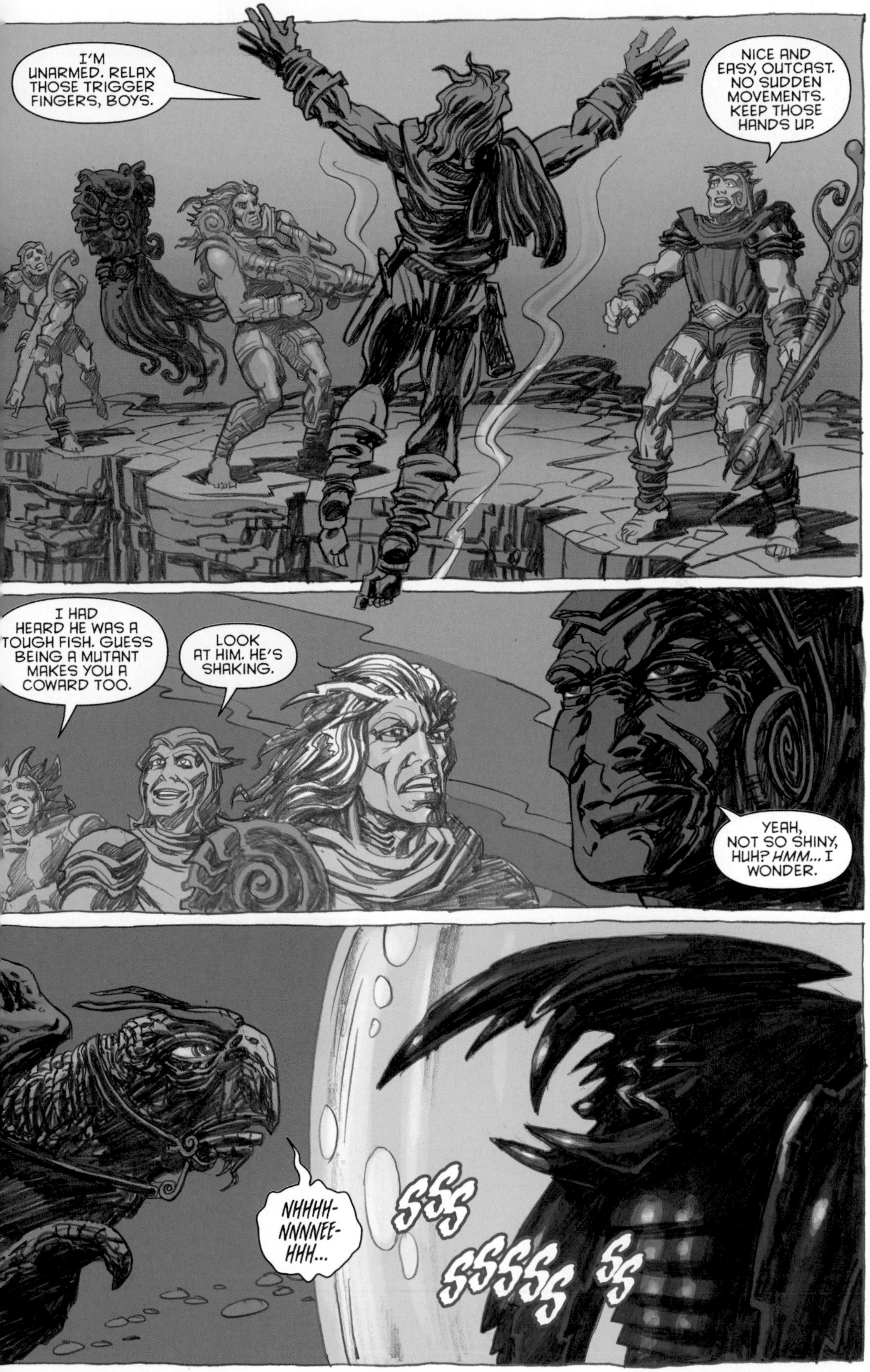
I'M UNARMED. RELAX THOSE TRIGGER FINGERS, BOYS.
NICE AND EASY, OUTCAST. NO SUDDEN MOVEMENTS. KEEP THOSE HANDS UP.
I HAD HEARD HE WAS A TOUGH FISH. GUESS BEING A MUTANT MAKES YOU A COWARD TOO.
LOOK AT HIM. HE'S SHAKING.
YEAH, NOT SO SHINY, HUH? *HMM...* I WONDER.
NHHHH-NNNNEE-HHH...
SSS
SSSSS SS

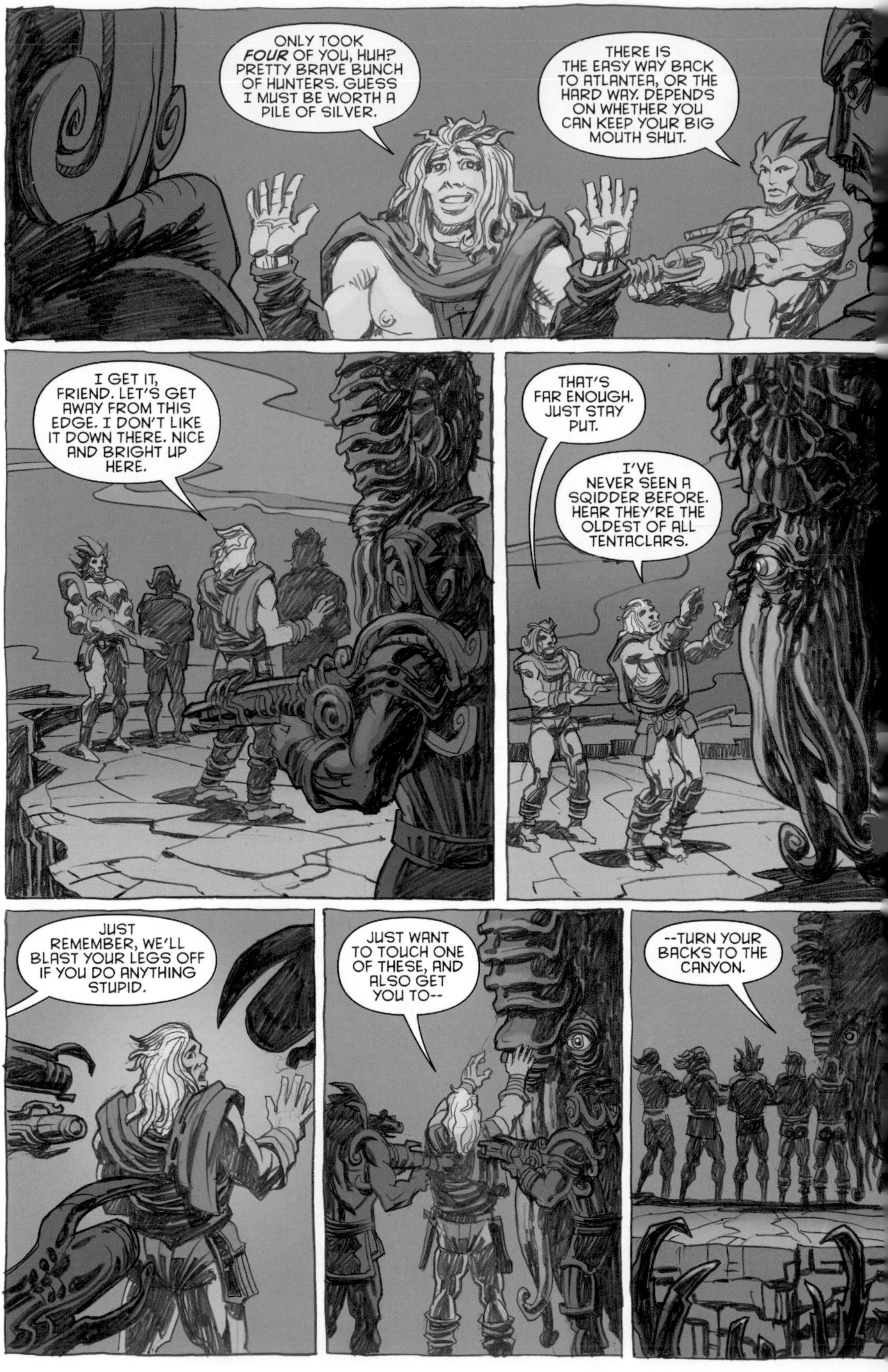
ONLY TOOK FOUR OF YOU, HUH? PRETTY BRAVE BUNCH OF HUNTERS. GUESS I MUST BE WORTH A PILE OF SILVER.
THERE IS THE EASY WAY BACK TO ATLANTEA, OR THE HARD WAY. DEPENDS ON WHETHER YOU CAN KEEP YOUR BIG MOUTH SHUT.
I GET IT, FRIEND. LET'S GET AWAY FROM THIS EDGE. I DON'T LIKE IT DOWN THERE. NICE AND BRIGHT UP HERE.
THAT'S FAR ENOUGH. JUST STAY PUT.
I'VE NEVER SEEN A SQIDDER BEFORE. HEAR THEY'RE THE OLDEST OF ALL TENTACLARS.
JUST REMEMBER, WE'LL BLAST YOUR LEGS OFF IF YOU DO ANYTHING STUPID.
JUST WANT TO TOUCH ONE OF THESE, AND ALSO GET YOU TO--
--TURN YOUR BACKS TO THE CANYON.

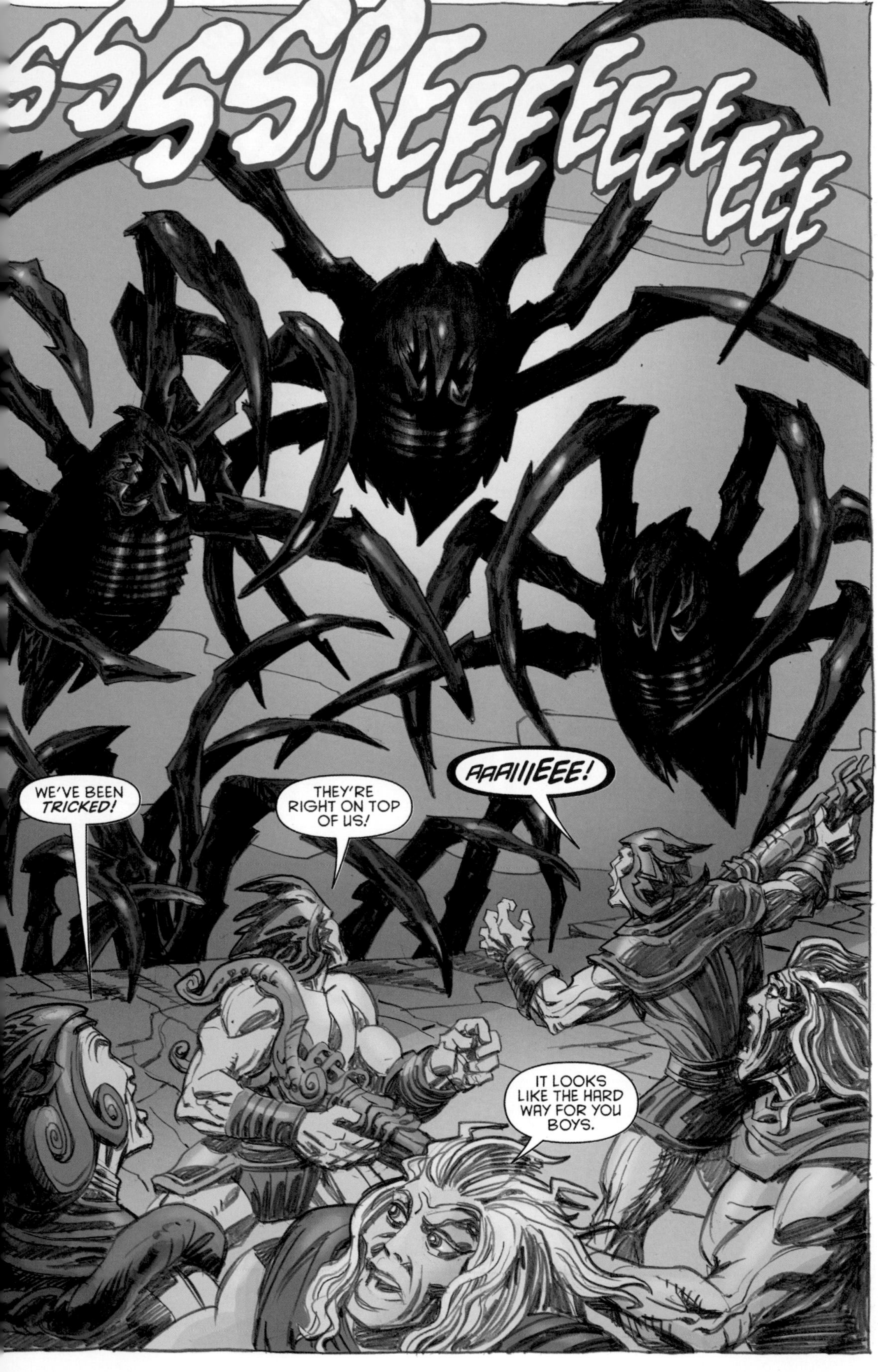
SSSSREEEEEEEEEEE
WE'VE BEEN TRICKED!
THEY'RE RIGHT ON TOP OF US!
AAAIIIEEE!
IT LOOKS LIKE THE HARD WAY FOR YOU BOYS.

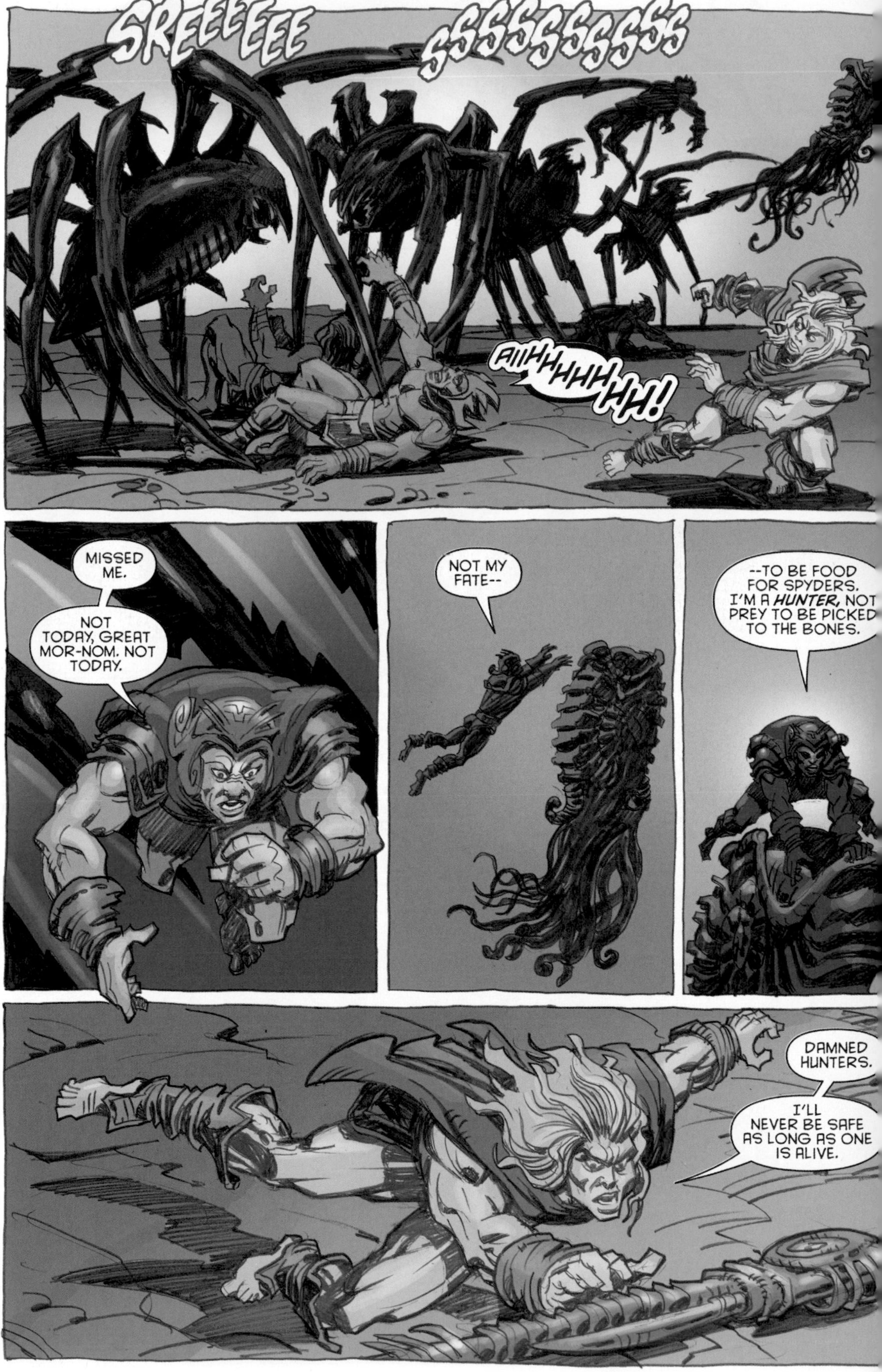
SREEEEEE
SSSSSSSSSS
AIIHHHHHHH!
MISSED ME.
NOT TODAY, GREAT MOR-NOM. NOT TODAY.
NOT MY FATE--
--TO BE FOOD FOR SPYDERS. I'M A *HUNTER,* NOT PREY TO BE PICKED TO THE BONES.
DAMNED HUNTERS.
I'LL NEVER BE SAFE AS LONG AS ONE IS ALIVE.

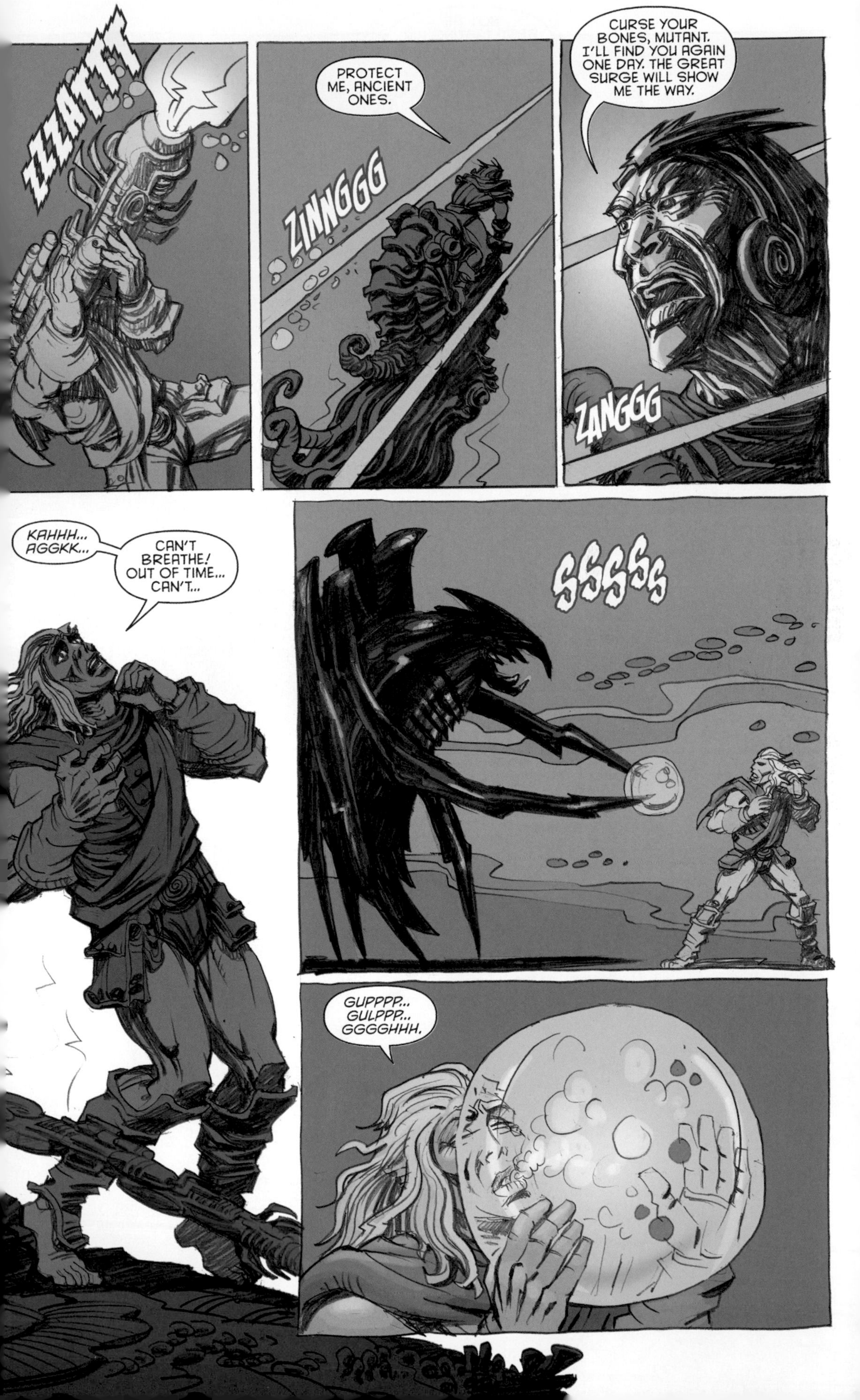

ZZZATTT
PROTECT ME, ANCIENT ONES.
ZINNGGG
CURSE YOUR BONES, MUTANT. I'LL FIND YOU AGAIN ONE DAY. THE GREAT SURGE WILL SHOW ME THE WAY.
ZANGGG
KAHHH... AGGKK...
CAN'T BREATHE! OUT OF TIME... CAN'T...
SSSSS
GUPPPP... GULPPP... GGGGHHH.

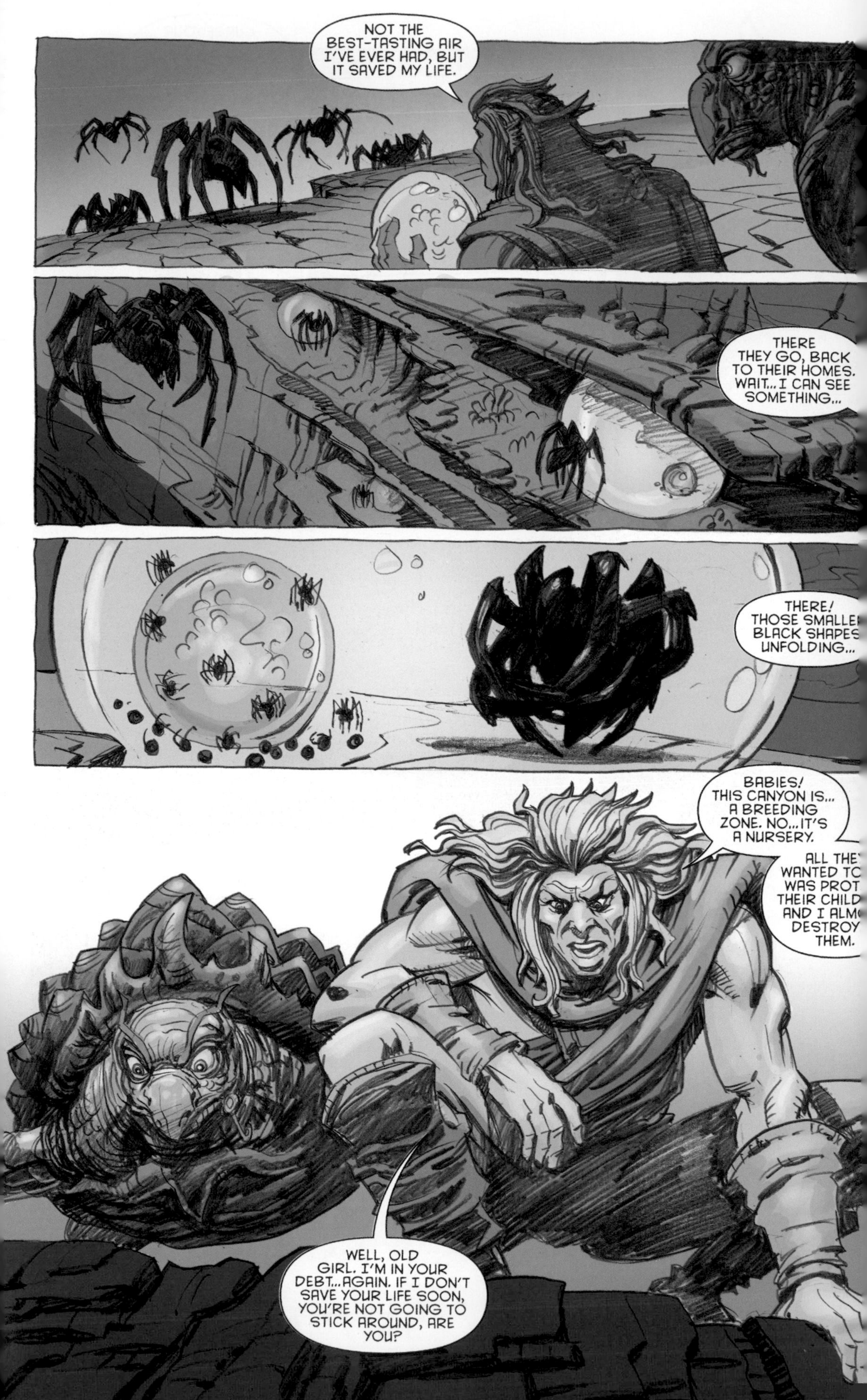
NOT THE BEST-TASTING AIR I'VE EVER HAD, BUT IT SAVED MY LIFE.
THERE THEY GO, BACK TO THEIR HOMES. WAIT... I CAN SEE SOMETHING...
THERE! THOSE SMALLE BLACK SHAPES UNFOLDING...
BABIES! THIS CANYON IS... A BREEDING ZONE. NO... IT'S A NURSERY.
ALL THE WANTED TO WAS PROT THEIR CHILD AND I ALM DESTROY THEM.
WELL, OLD GIRL. I'M IN YOUR DEBT... AGAIN. IF I DON'T SAVE YOUR LIFE SOON, YOU'RE NOT GOING TO STICK AROUND, ARE YOU?

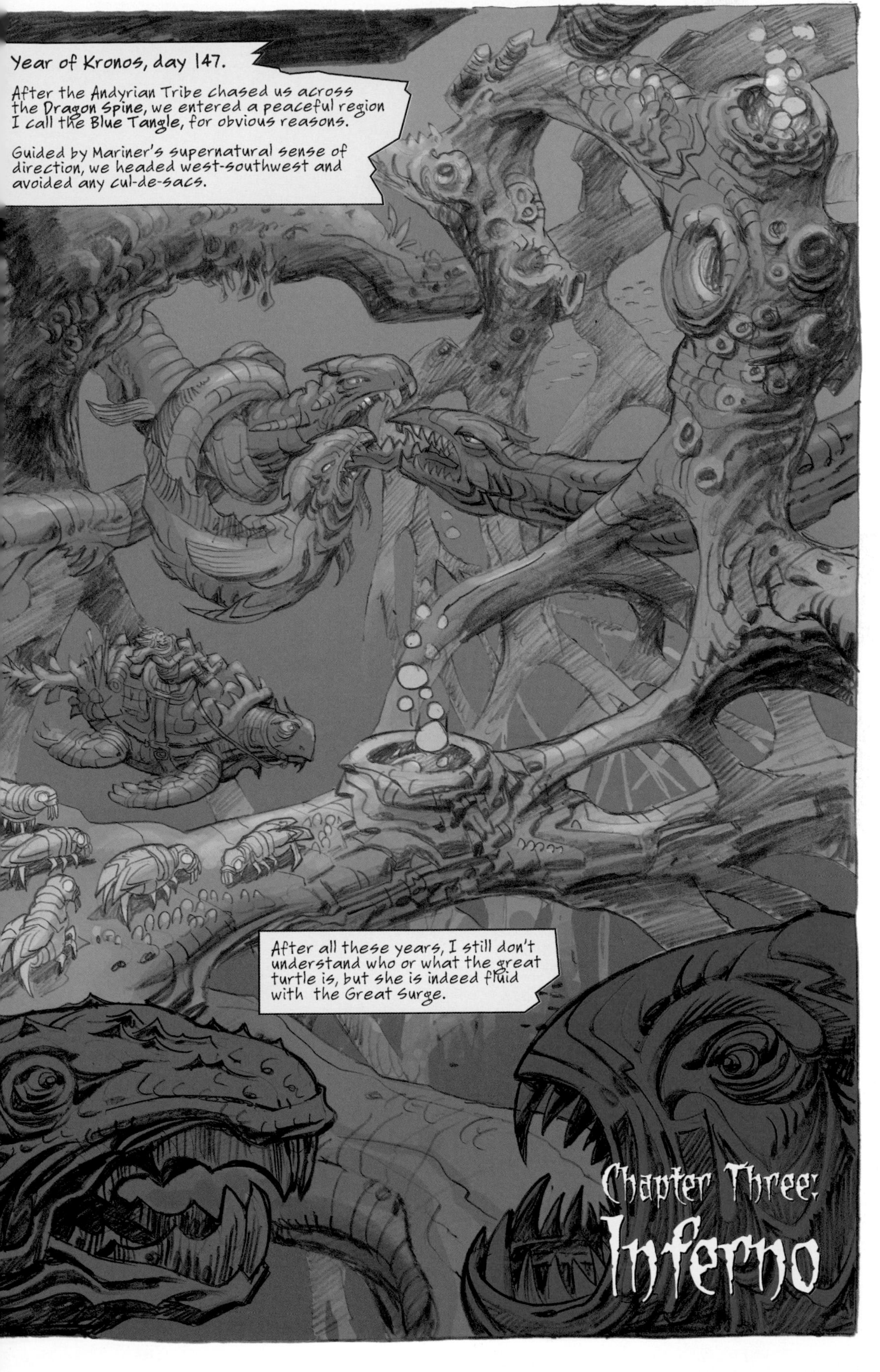

Year of Kronos, day 147.
After the Andyrian Tribe chased us across the Dragon Spine, we entered a peaceful region I call the Blue Tangle, for obvious reasons.
Guided by Mariner's supernatural sense of direction, we headed west-southwest and avoided any cul-de-sacs.
After all these years, I still don't understand who or what the great turtle is, but she is indeed fluid with the Great Surge.
Chapter Three:
Inferno

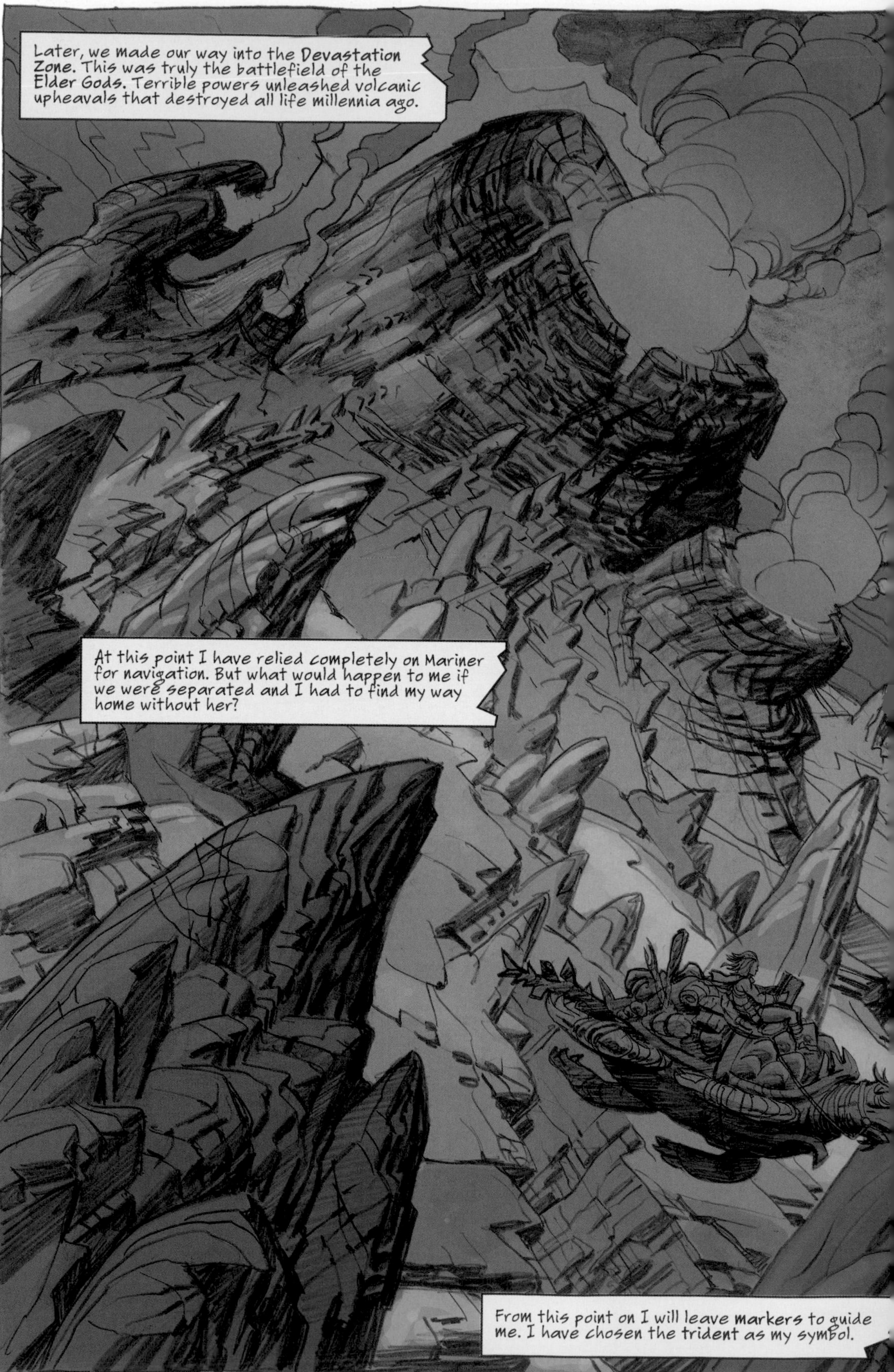
Later, we made our way into the Devastation Zone. This was truly the battlefield of the Elder Gods. Terrible powers unleashed volcanic upheavals that destroyed all life millennia ago.
At this point I have relied completely on Mariner for navigation. But what would happen to me if we were separated and I had to find my way home without her?
From this point on I will leave markers to guide me. I have chosen the trident as my symbol.

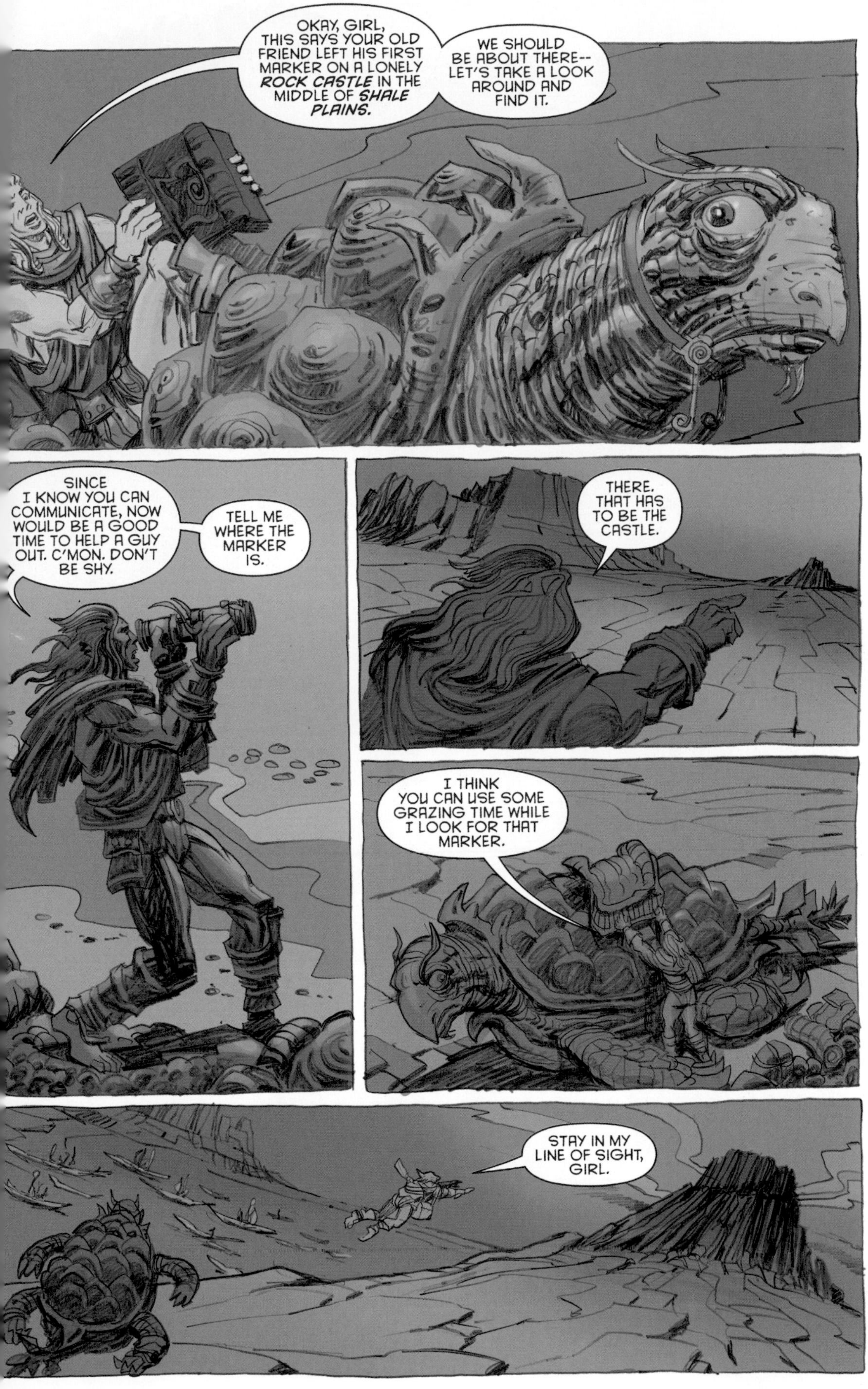
OKAY, GIRL, THIS SAYS YOUR OLD FRIEND LEFT HIS FIRST MARKER ON A LONELY ROCK CASTLE IN THE MIDDLE OF SHALE PLAINS.
WE SHOULD BE ABOUT THERE-- LET'S TAKE A LOOK AROUND AND FIND IT.
SINCE I KNOW YOU CAN COMMUNICATE, NOW WOULD BE A GOOD TIME TO HELP A GUY OUT. C'MON. DON'T BE SHY.
TELL ME WHERE THE MARKER IS.
THERE. THAT HAS TO BE THE CASTLE.
I THINK YOU CAN USE SOME GRAZING TIME WHILE I LOOK FOR THAT MARKER.
STAY IN MY LINE OF SIGHT, GIRL.

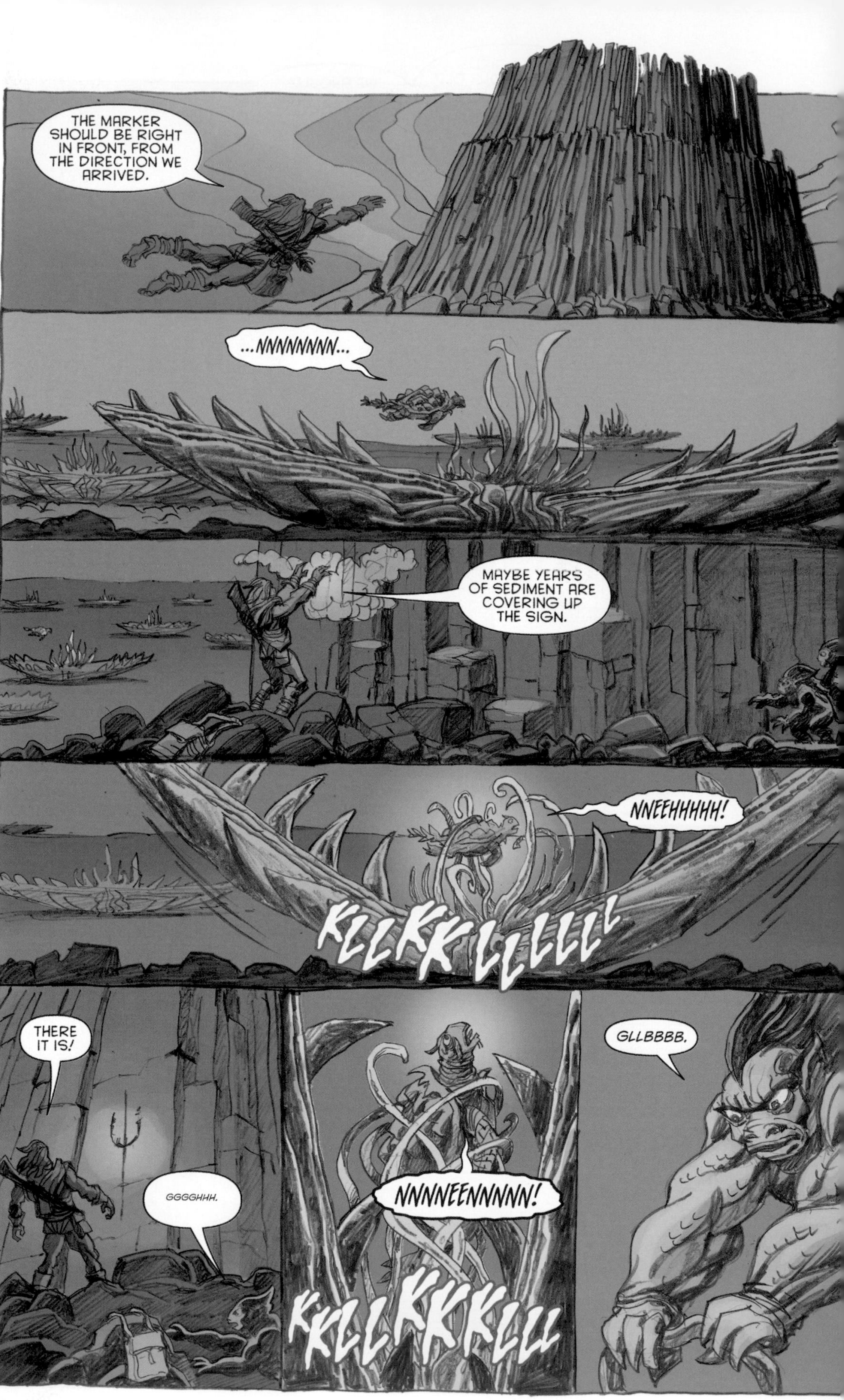
THE MARKER SHOULD BE RIGHT IN FRONT, FROM THE DIRECTION WE ARRIVED.
...NNNNNNN...
MAYBE YEARS OF SEDIMENT ARE COVERING UP THE SIGN.
NNEEHHHHH!
KLLKKLLLLL
THERE IT IS!
GGGGHHH.
NNNNEENNNNN!
KKLLKKKLLL
GLLBBBB.

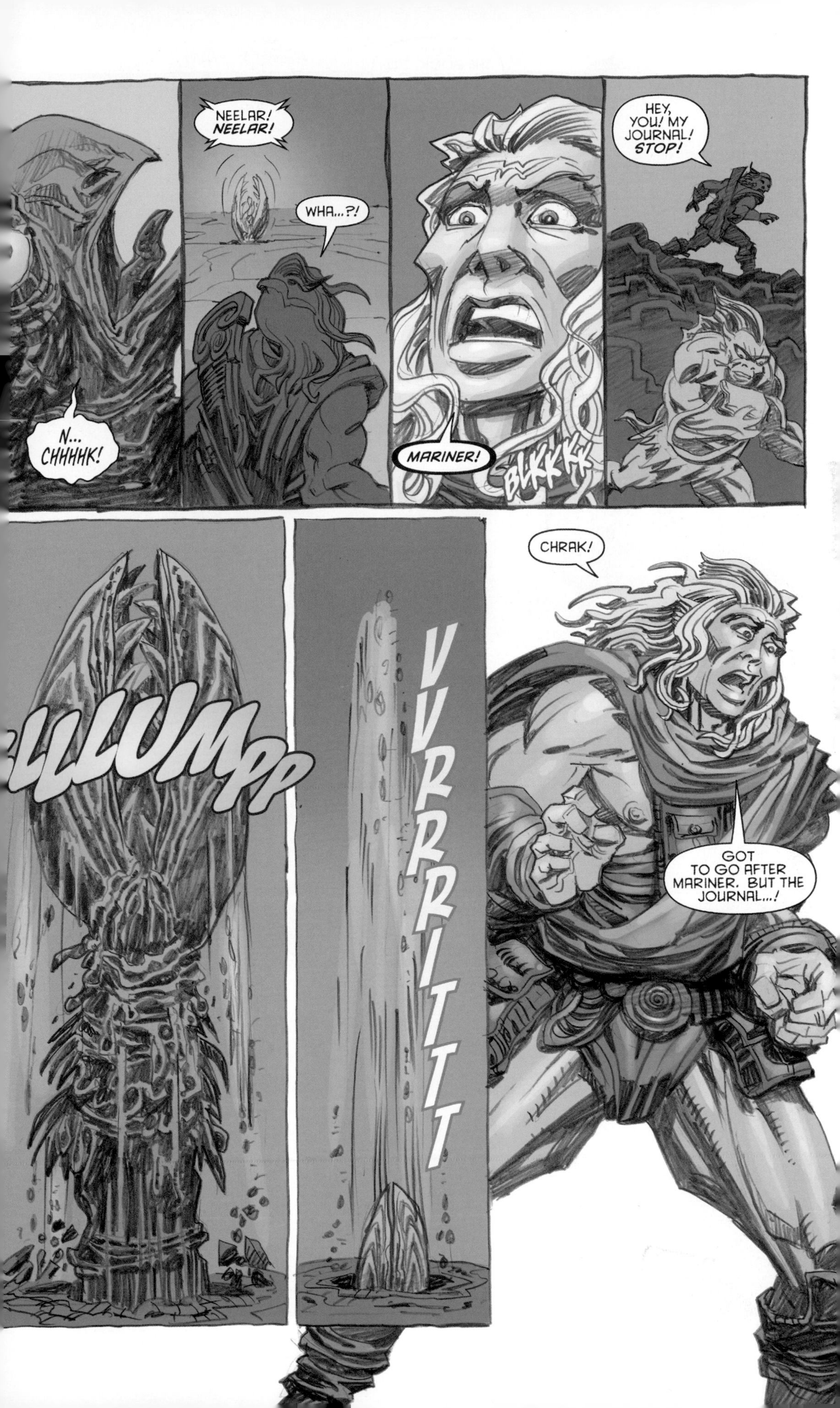
N... CHHHHK!
NEELAR! NEELAR!
WHA...?!
MARINER!
BLKKKK
HEY, YOU! MY JOURNAL! STOP!
LLUMPP
VVRRRITTT
CHRAK!
GOT TO GO AFTER MARINER. BUT THE JOURNAL...!

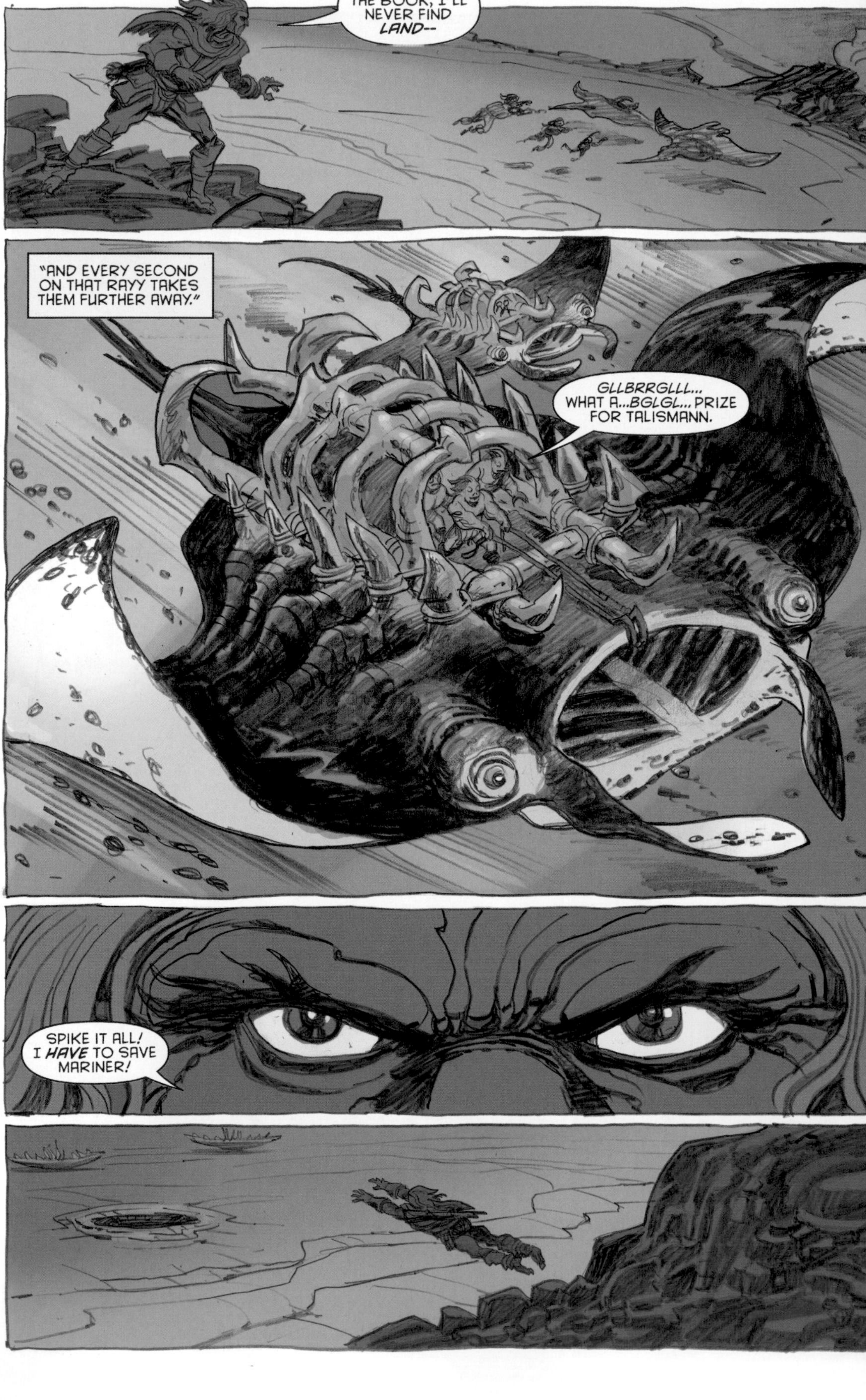
IF I LOSE THE BOOK, I'LL NEVER FIND *LAND--*
"AND EVERY SECOND ON THAT RAYY TAKES THEM FURTHER AWAY."
GLLBRRGLLL... WHAT A...*BGLGL*... PRIZE FOR TALISMANN.
SPIKE IT ALL! I *HAVE* TO SAVE MARINER!

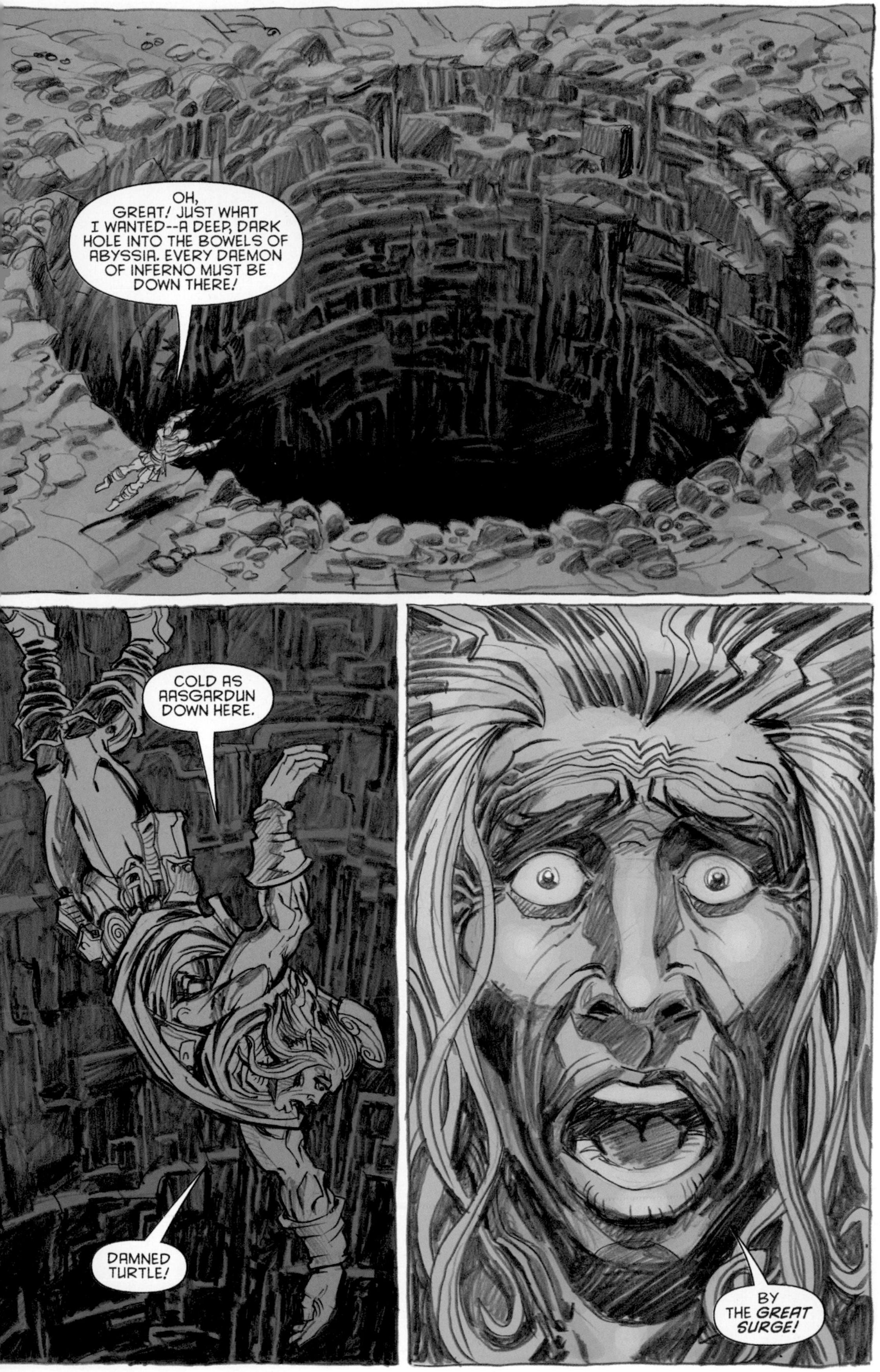

OH, GREAT! JUST WHAT I WANTED--A DEEP, DARK HOLE INTO THE BOWELS OF ABYSSIA. EVERY DAEMON OF INFERNO MUST BE DOWN THERE!
COLD AS AASGARDUN DOWN HERE.
DAMNED TURTLE!
BY THE GREAT SURGE!

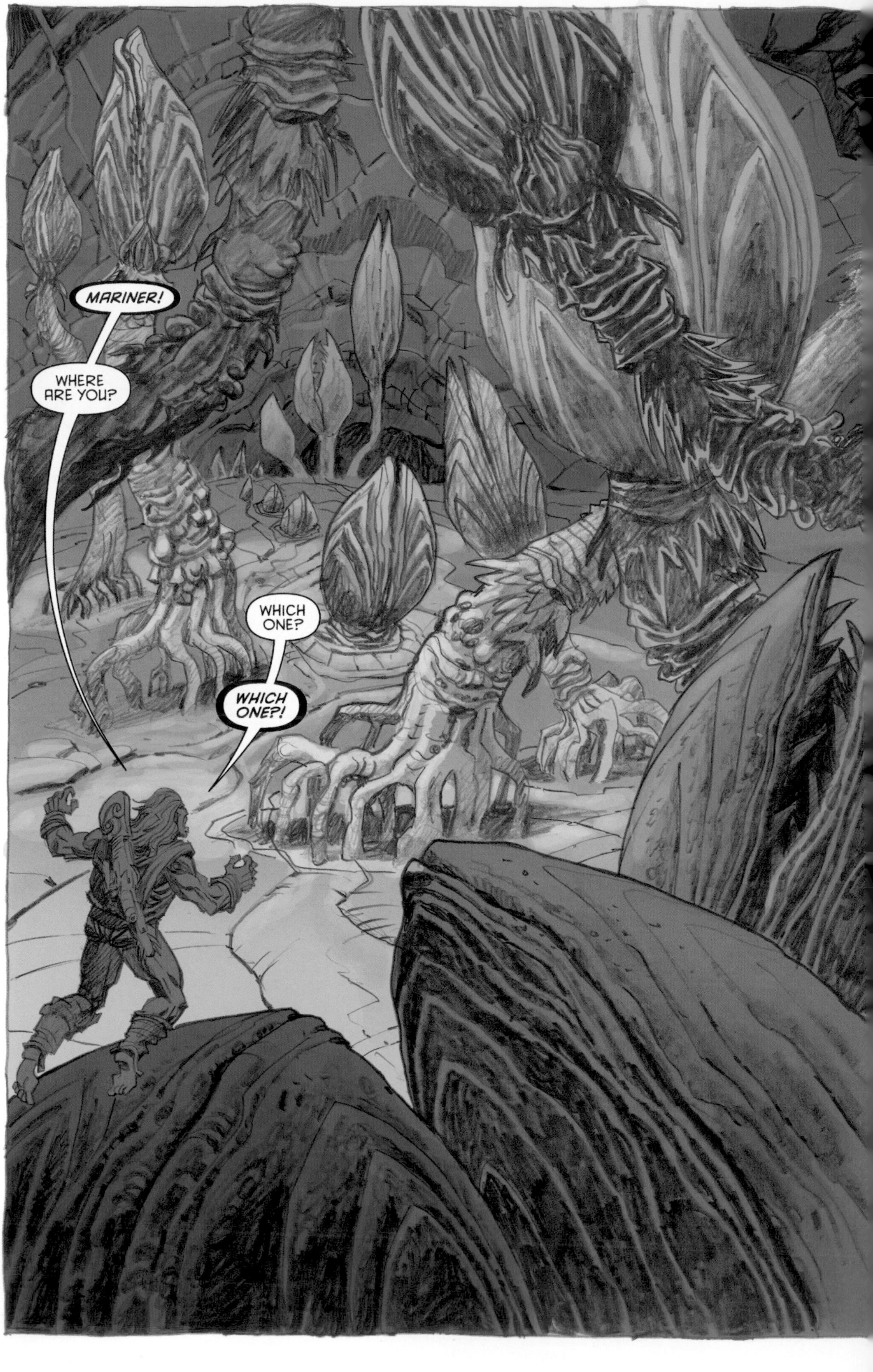
MARINER!
WHERE ARE YOU?
WHICH ONE?
WHICH ONE?!

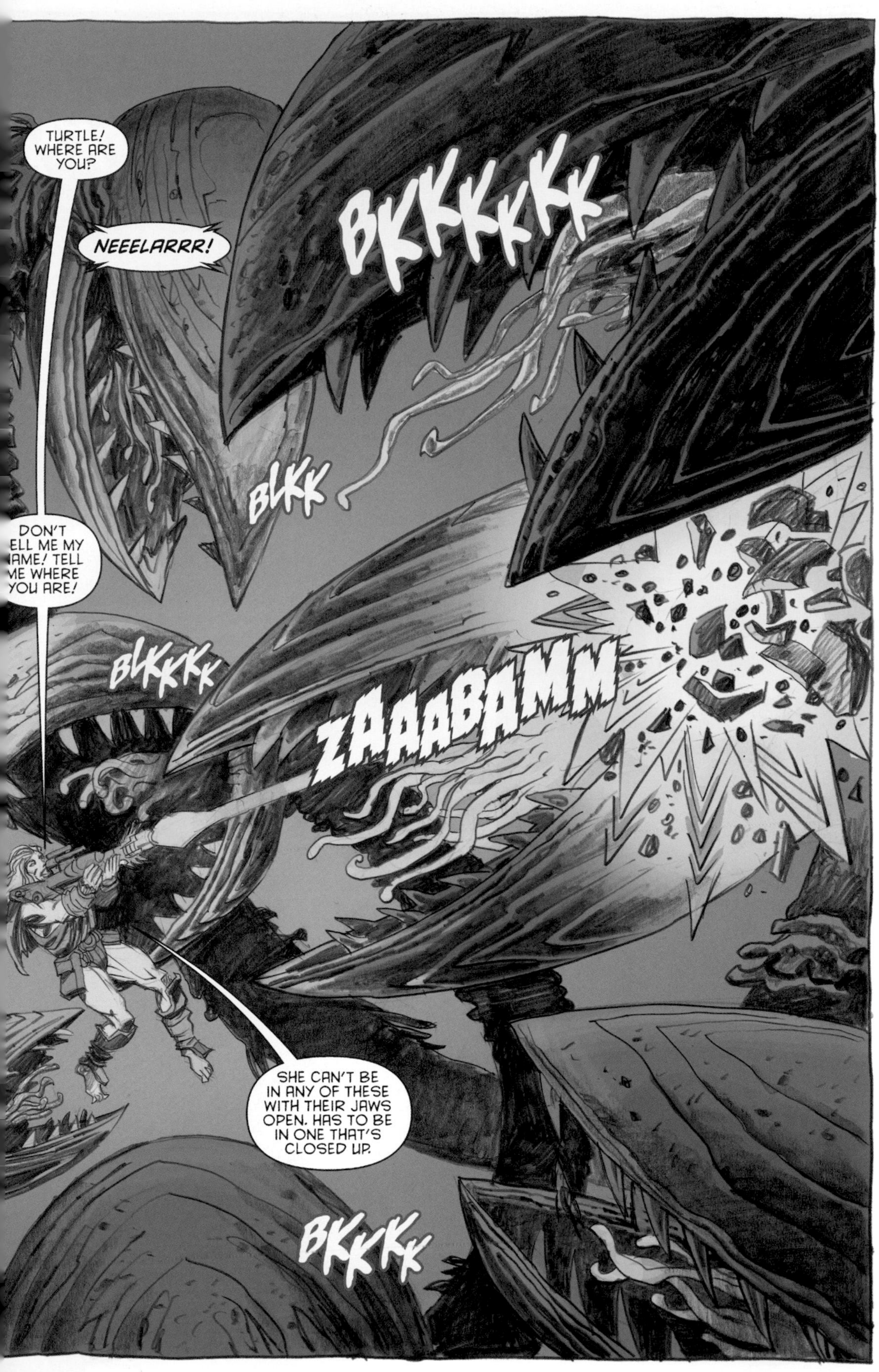
TURTLE! WHERE ARE YOU?
NEEELARRR!
BKKKKKK
BLKK
DON'T ELL ME MY AME! TELL ME WHERE YOU ARE!
BLKKKK
ZAAABAMM
SHE CAN'T BE IN ANY OF THESE WITH THEIR JAWS OPEN. HAS TO BE IN ONE THAT'S CLOSED UP.
BKKKK

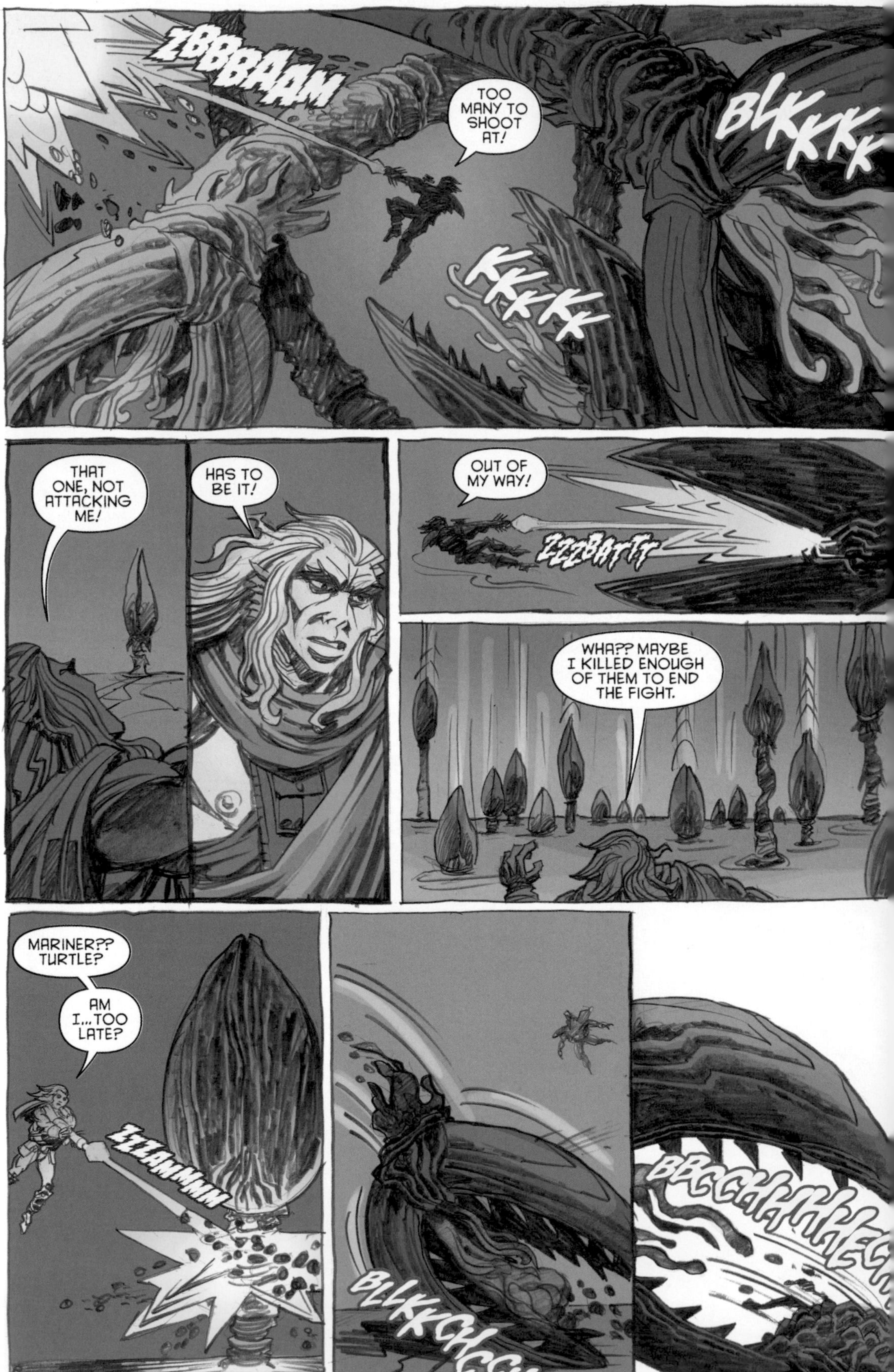
ZBBBAAM
TOO MANY TO SHOOT AT!
BLKKKK
KKKKK
THAT ONE, NOT ATTACKING ME!
HAS TO BE IT!
OUT OF MY WAY!
ZZZBATTT
WHA?? MAYBE I KILLED ENOUGH OF THEM TO END THE FIGHT.
MARINER?? TURTLE?
AM I...TOO LATE?
ZZZAMMMM
BLLKKCHCCH
BBCCHHHHEG

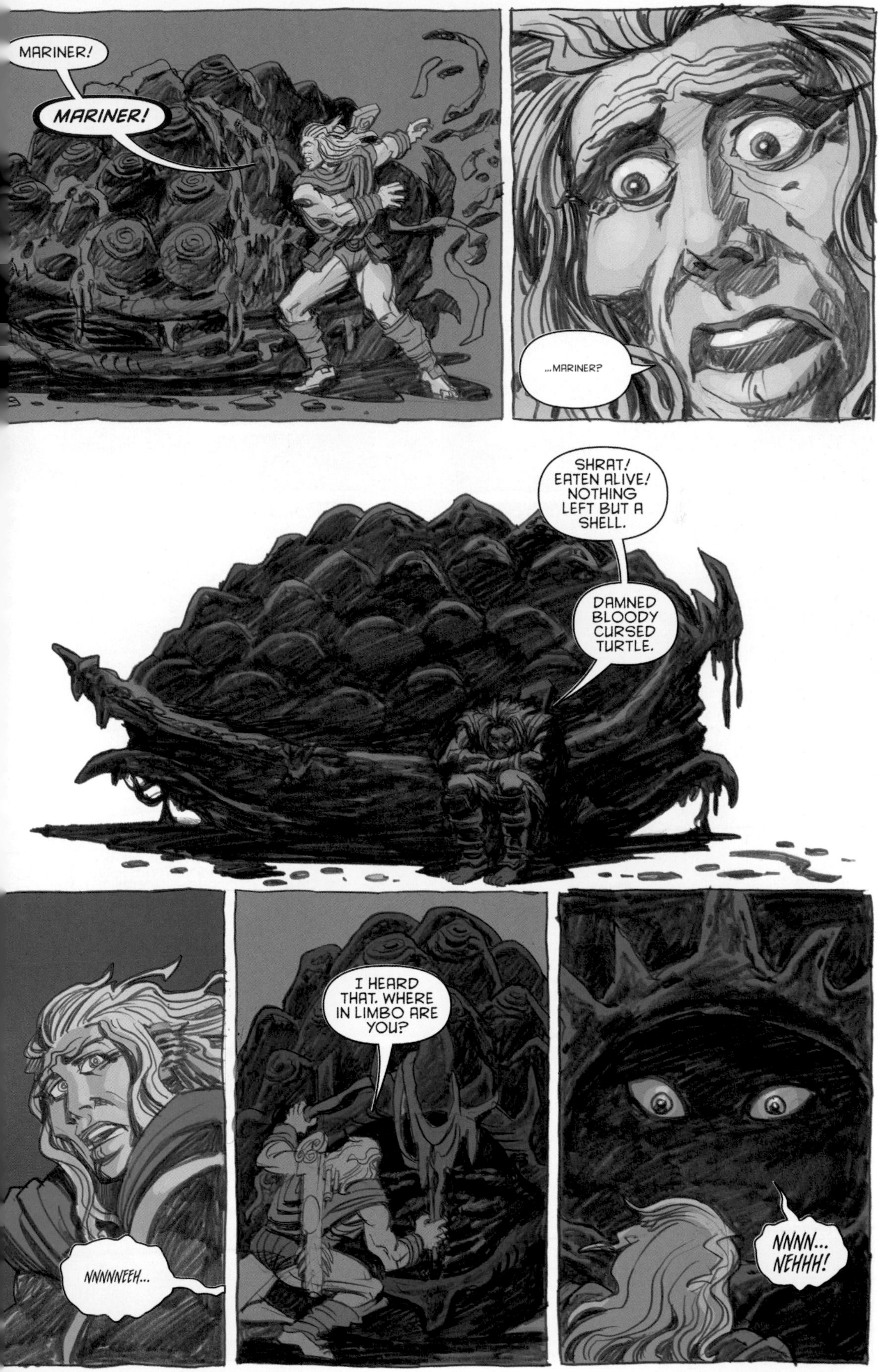
MARINER!
MARINER!
...MARINER?
SHRAT! EATEN ALIVE! NOTHING LEFT BUT A SHELL.
DAMNED BLOODY CURSED TURTLE.
NNNNNEEH...
I HEARD THAT. WHERE IN LIMBO ARE YOU?
NNNN... NEHHH!

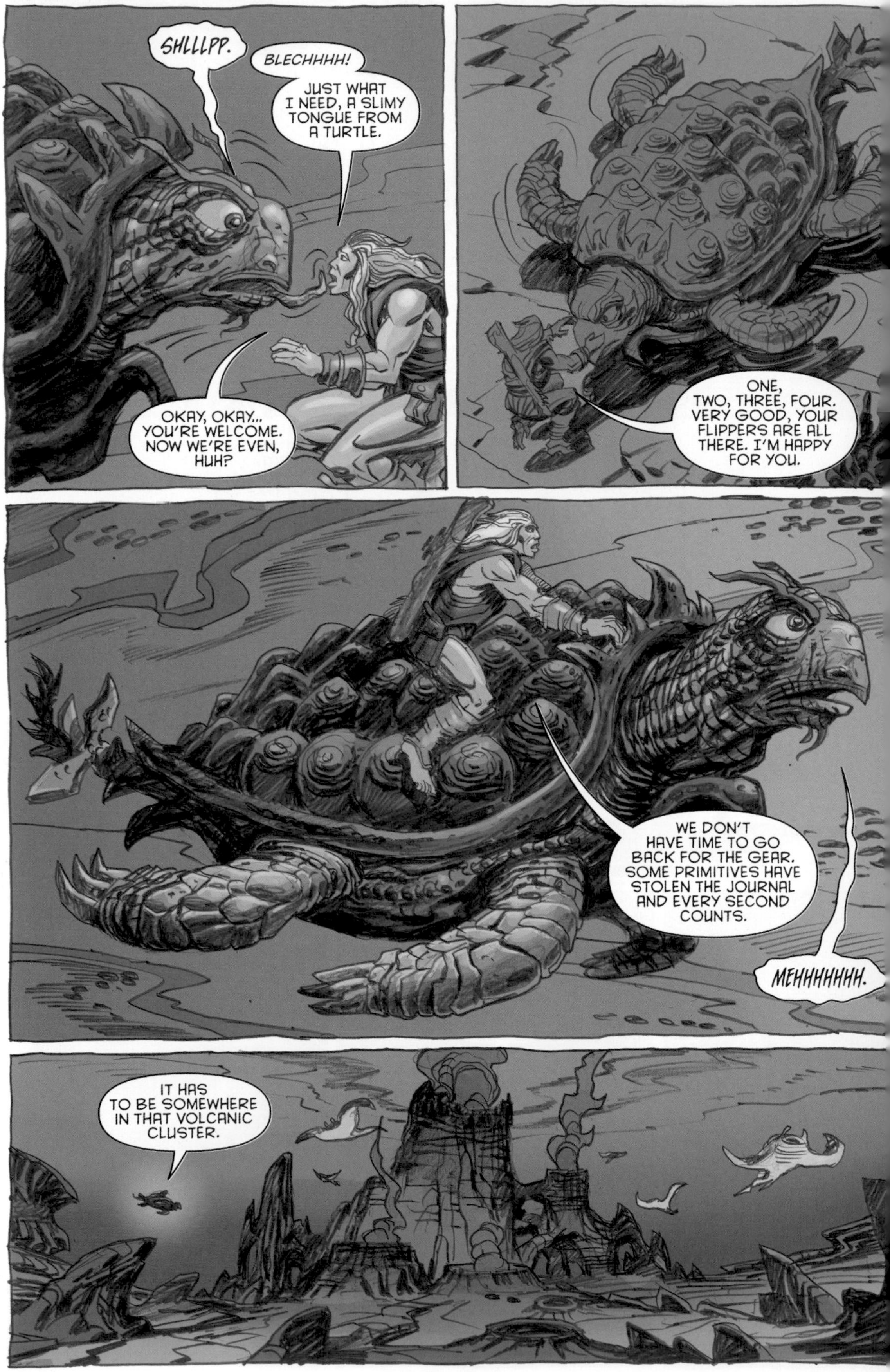
SHLLLPP.
BLECHHHH!
JUST WHAT I NEED, A SLIMY TONGUE FROM A TURTLE.
OKAY, OKAY... YOU'RE WELCOME. NOW WE'RE EVEN, HUH?
ONE, TWO, THREE, FOUR. VERY GOOD, YOUR FLIPPERS ARE ALL THERE. I'M HAPPY FOR YOU.
WE DON'T HAVE TIME TO GO BACK FOR THE GEAR. SOME PRIMITIVES HAVE STOLEN THE JOURNAL AND EVERY SECOND COUNTS.
MEHHHHHHH.
IT HAS TO BE SOMEWHERE IN THAT VOLCANIC CLUSTER.

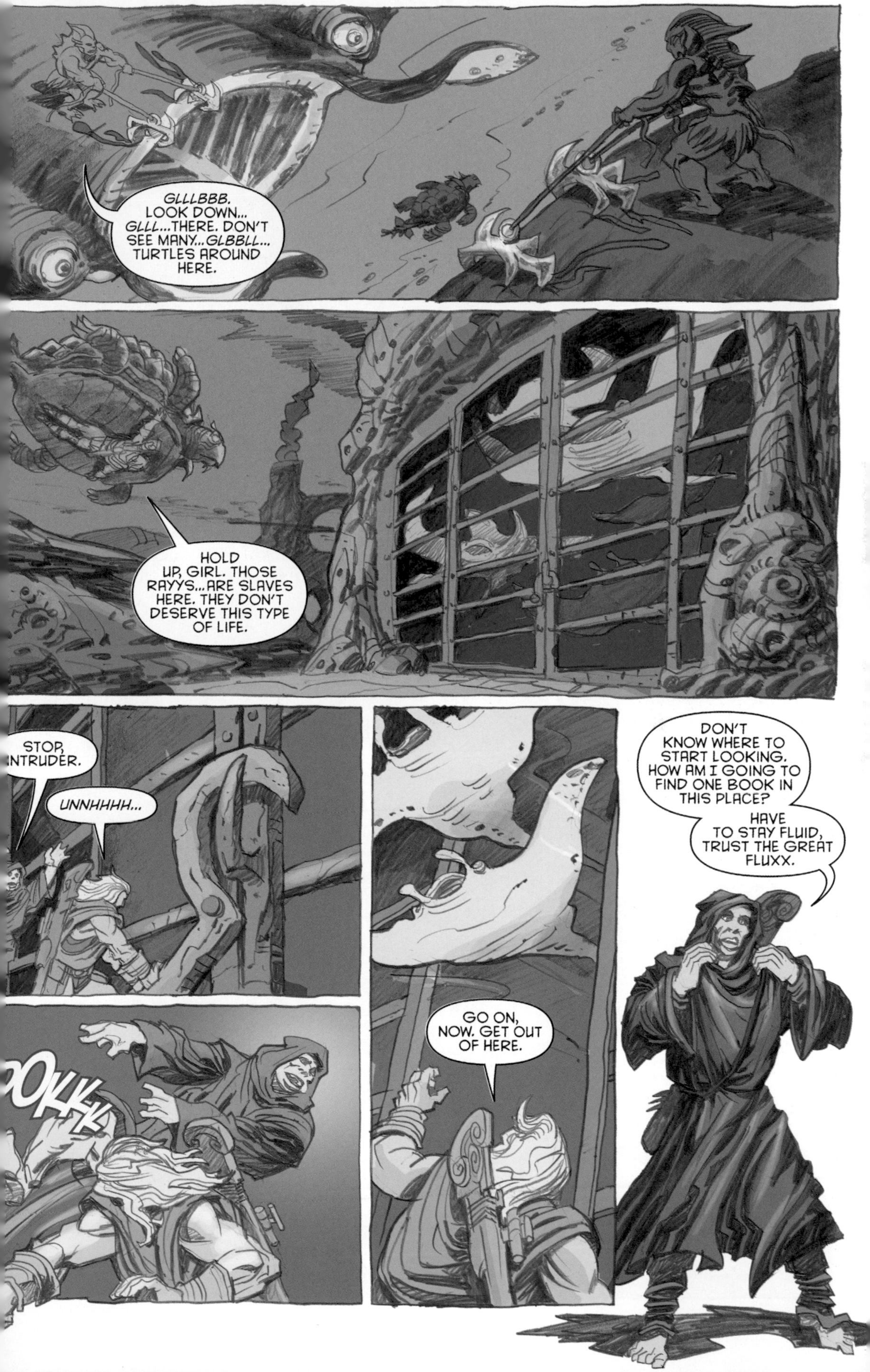
GLLLBBB. LOOK DOWN... GLLL...THERE. DON'T SEE MANY...GLBBLL... TURTLES AROUND HERE.
HOLD UP, GIRL. THOSE RAYYS...ARE SLAVES HERE. THEY DON'T DESERVE THIS TYPE OF LIFE.
STOP, INTRUDER.
UNNHHHH...
OOKKK
GO ON, NOW. GET OUT OF HERE.
DON'T KNOW WHERE TO START LOOKING. HOW AM I GOING TO FIND ONE BOOK IN THIS PLACE?
HAVE TO STAY FLUID, TRUST THE GREAT FLUXX.

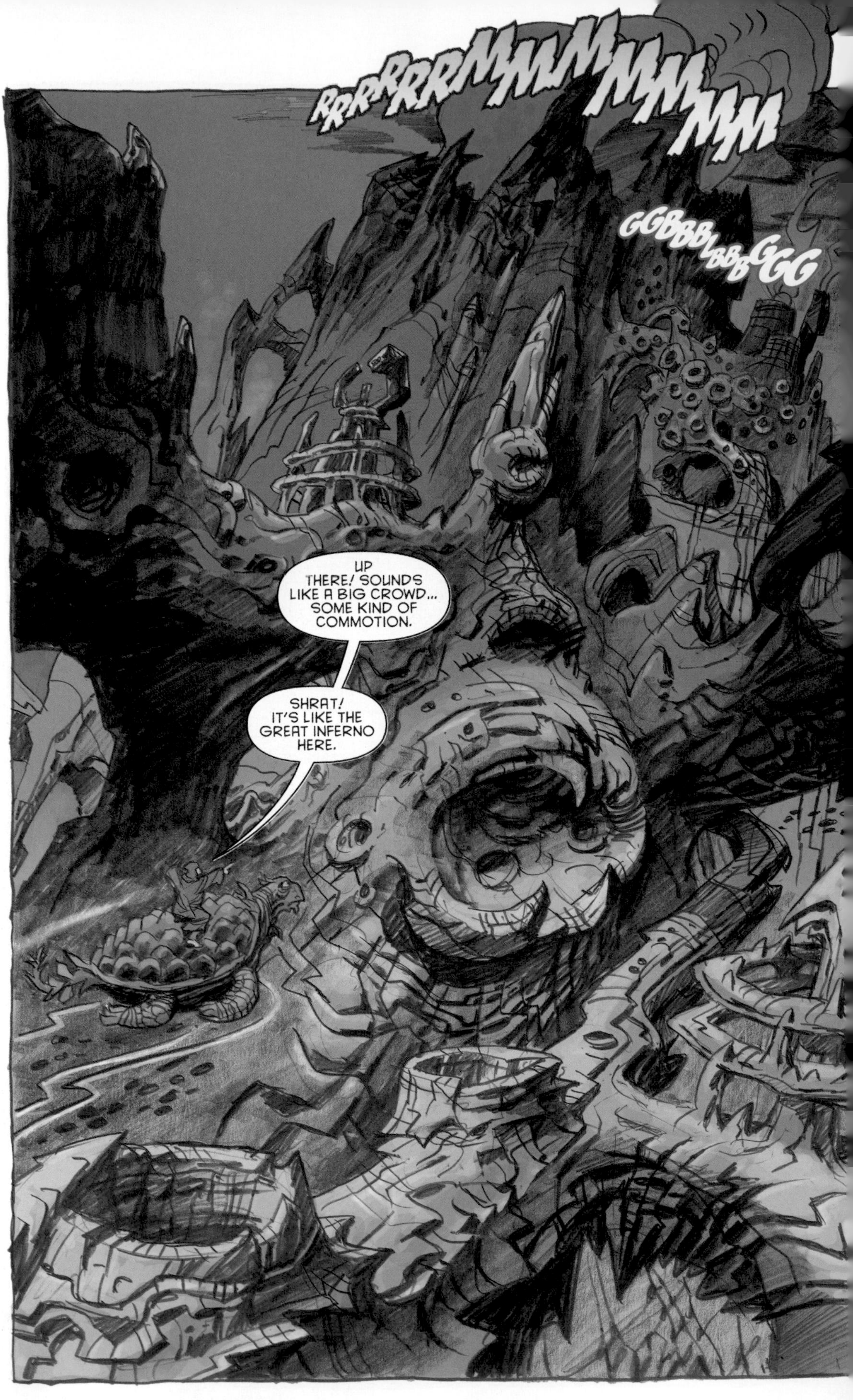
RRRRRRRMMMMMMMMM
GGBBBLBBBGGG
UP THERE! SOUNDS LIKE A BIG CROWD... SOME KIND OF COMMOTION.
SHRAT! IT'S LIKE THE GREAT INFERNO HERE.

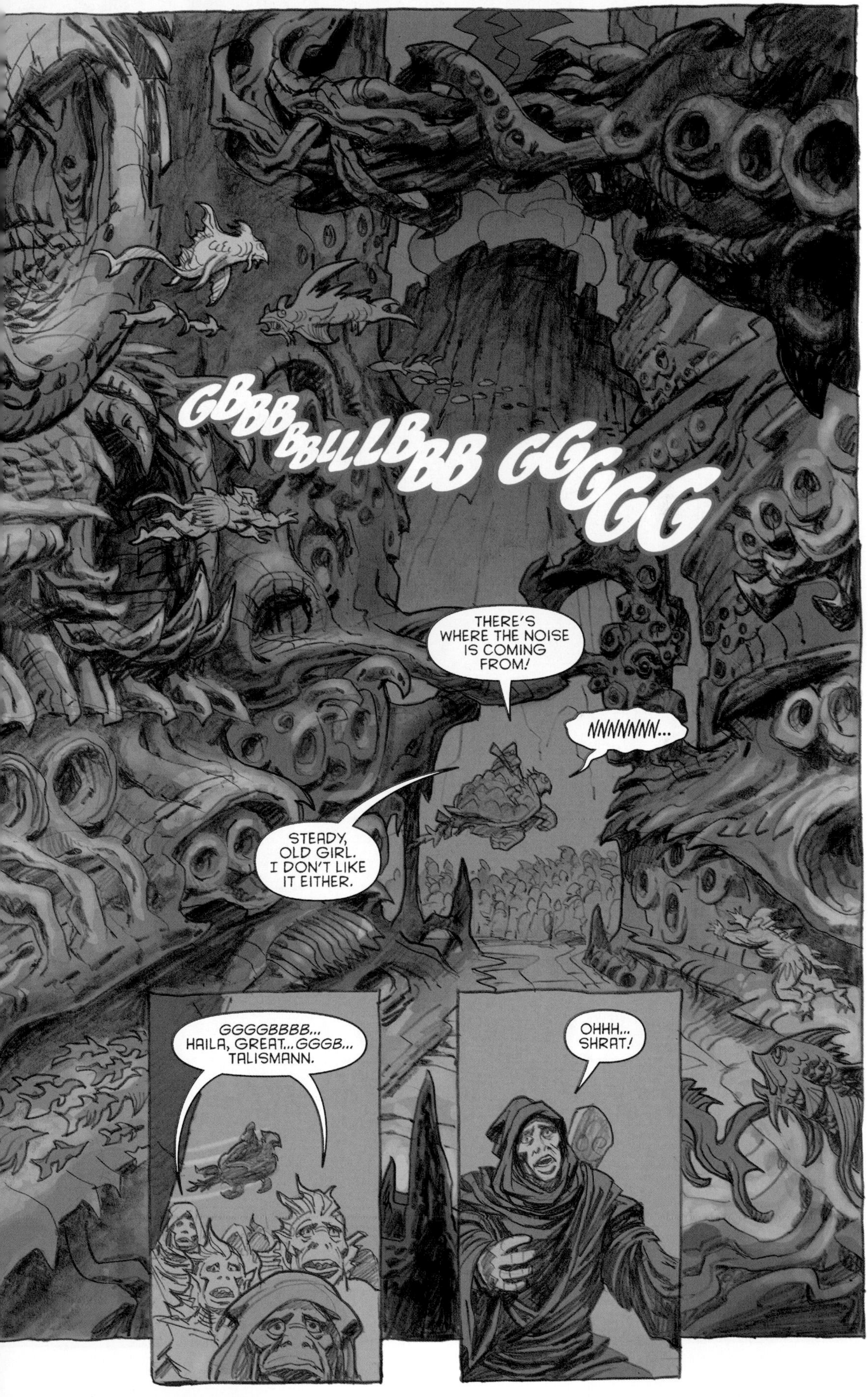
GBBBBBLLLBBB GGGGGG
THERE'S WHERE THE NOISE IS COMING FROM!
NNNNNNN...
STEADY, OLD GIRL. I DON'T LIKE IT EITHER.
GGGGBBBB... HAILA, GREAT...GGGB... TALISMANN.
OHHH... SHRAT!

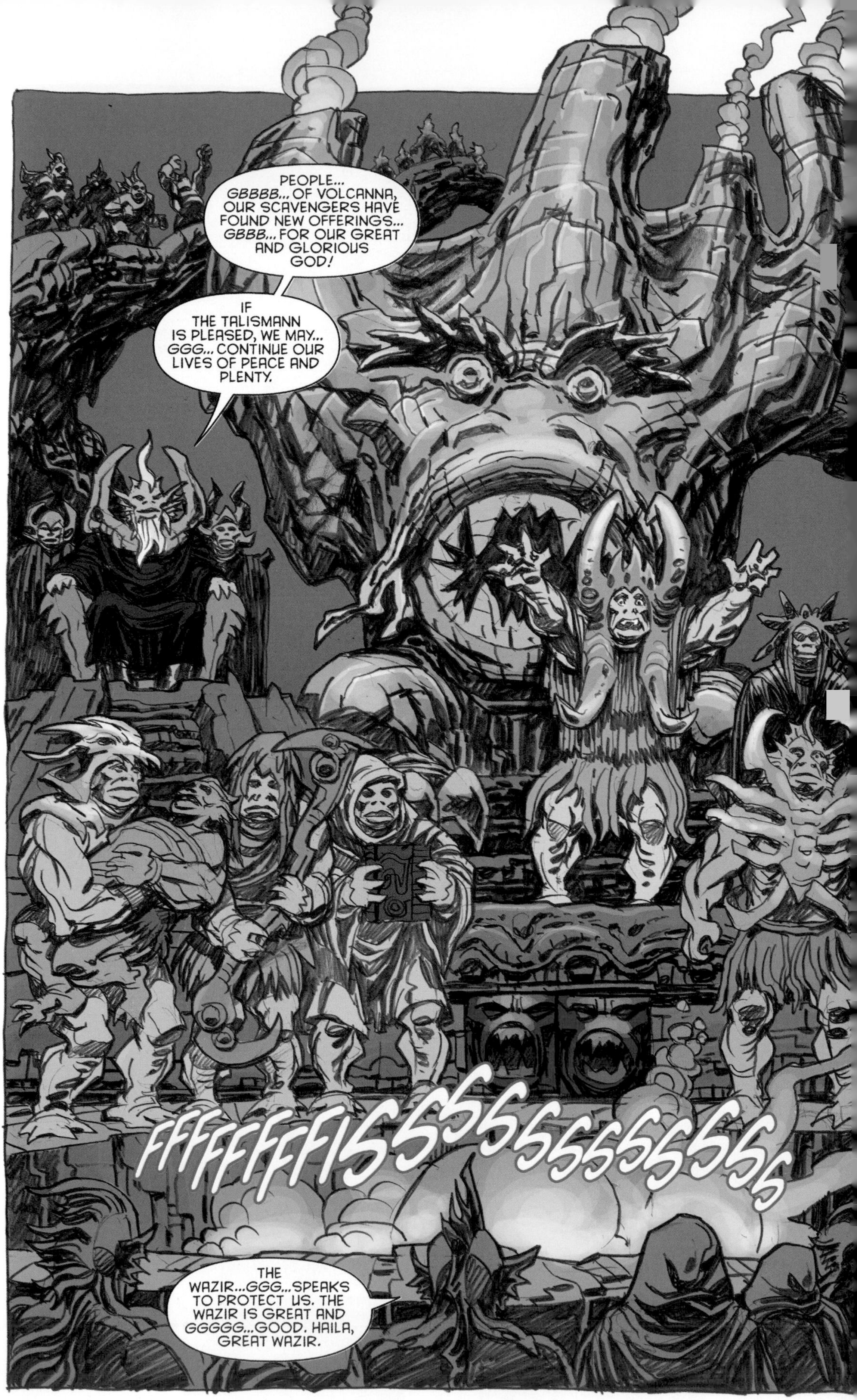
PEOPLE... GBBBB... OF VOLCANNA, OUR SCAVENGERS HAVE FOUND NEW OFFERINGS... GBBB... FOR OUR GREAT AND GLORIOUS GOD!
IF THE TALISMANN IS PLEASED, WE MAY... GGG... CONTINUE OUR LIVES OF PEACE AND PLENTY.
FFFFFFFFISSSSSSSSSSSSSS
THE WAZIR...GGG...SPEAKS TO PROTECT US. THE WAZIR IS GREAT AND GGGGG...GOOD. HAILA, GREAT WAZIR.

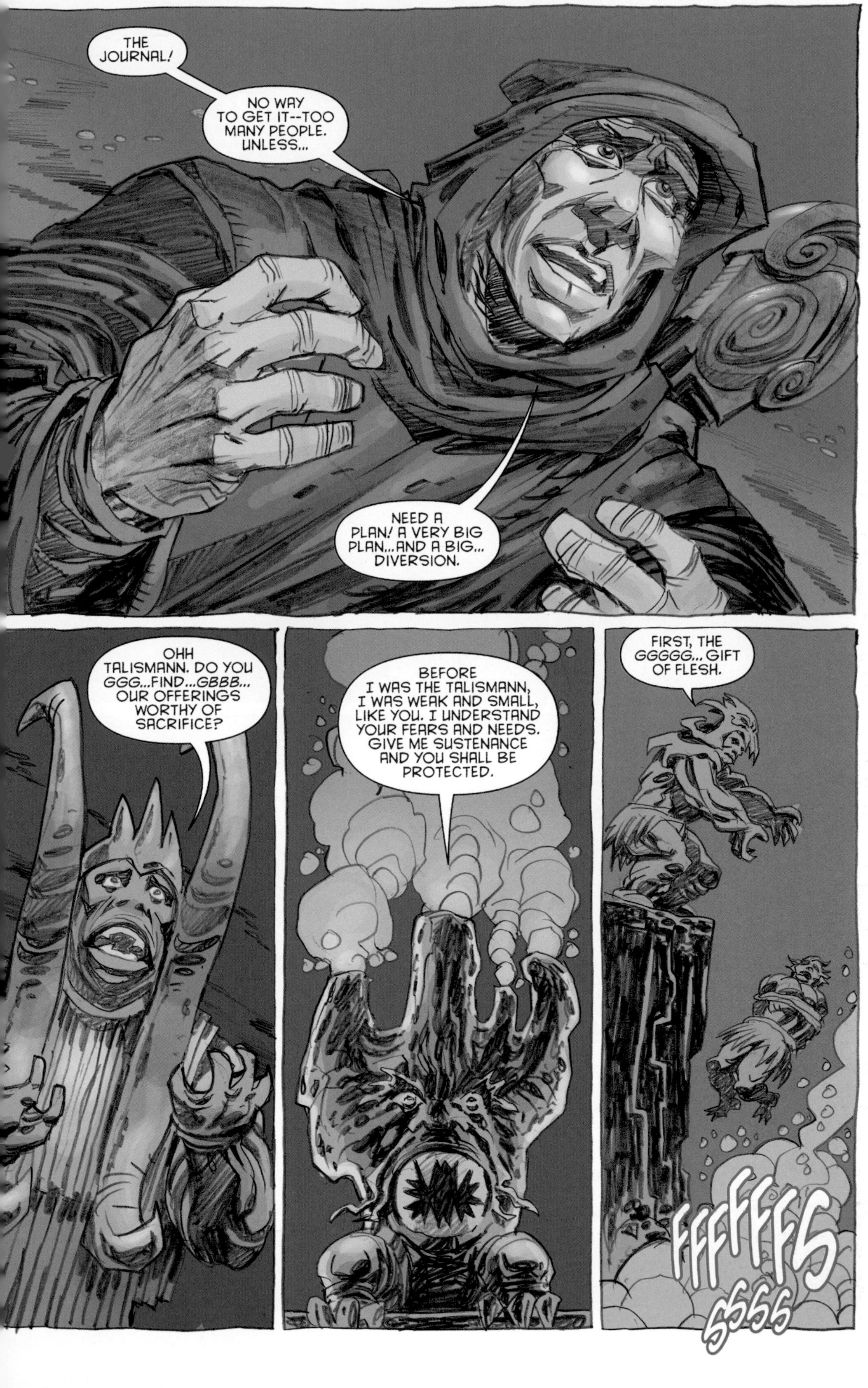
THE JOURNAL!
NO WAY TO GET IT--TOO MANY PEOPLE. UNLESS...
NEED A PLAN! A VERY BIG PLAN...AND A BIG... DIVERSION.
OHH TALISMANN. DO YOU GGG...FIND...GBBB... OUR OFFERINGS WORTHY OF SACRIFICE?
BEFORE I WAS THE TALISMANN, I WAS WEAK AND SMALL, LIKE YOU. I UNDERSTAND YOUR FEARS AND NEEDS. GIVE ME SUSTENANCE AND YOU SHALL BE PROTECTED.
FIRST, THE GGGGG... GIFT OF FLESH.
FFFFFS SSSS

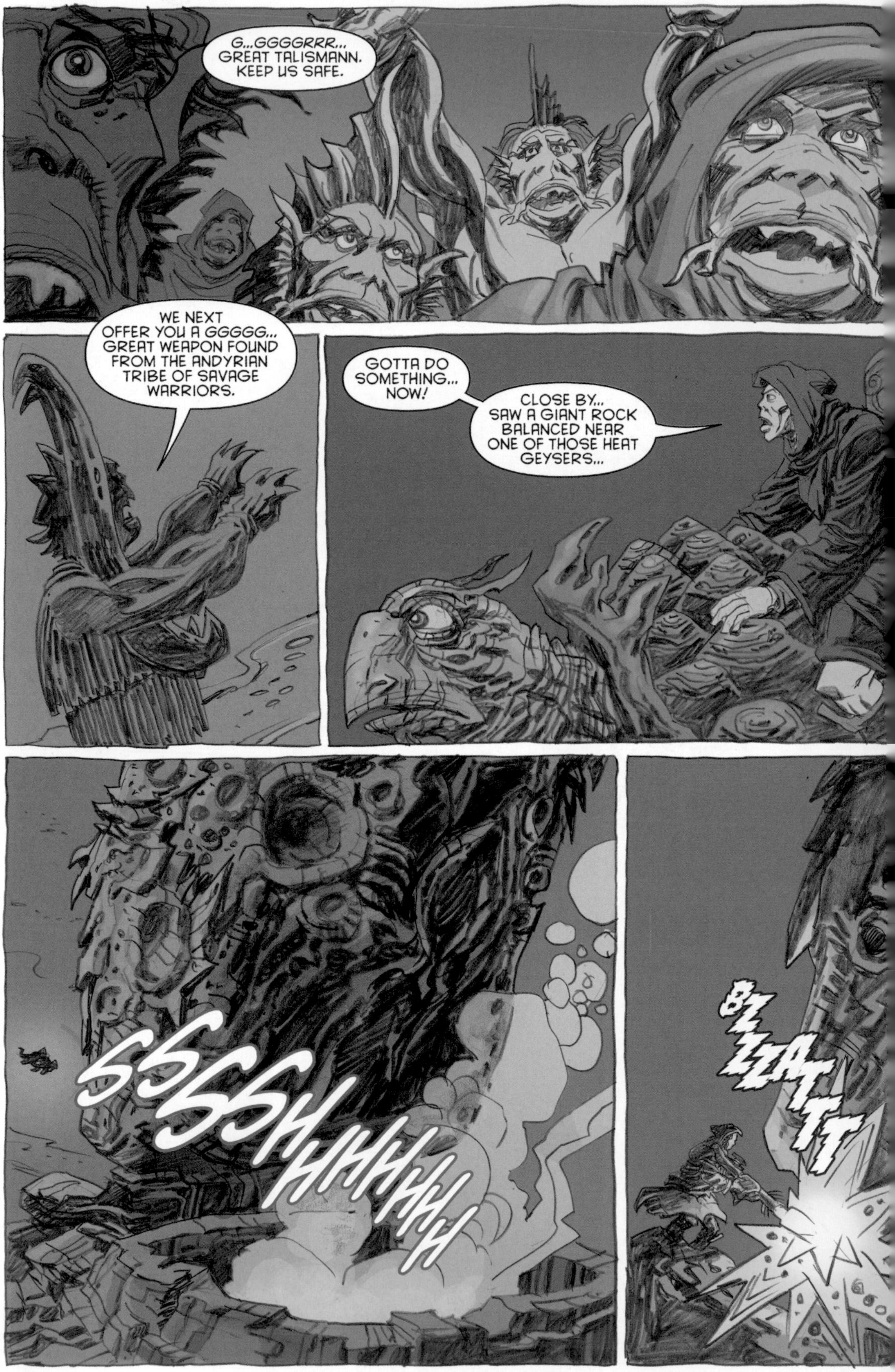

G...GGGGRRR...
GREAT TALISMANN.
KEEP US SAFE.
WE NEXT OFFER YOU A GGGGG... GREAT WEAPON FOUND FROM THE ANDYRIAN TRIBE OF SAVAGE WARRIORS.
GOTTA DO SOMETHING... NOW!
CLOSE BY... SAW A GIANT ROCK BALANCED NEAR ONE OF THOSE HEAT GEYSERS...
SSSSHHHHHHH
BZZZATTT

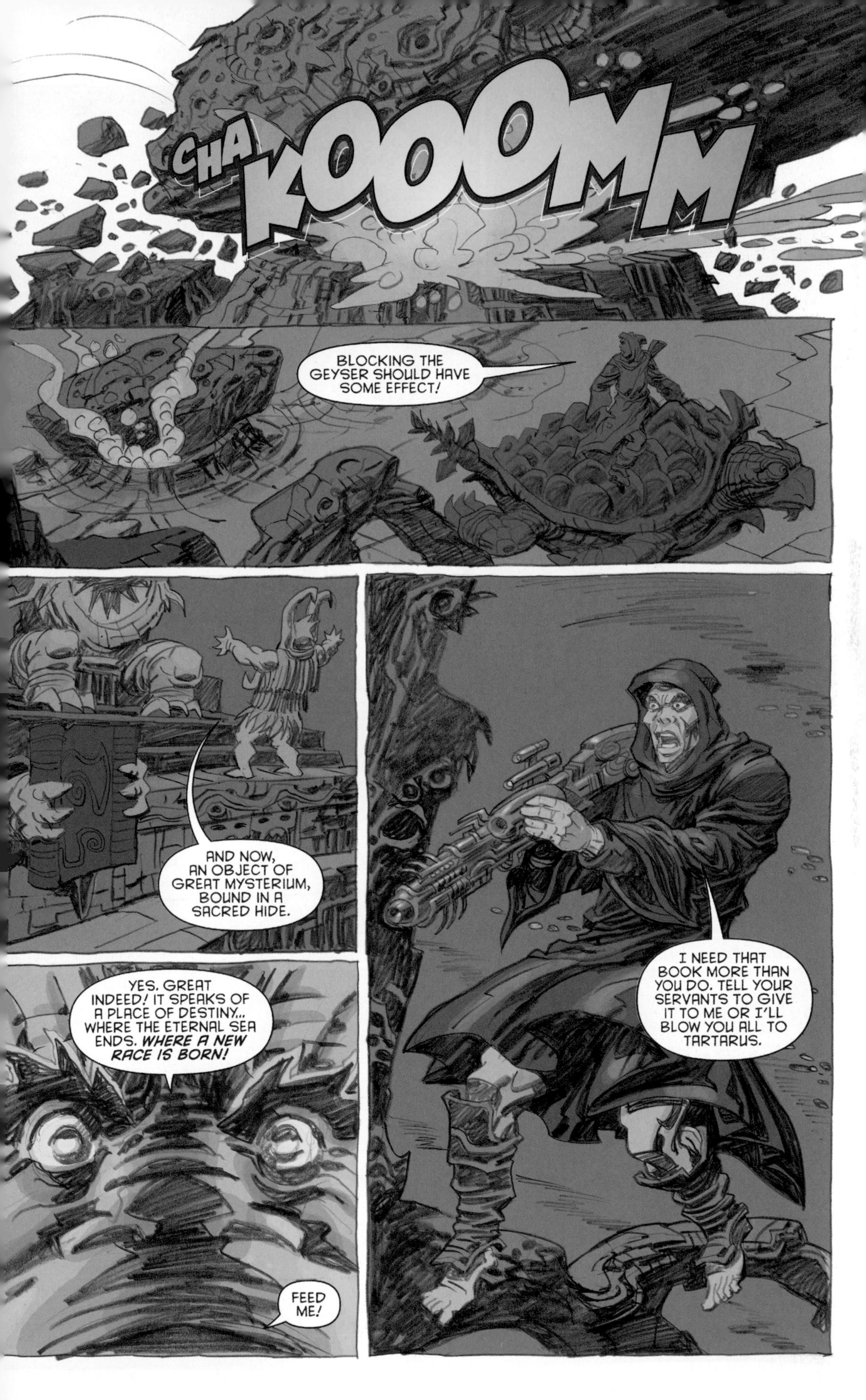
CHA KOOOMM
BLOCKING THE GEYSER SHOULD HAVE SOME EFFECT!
AND NOW, AN OBJECT OF GREAT MYSTERIUM, BOUND IN A SACRED HIDE.
YES. GREAT INDEED! IT SPEAKS OF A PLACE OF DESTINY... WHERE THE ETERNAL SEA ENDS. *WHERE A NEW RACE IS BORN!*
FEED ME!
I NEED THAT BOOK MORE THAN YOU DO. TELL YOUR SERVANTS TO GIVE IT TO ME OR I'LL BLOW YOU ALL TO TARTARUS.

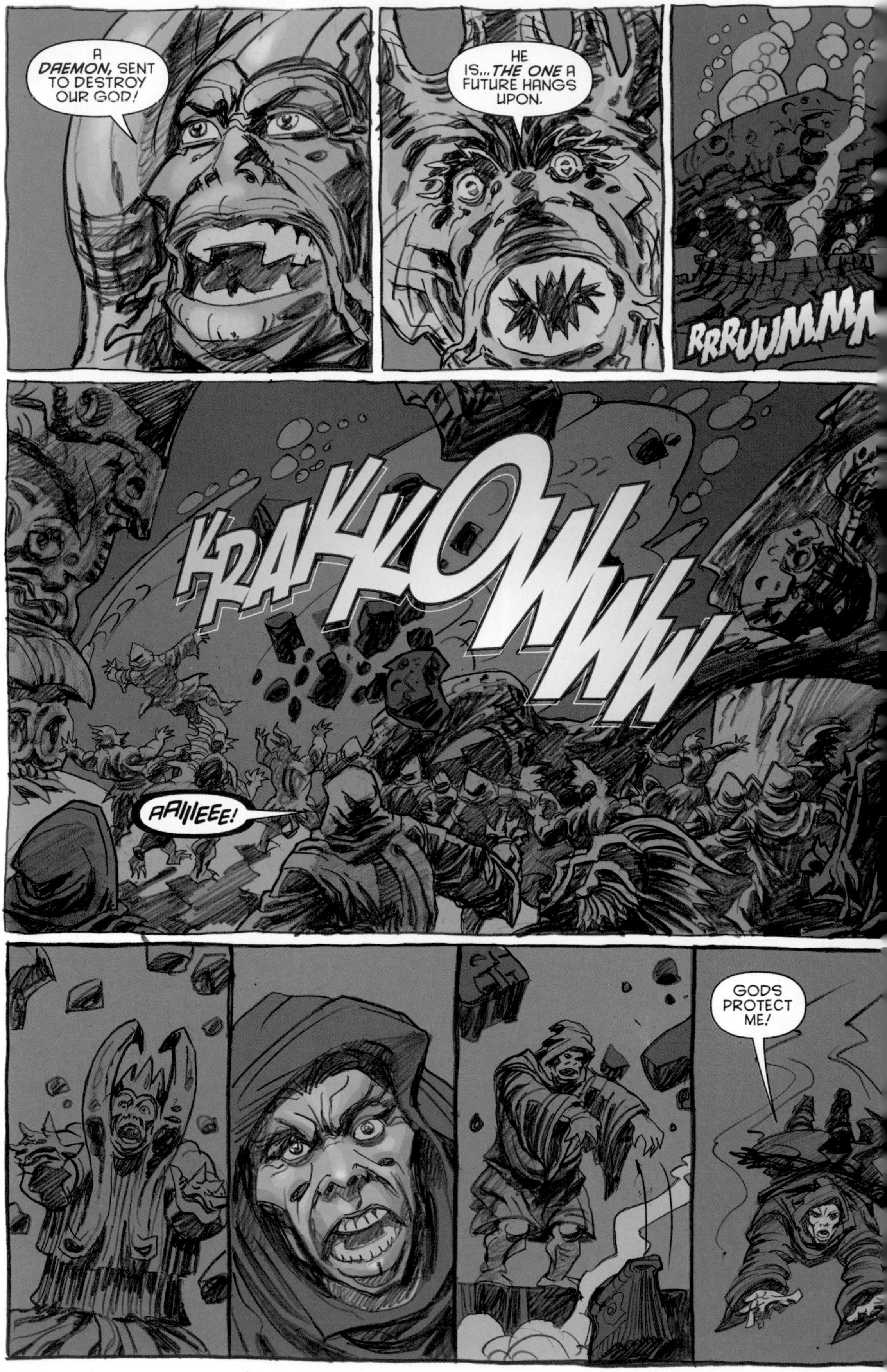
A DAEMON, SENT TO DESTROY OUR GOD!
HE IS...THE ONE A FUTURE HANGS UPON.
RRRUUMMM
KRAKKOWWWW
AAIIIEEE!
GODS PROTECT ME!

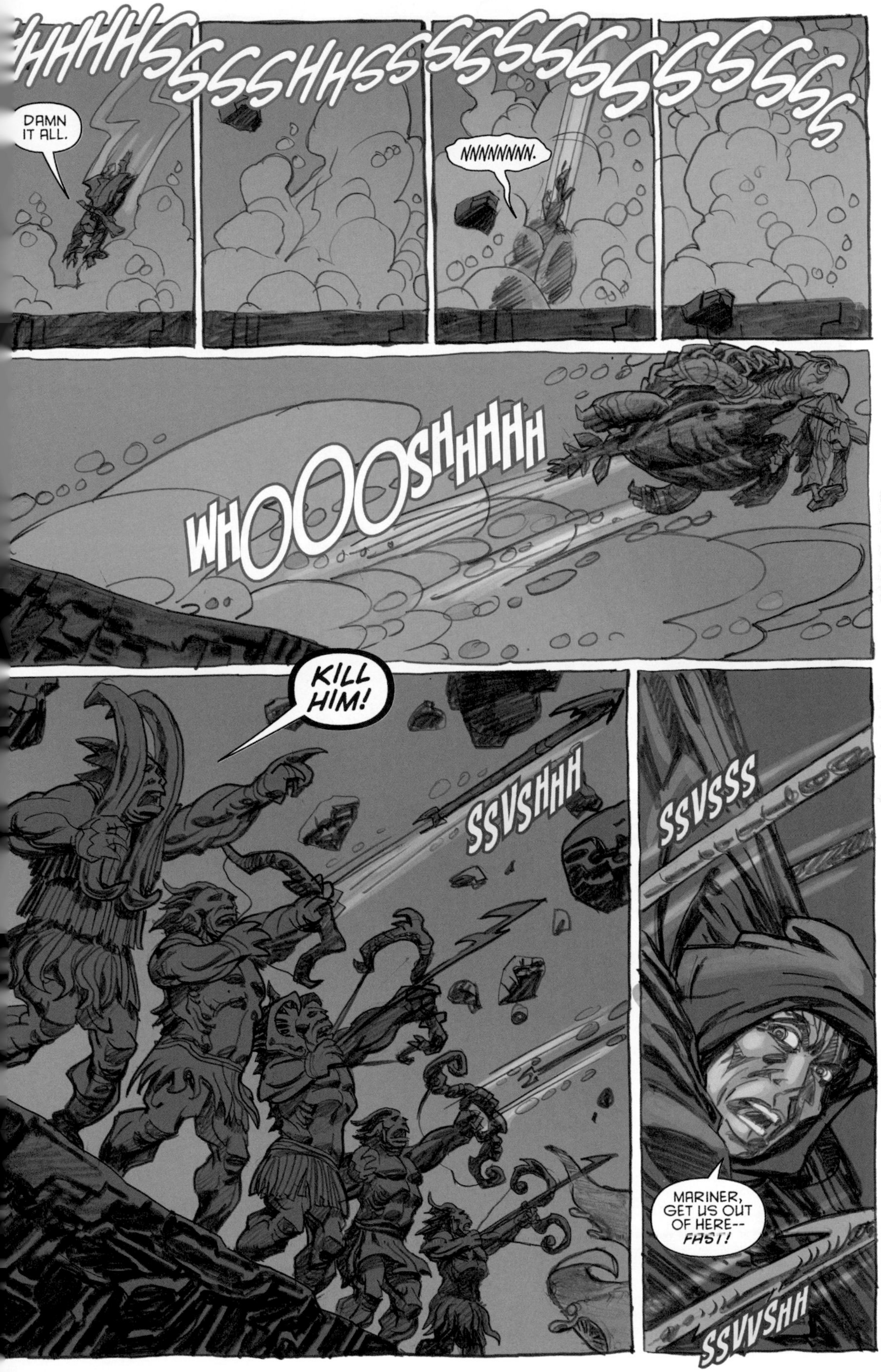
HHHHHSSSSHHSSSSSSSSSSSSSSS
DAMN IT ALL.
NNNNNNNN.
WHOOOOSHHHHH
KILL HIM!
SSVSHHH
SSVSSS
MARINER, GET US OUT OF HERE-- FAST!
SSVVSHH

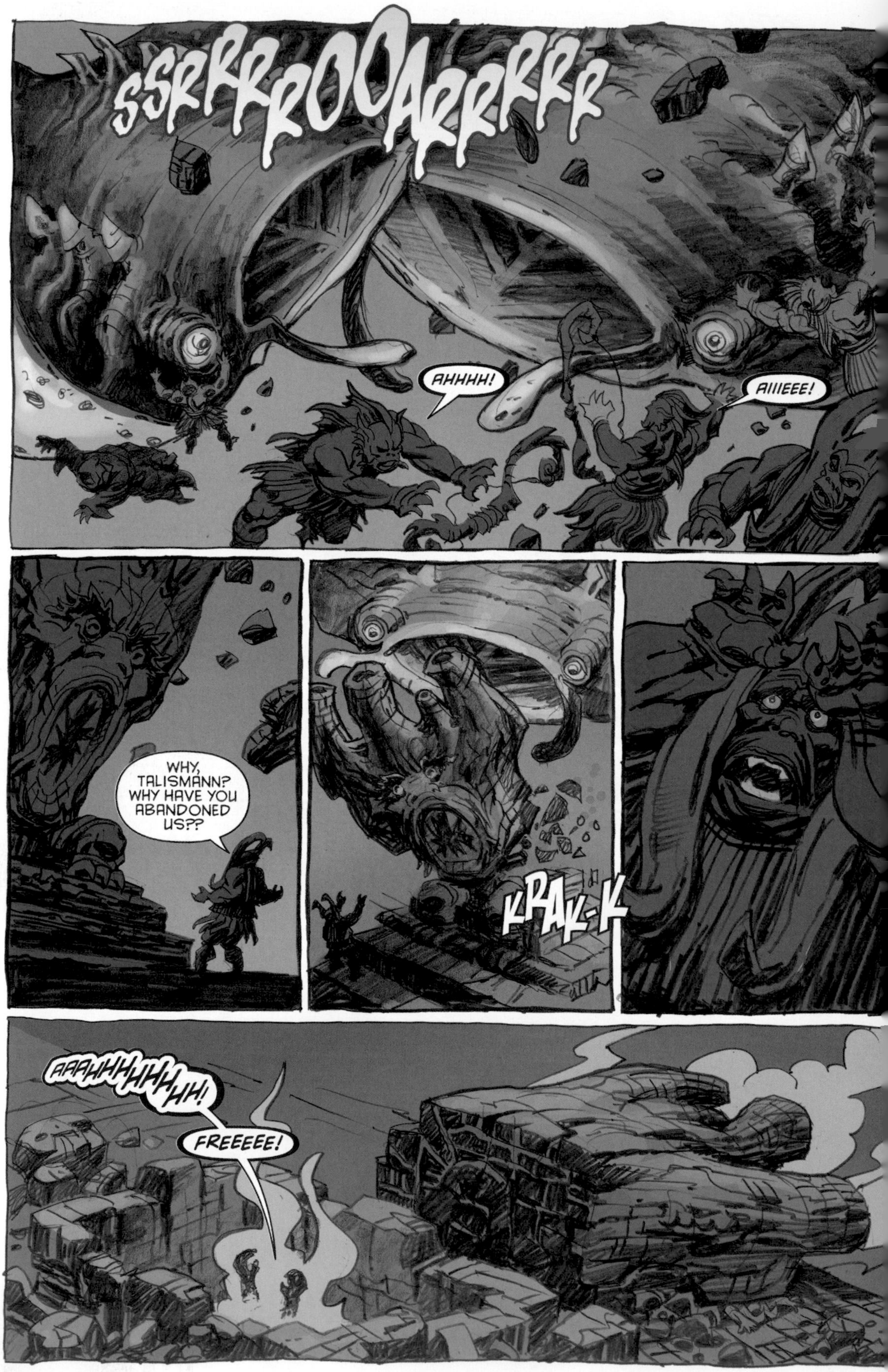
SSRRRROOOARRRRRR
AHHHH!
AIIIEEE!
WHY, TALISMANN? WHY HAVE YOU ABANDONED US??
KRAK-K
AAAHHHHHHHH!
FREEEEE!

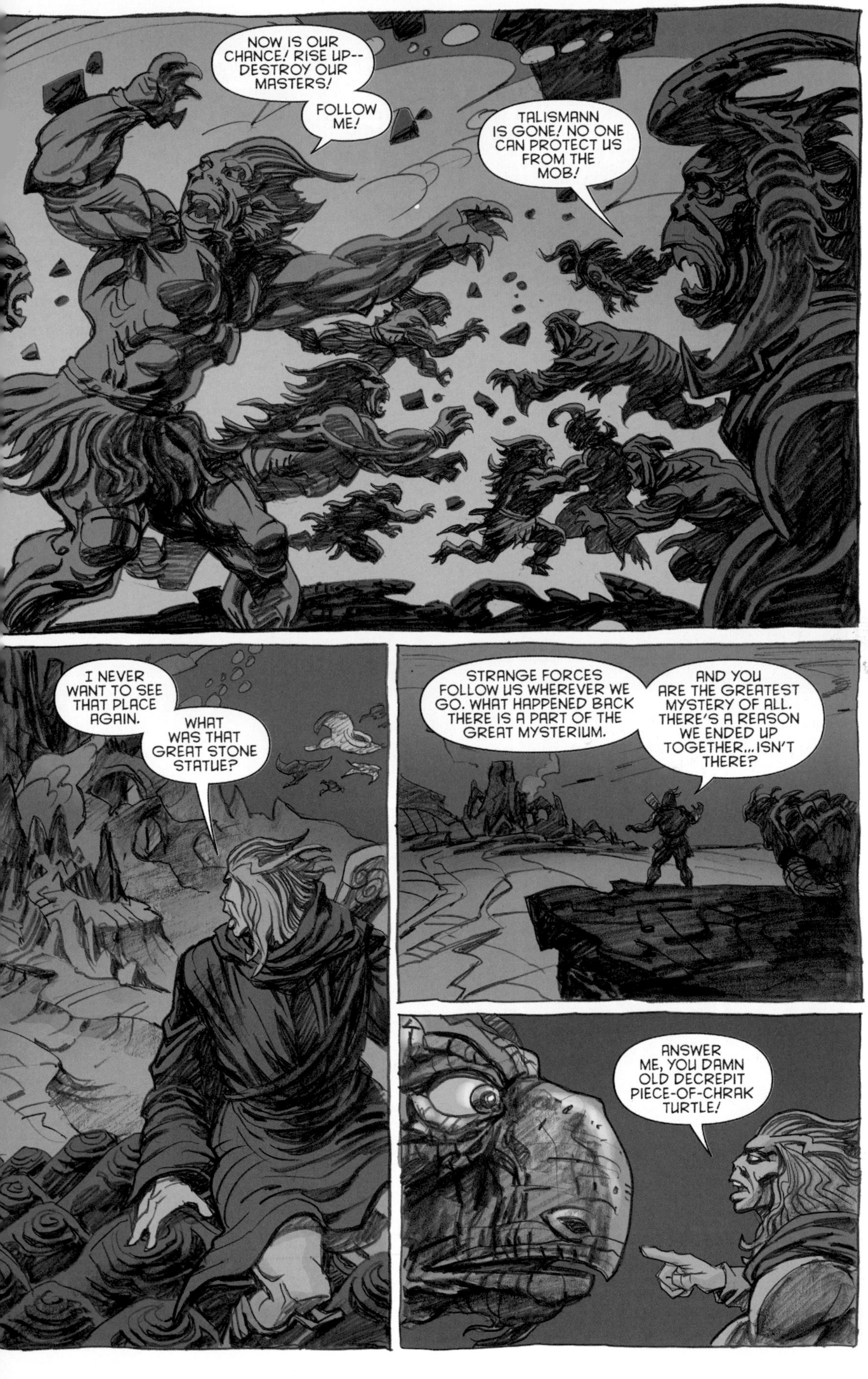
NOW IS OUR CHANCE! RISE UP-- DESTROY OUR MASTERS!
FOLLOW ME!
TALISMANN IS GONE! NO ONE CAN PROTECT US FROM THE MOB!
I NEVER WANT TO SEE THAT PLACE AGAIN.
WHAT WAS THAT GREAT STONE STATUE?
STRANGE FORCES FOLLOW US WHEREVER WE GO. WHAT HAPPENED BACK THERE IS A PART OF THE GREAT MYSTERIUM.
AND YOU ARE THE GREATEST MYSTERY OF ALL. THERE'S A REASON WE ENDED UP TOGETHER...ISN'T THERE?
ANSWER ME, YOU DAMN OLD DECREPIT PIECE-OF-CHRAK TURTLE!

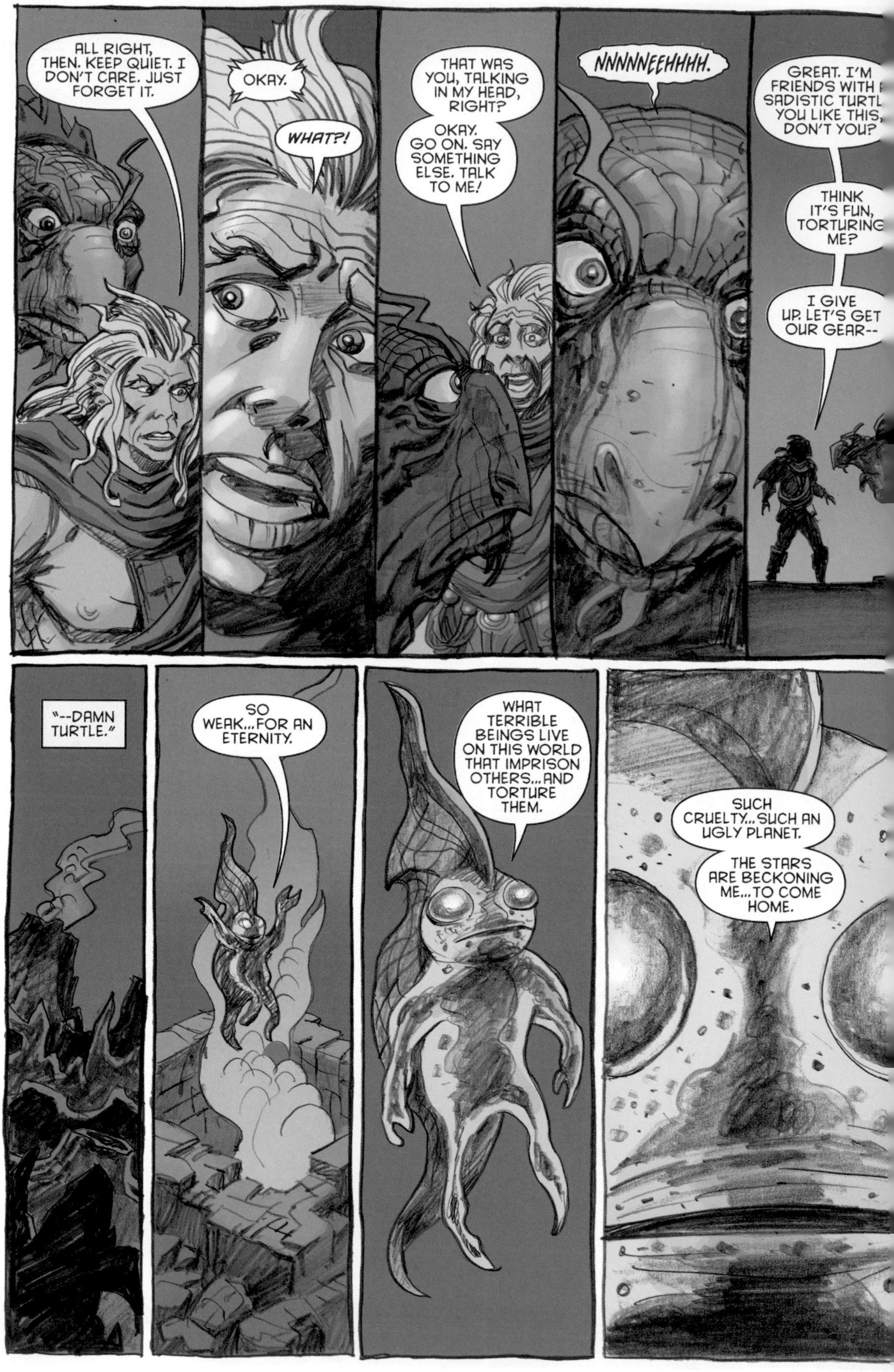
ALL RIGHT, THEN. KEEP QUIET. I DON'T CARE. JUST FORGET IT.
OKAY.
WHAT?!
THAT WAS YOU, TALKING IN MY HEAD, RIGHT?
OKAY. GO ON. SAY SOMETHING ELSE. TALK TO ME!
NNNNNEEHHHH.
GREAT. I'M FRIENDS WITH
SADISTIC TURTL
YOU LIKE THIS,
DON'T YOU?
THINK IT'S FUN, TORTURING ME?
I GIVE UP. LET'S GET OUR GEAR--
"--DAMN TURTLE."
SO WEAK...FOR AN ETERNITY.
WHAT TERRIBLE BEINGS LIVE ON THIS WORLD THAT IMPRISON OTHERS...AND TORTURE THEM.
SUCH CRUELTY...SUCH AN UGLY PLANET.
THE STARS ARE BECKONING ME...TO COME HOME.

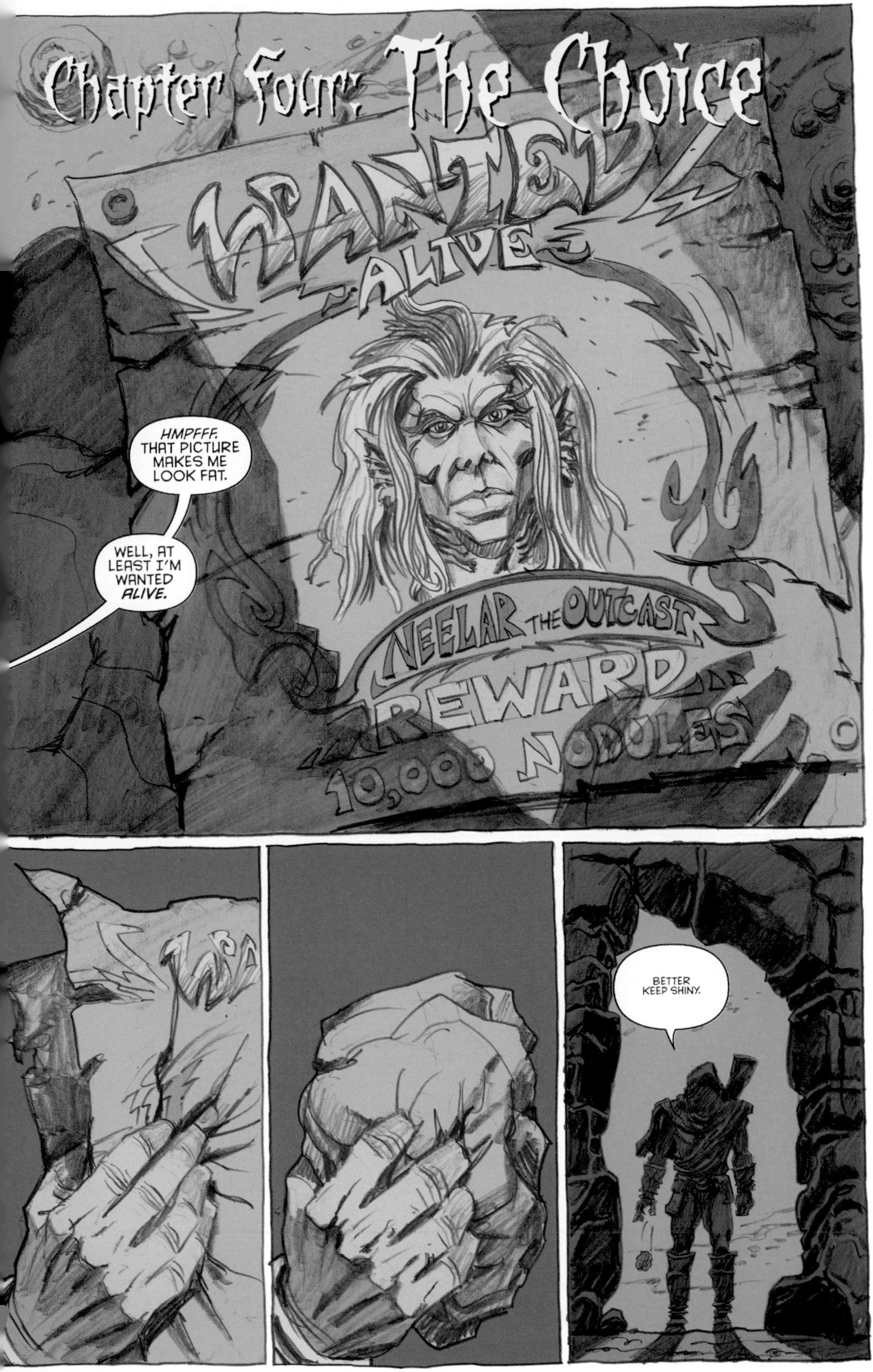
Chapter Four: The Choice
WANTED
ALIVE
HMPFFF. THAT PICTURE MAKES ME LOOK FAT.
WELL, AT LEAST I'M WANTED ALIVE.
NEELAR THE OUTCAST
REWARD
10,000 NODULES
BETTER KEEP SHINY.

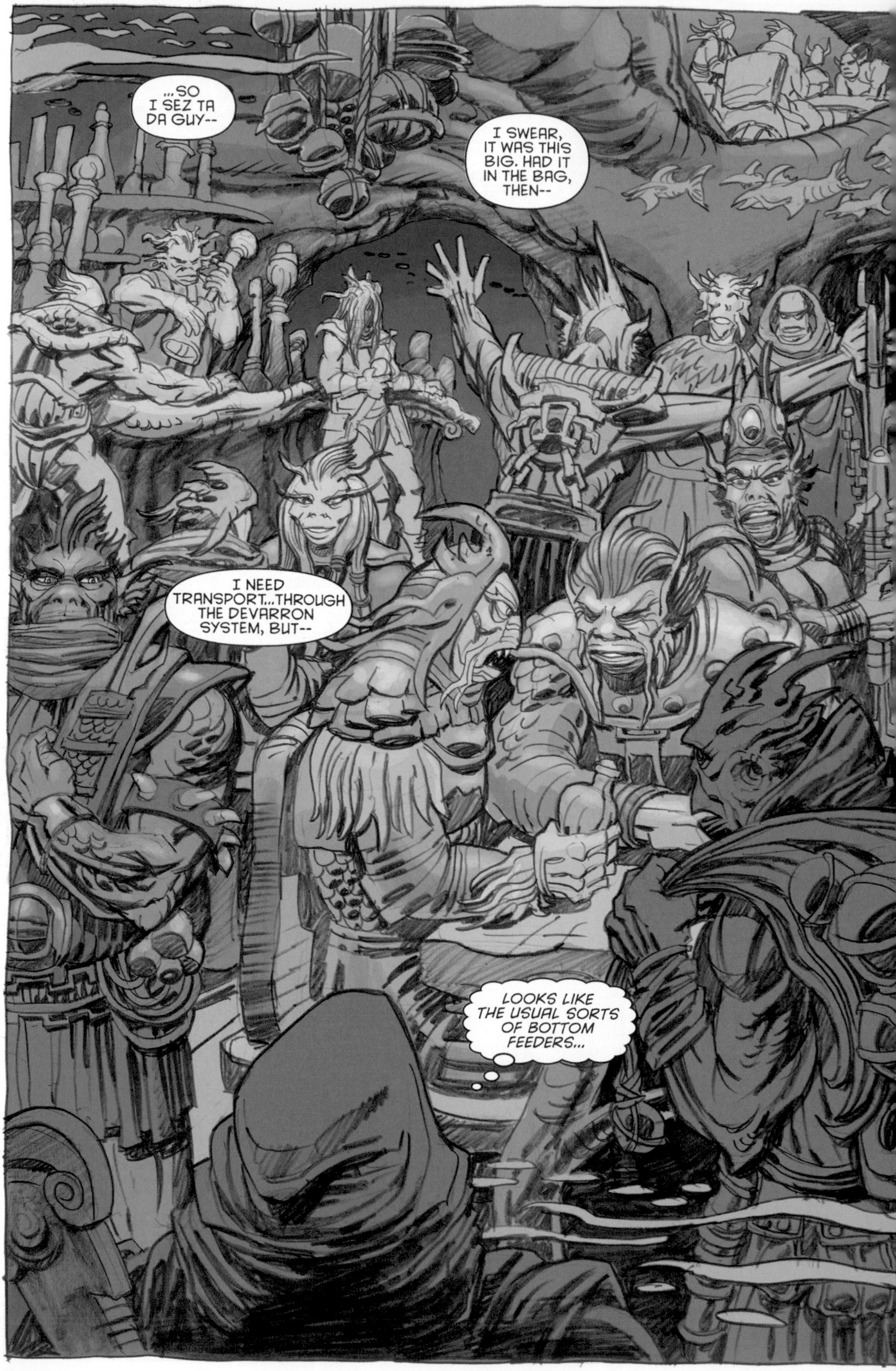
...SO I SEZ TA DA GUY--
I SWEAR, IT WAS THIS BIG. HAD IT IN THE BAG, THEN--
I NEED TRANSPORT...THROUGH THE DEVARRON SYSTEM, BUT--
LOOKS LIKE THE USUAL SORTS OF BOTTOM FEEDERS...

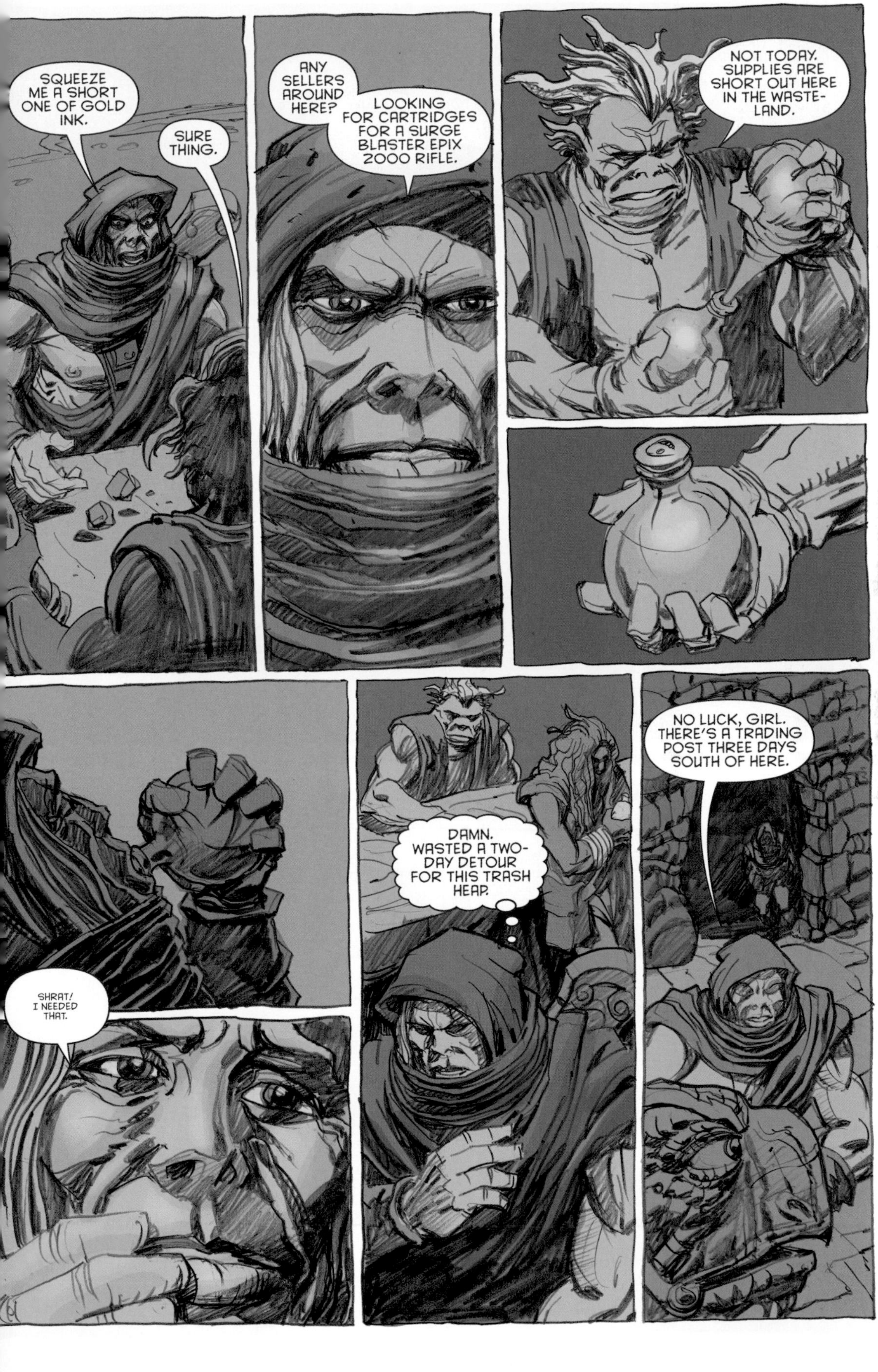
SQUEEZE ME A SHORT ONE OF GOLD INK.
SURE THING.
ANY SELLERS AROUND HERE?
LOOKING FOR CARTRIDGES FOR A SURGE BLASTER EPIX 2000 RIFLE.
NOT TODAY. SUPPLIES ARE SHORT OUT HERE IN THE WASTE-LAND.
SHRAT! I NEEDED THAT.
DAMN. WASTED A TWO-DAY DETOUR FOR THIS TRASH HEAP.
NO LUCK, GIRL. THERE'S A TRADING POST THREE DAYS SOUTH OF HERE.

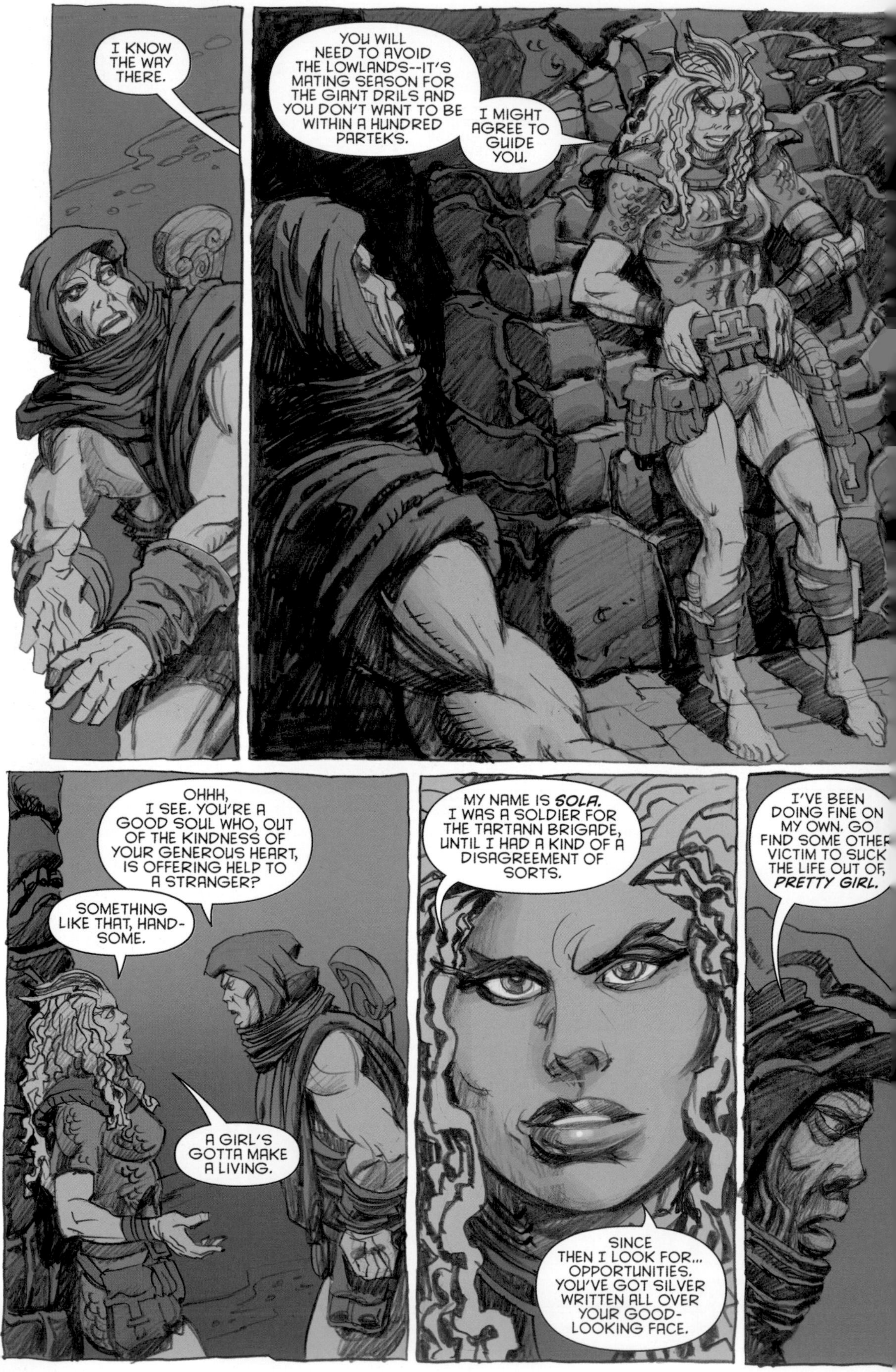
I KNOW THE WAY THERE.
YOU WILL NEED TO AVOID THE LOWLANDS--IT'S MATING SEASON FOR THE GIANT DRILS AND YOU DON'T WANT TO BE WITHIN A HUNDRED PARTEKS.
I MIGHT AGREE TO GUIDE YOU.
OHHH, I SEE. YOU'RE A GOOD SOUL WHO, OUT OF THE KINDNESS OF YOUR GENEROUS HEART, IS OFFERING HELP TO A STRANGER?
SOMETHING LIKE THAT, HAND-SOME.
A GIRL'S GOTTA MAKE A LIVING.
MY NAME IS *SOLA*. I WAS A SOLDIER FOR THE TARTANN BRIGADE, UNTIL I HAD A KIND OF A DISAGREEMENT OF SORTS.
SINCE THEN I LOOK FOR... OPPORTUNITIES. YOU'VE GOT SILVER WRITTEN ALL OVER YOUR GOOD-LOOKING FACE.
I'VE BEEN DOING FINE ON MY OWN. GO FIND SOME OTHER VICTIM TO SUCK THE LIFE OUT OF, *PRETTY GIRL.*

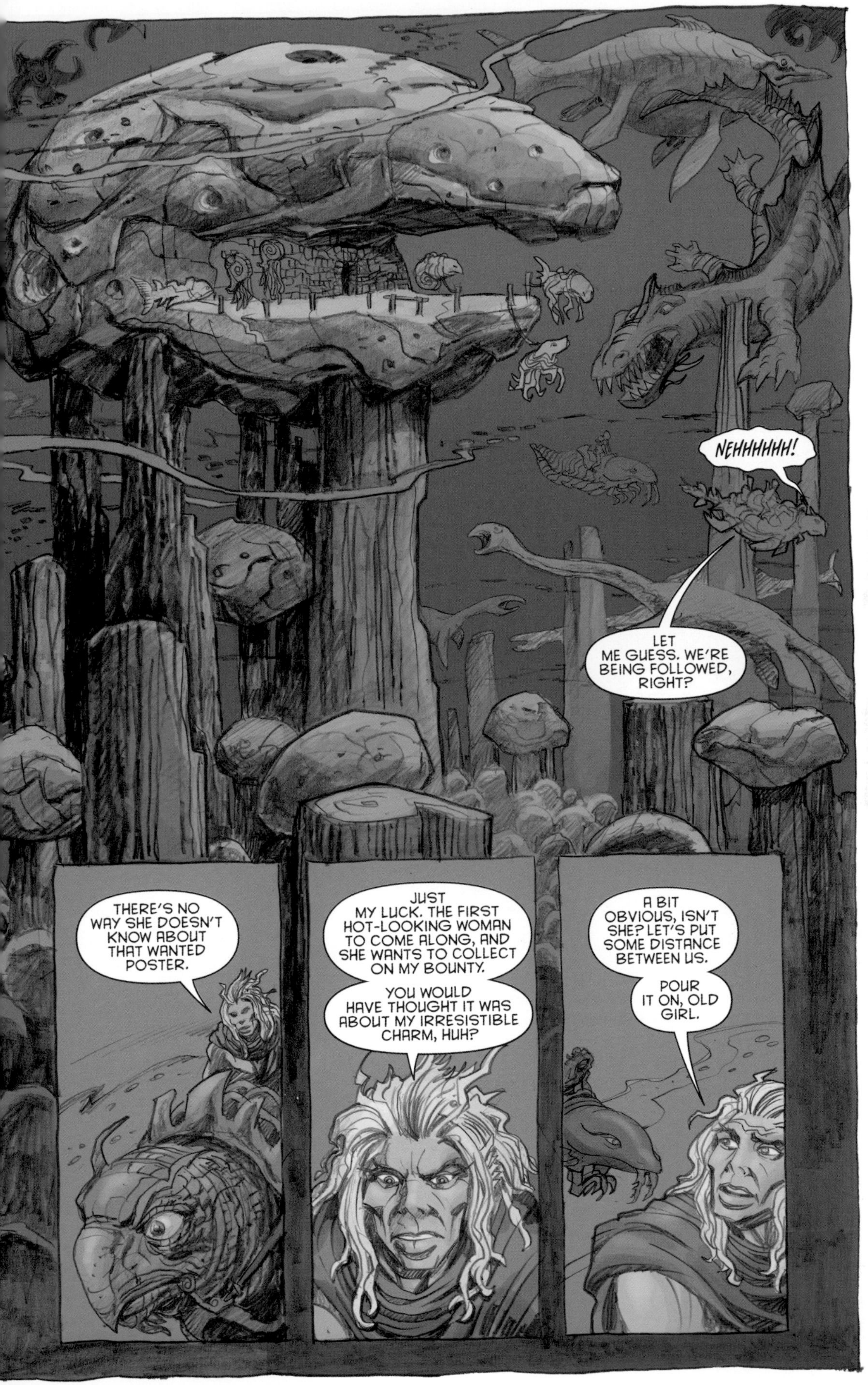
NEHHHHHH!
LET ME GUESS. WE'RE BEING FOLLOWED, RIGHT?
THERE'S NO WAY SHE DOESN'T KNOW ABOUT THAT WANTED POSTER.
JUST MY LUCK. THE FIRST HOT-LOOKING WOMAN TO COME ALONG, AND SHE WANTS TO COLLECT ON MY BOUNTY.
YOU WOULD HAVE THOUGHT IT WAS ABOUT MY IRRESISTIBLE CHARM, HUH?
A BIT OBVIOUS, ISN'T SHE? LET'S PUT SOME DISTANCE BETWEEN US.
POUR IT ON, OLD GIRL.

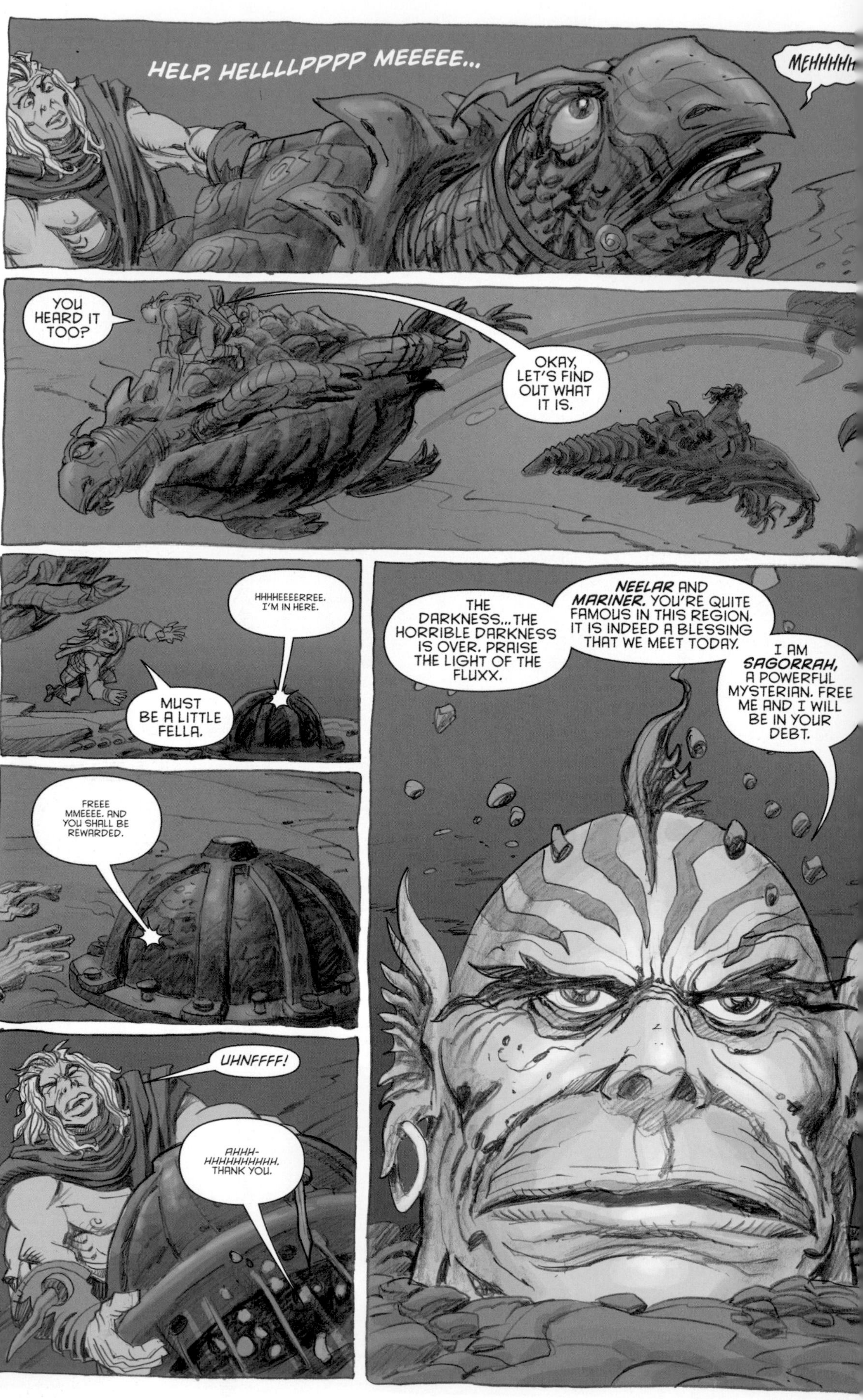

HELP. HELLLLPPPP MEEEEE...
MEHHHHH
YOU HEARD IT TOO?
OKAY, LET'S FIND OUT WHAT IT IS.
HHHHEEEERREE. I'M IN HERE.
MUST BE A LITTLE FELLA.
FREEE MMEEEE. AND YOU SHALL BE REWARDED.
UHNFFFF!
AHHH-HHHHHHHHHH. THANK YOU.
THE DARKNESS... THE HORRIBLE DARKNESS IS OVER. PRAISE THE LIGHT OF THE FLUXX.
NEELAR AND MARINER. YOU'RE QUITE FAMOUS IN THIS REGION. IT IS INDEED A BLESSING THAT WE MEET TODAY.
I AM SAGORRAH, A POWERFUL MYSTERIAN. FREE ME AND I WILL BE IN YOUR DEBT.

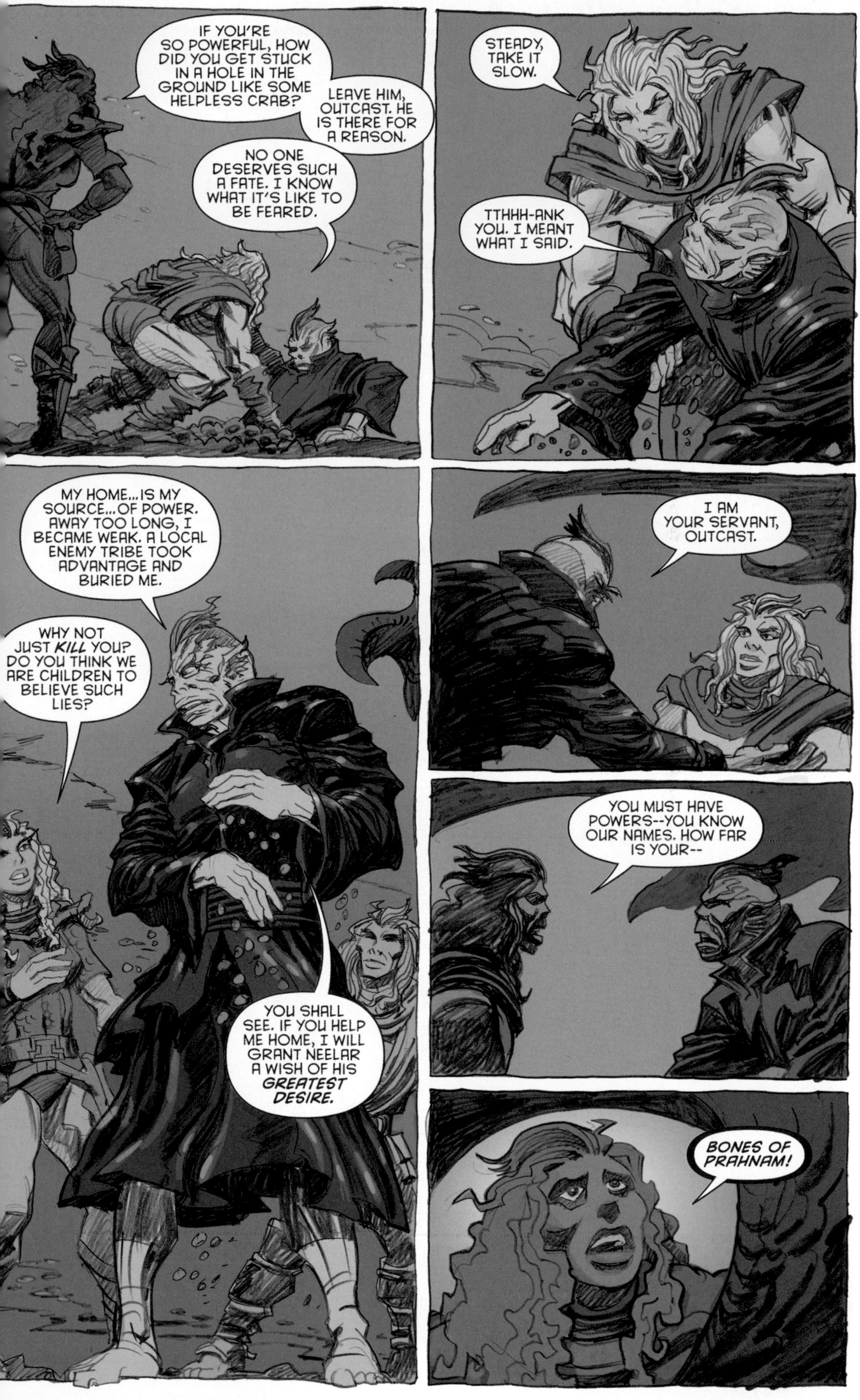
IF YOU'RE SO POWERFUL, HOW DID YOU GET STUCK IN A HOLE IN THE GROUND LIKE SOME HELPLESS CRAB?
LEAVE HIM, OUTCAST. HE IS THERE FOR A REASON.
NO ONE DESERVES SUCH A FATE. I KNOW WHAT IT'S LIKE TO BE FEARED.
STEADY, TAKE IT SLOW.
TTHHH-ANK YOU. I MEANT WHAT I SAID.
MY HOME...IS MY SOURCE...OF POWER. AWAY TOO LONG, I BECAME WEAK. A LOCAL ENEMY TRIBE TOOK ADVANTAGE AND BURIED ME.
WHY NOT JUST KILL YOU? DO YOU THINK WE ARE CHILDREN TO BELIEVE SUCH LIES?
YOU SHALL SEE. IF YOU HELP ME HOME, I WILL GRANT NEELAR A WISH OF HIS GREATEST DESIRE.
I AM YOUR SERVANT, OUTCAST.
YOU MUST HAVE POWERS--YOU KNOW OUR NAMES. HOW FAR IS YOUR--
BONES OF PRAHNAM!

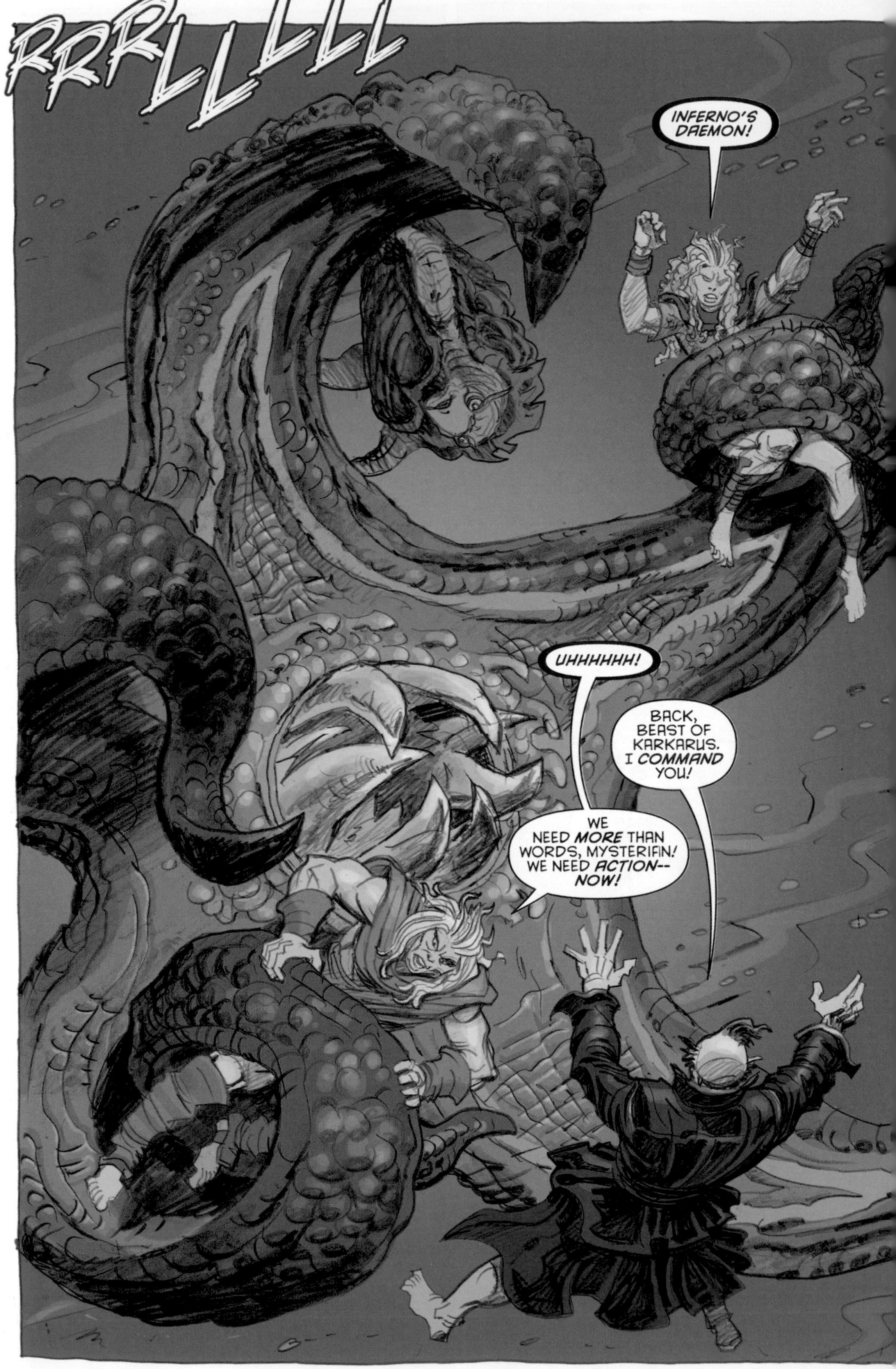
RRRLLLLL
INFERNO'S DAEMON!
UHHHHHH!
BACK, BEAST OF KARKARUS. I COMMAND YOU!
WE NEED MORE THAN WORDS, MYSTERIAN! WE NEED ACTION-- NOW!

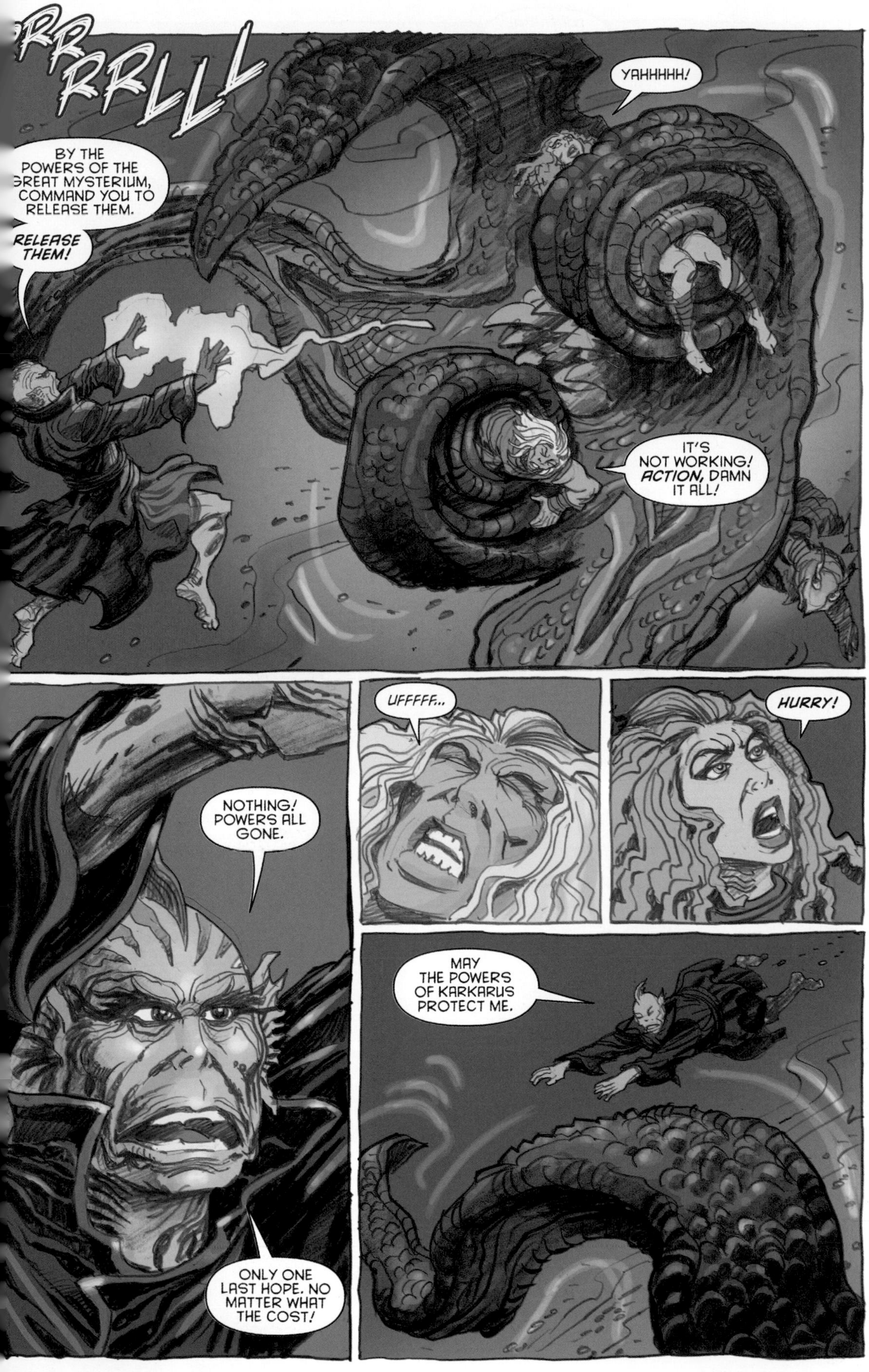
RRRRRLLL
YAHHHHH!
BY THE POWERS OF THE GREAT MYSTERIUM, COMMAND YOU TO RELEASE THEM.
RELEASE THEM!
IT'S NOT WORKING! ACTION, DAMN IT ALL!
NOTHING! POWERS ALL GONE.
UFFFFF...
HURRY!
ONLY ONE LAST HOPE. NO MATTER WHAT THE COST!
MAY THE POWERS OF KARKARUS PROTECT ME.

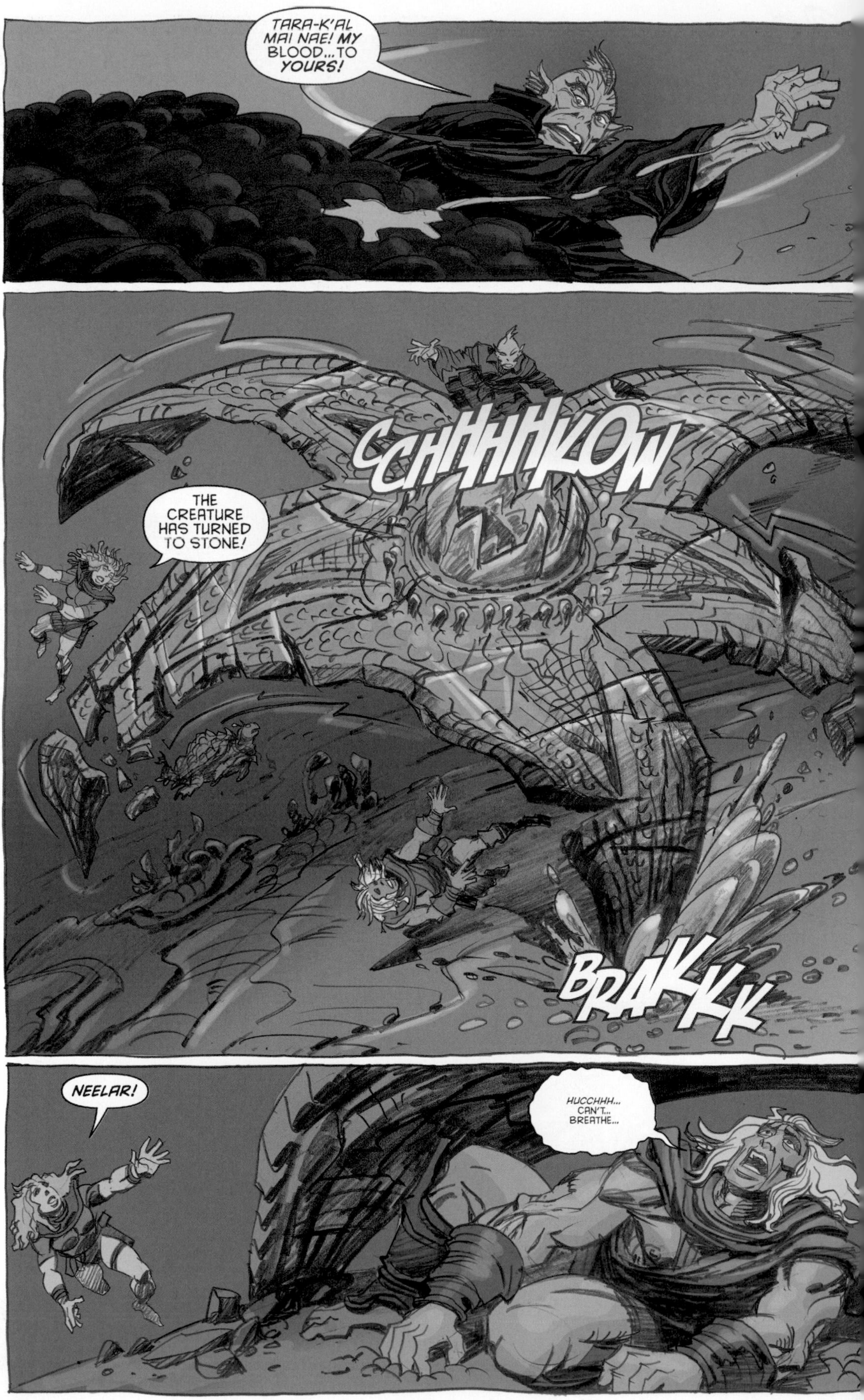
TARA-K'AL MAI NAE! MY BLOOD...TO YOURS!
CCHHHHKOW
THE CREATURE HAS TURNED TO STONE!
BRAKKK
NEELAR!
HUCCHHH... CAN'T... BREATHE...

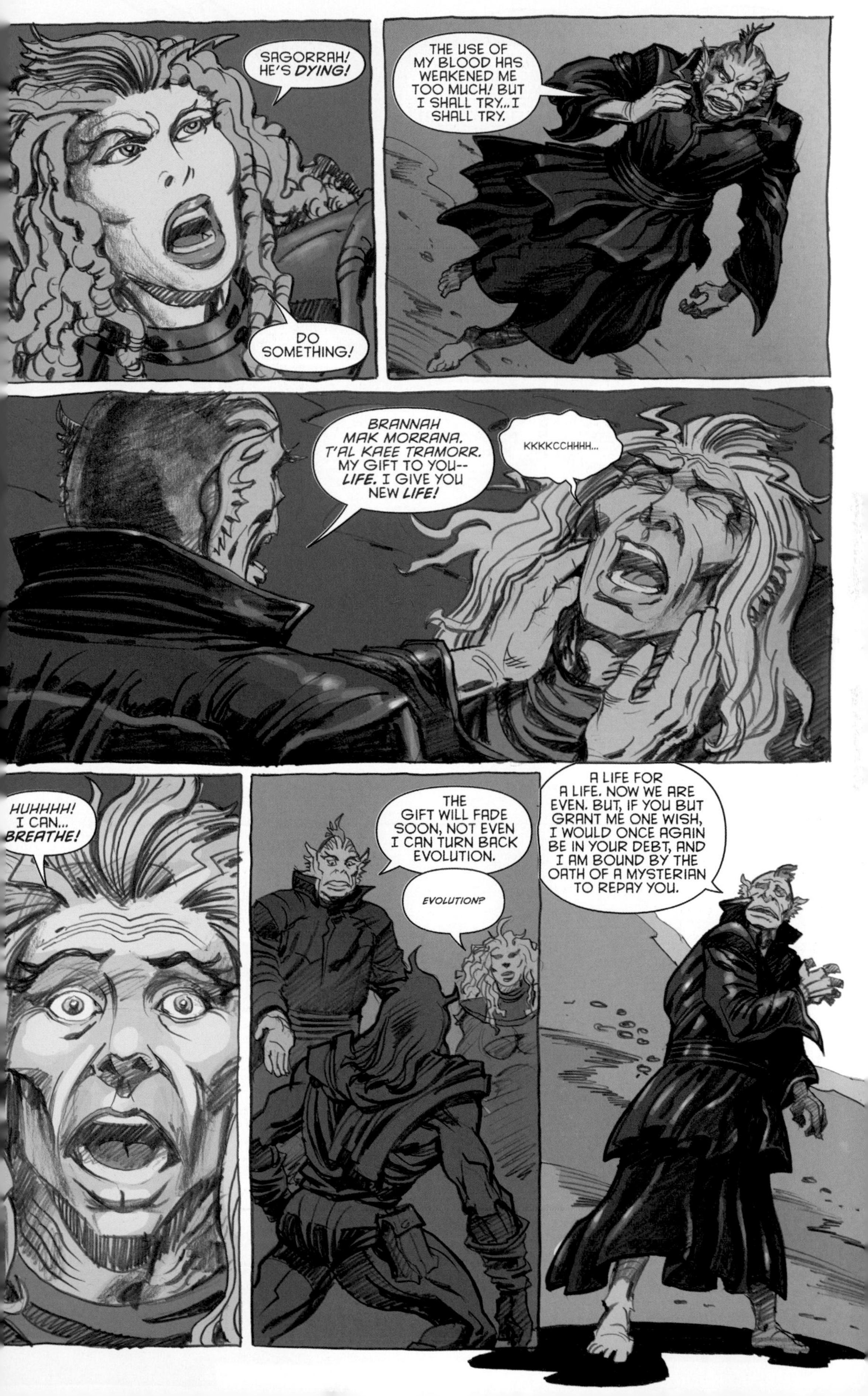

SAGORRAH! HE'S *DYING!*
DO SOMETHING!
THE USE OF MY BLOOD HAS WEAKENED ME TOO MUCH! BUT I SHALL TRY... I SHALL TRY.
BRANNAH MAK MORRANA. T'AL KAEE TRAMORR. MY GIFT TO YOU-- ***LIFE.*** I GIVE YOU NEW ***LIFE!***
KKKKCCHHHH...
HUHHHH! I CAN... ***BREATHE!***
THE GIFT WILL FADE SOON, NOT EVEN I CAN TURN BACK EVOLUTION.
EVOLUTION?
A LIFE FOR A LIFE. NOW WE ARE EVEN. BUT, IF YOU BUT GRANT ME ONE WISH, I WOULD ONCE AGAIN BE IN YOUR DEBT, AND I AM BOUND BY THE OATH OF A MYSTERIAN TO REPAY YOU.

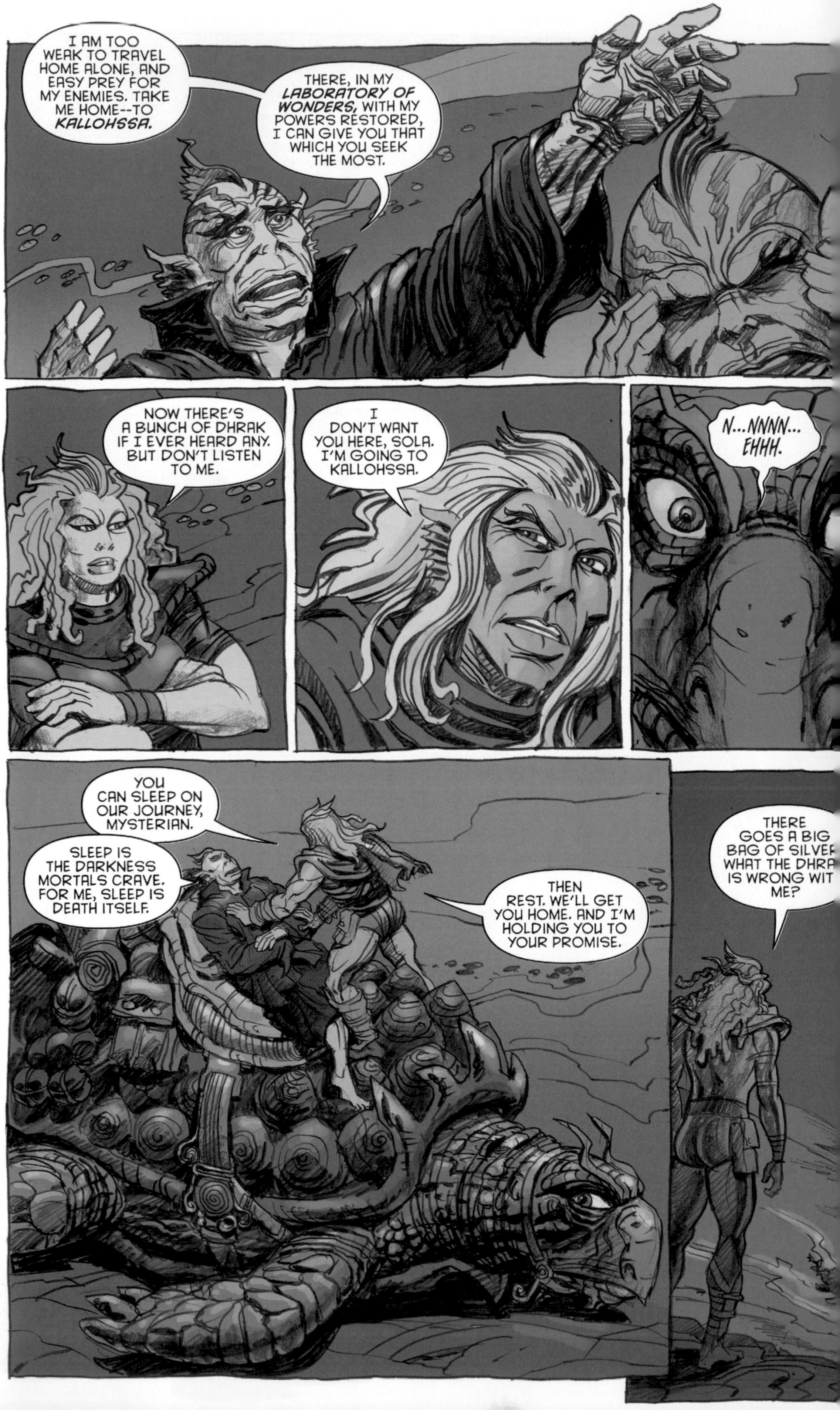

I AM TOO WEAK TO TRAVEL HOME ALONE, AND EASY PREY FOR MY ENEMIES. TAKE ME HOME--TO KALLOHSSA.
THERE, IN MY LABORATORY OF WONDERS, WITH MY POWERS RESTORED, I CAN GIVE YOU THAT WHICH YOU SEEK THE MOST.
NOW THERE'S A BUNCH OF DHRAK IF I EVER HEARD ANY. BUT DON'T LISTEN TO ME.
I DON'T WANT YOU HERE, SOLA. I'M GOING TO KALLOHSSA.
N...NNNN... EHHH.
YOU CAN SLEEP ON OUR JOURNEY, MYSTERIAN.
SLEEP IS THE DARKNESS MORTALS CRAVE. FOR ME, SLEEP IS DEATH ITSELF.
THEN REST. WE'LL GET YOU HOME. AND I'M HOLDING YOU TO YOUR PROMISE.

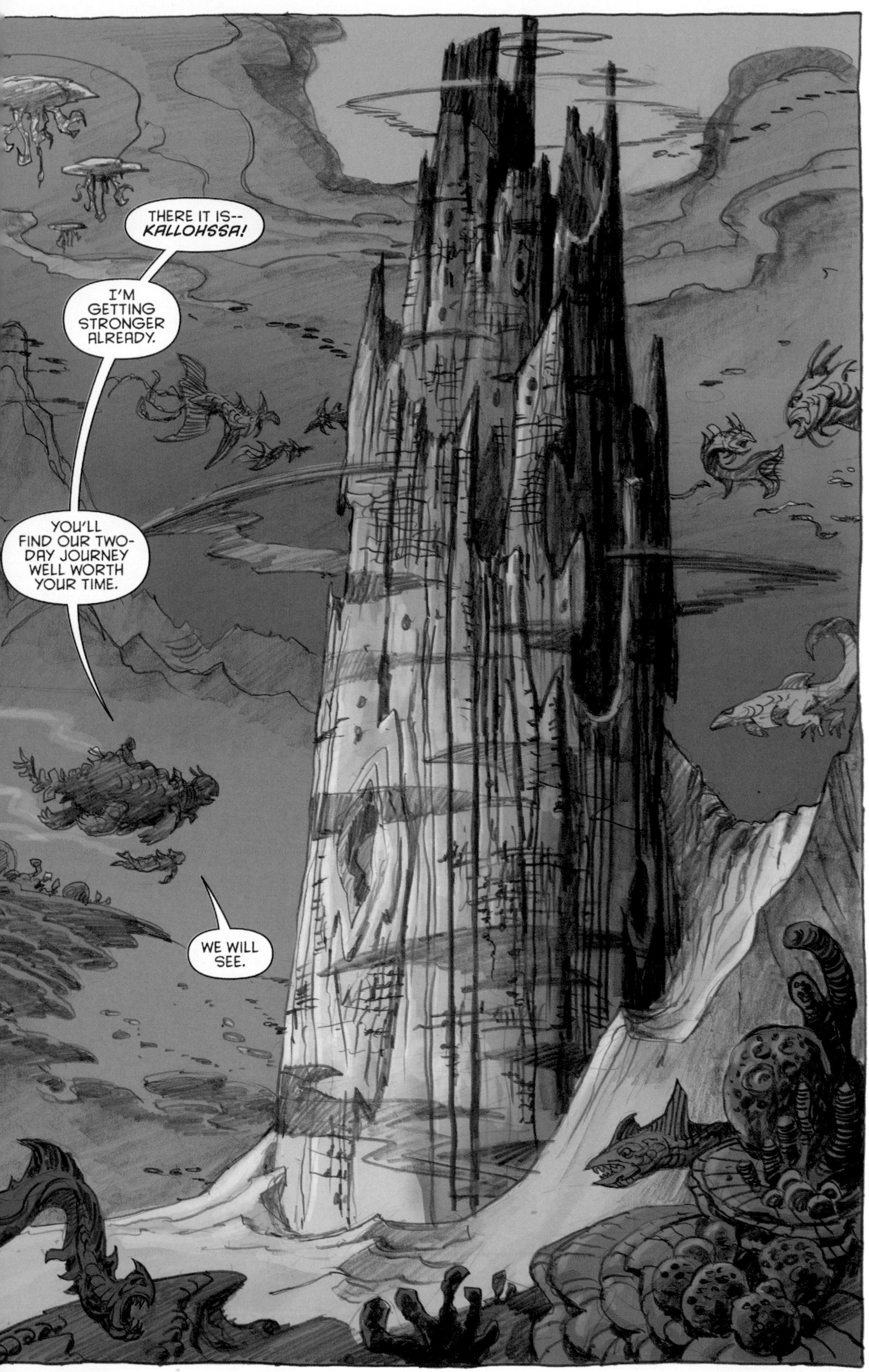
THERE IT IS--
KALLOHSSA!
I'M GETTING STRONGER ALREADY.
YOU'LL FIND OUR TWO-DAY JOURNEY WELL WORTH YOUR TIME.
WE WILL SEE.

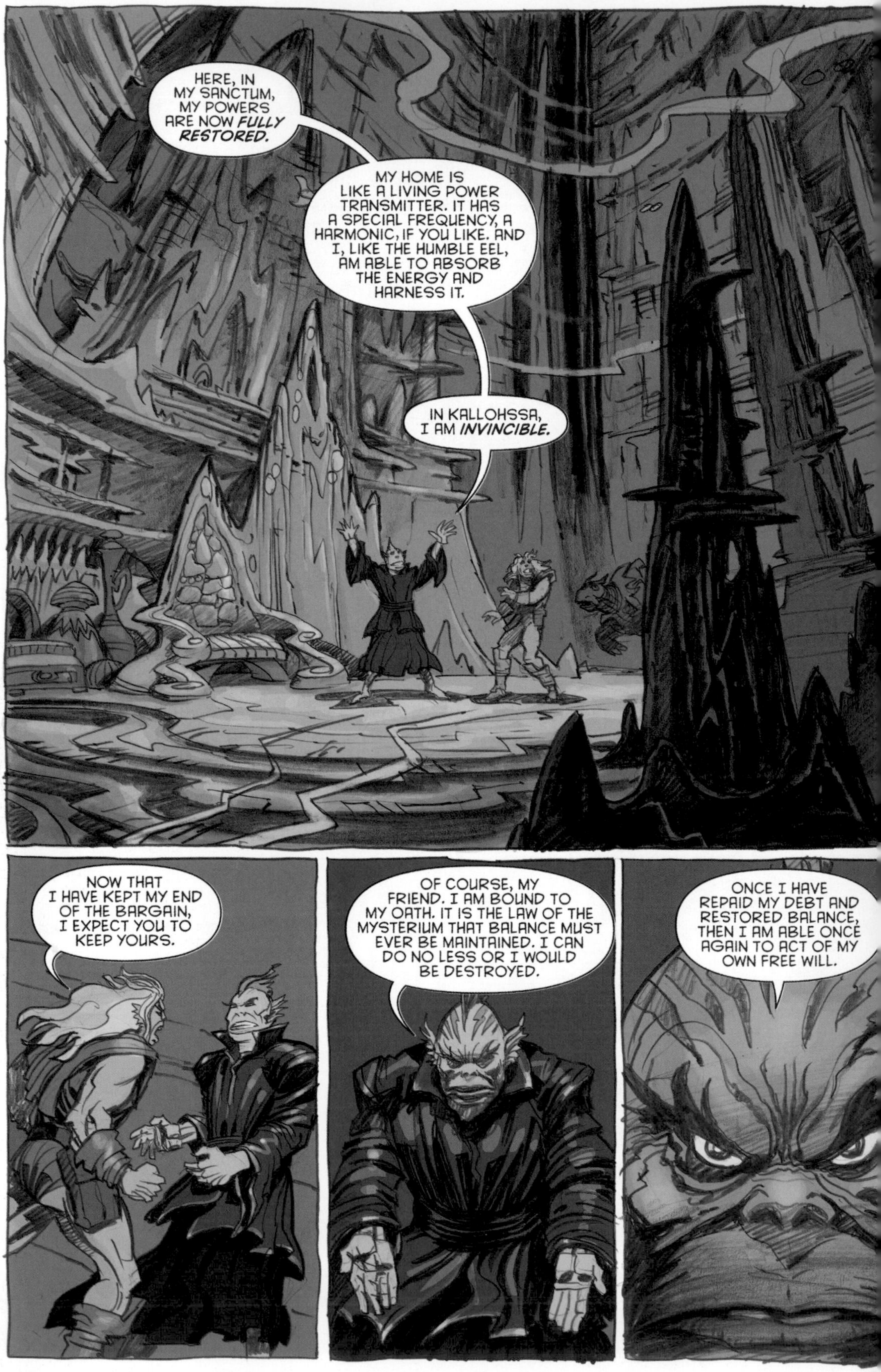
HERE, IN MY SANCTUM, MY POWERS ARE NOW *FULLY RESTORED.*
MY HOME IS LIKE A LIVING POWER TRANSMITTER. IT HAS A SPECIAL FREQUENCY, A HARMONIC, IF YOU LIKE. AND I, LIKE THE HUMBLE EEL, AM ABLE TO ABSORB THE ENERGY AND HARNESS IT.
IN KALLOHSSA, I AM *INVINCIBLE.*
NOW THAT I HAVE KEPT MY END OF THE BARGAIN, I EXPECT YOU TO KEEP YOURS.
OF COURSE, MY FRIEND. I AM BOUND TO MY OATH. IT IS THE LAW OF THE MYSTERIUM THAT BALANCE MUST EVER BE MAINTAINED. I CAN DO NO LESS OR I WOULD BE DESTROYED.
ONCE I HAVE REPAID MY DEBT AND RESTORED BALANCE, THEN I AM ABLE ONCE AGAIN TO ACT OF MY OWN FREE WILL.

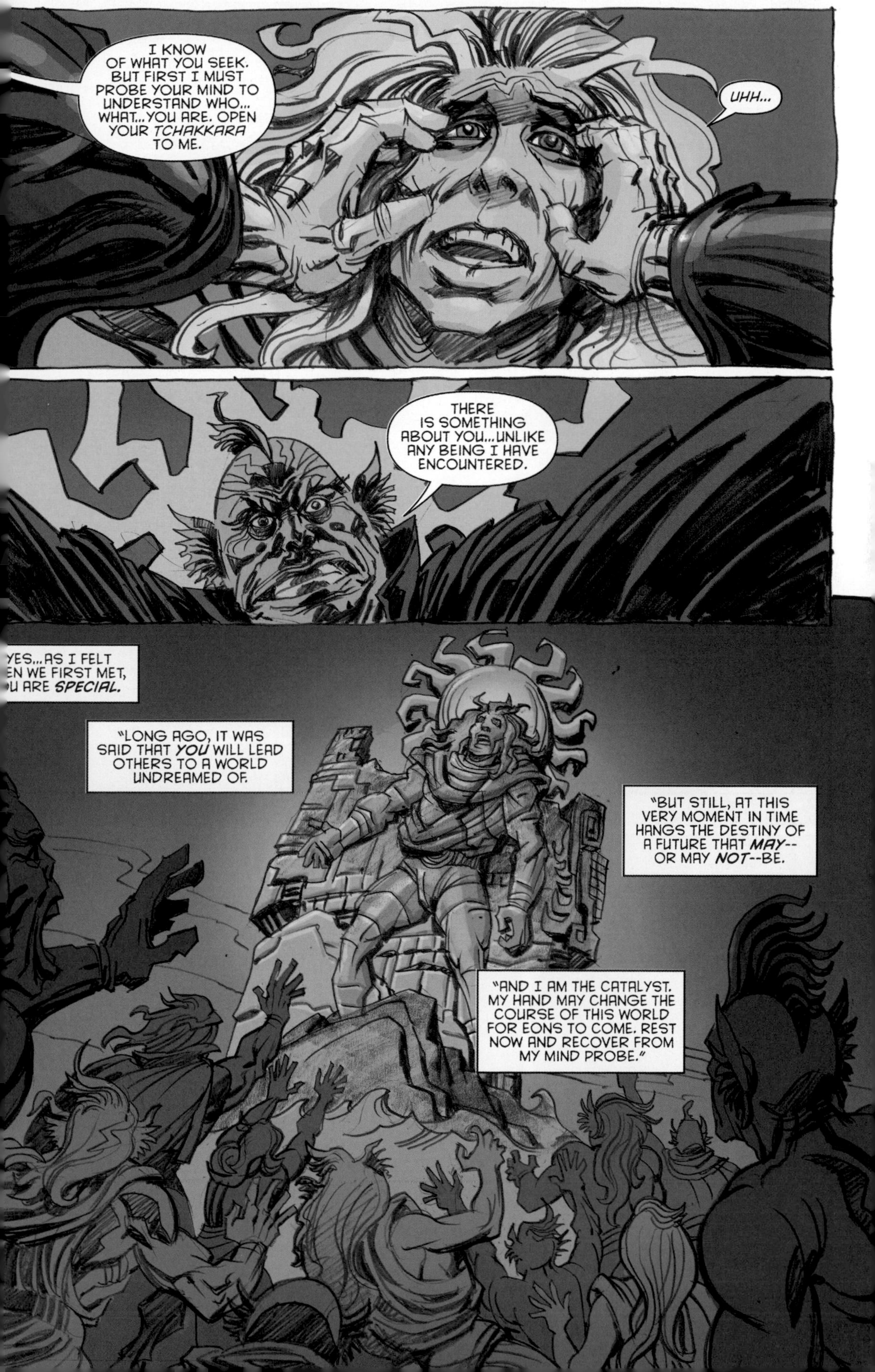
I KNOW OF WHAT YOU SEEK. BUT FIRST I MUST PROBE YOUR MIND TO UNDERSTAND WHO... WHAT...YOU ARE. OPEN YOUR *TCHAKKARA* TO ME.
UHH...
THERE IS SOMETHING ABOUT YOU...UNLIKE ANY BEING I HAVE ENCOUNTERED.
YES...AS I FELT
EN WE FIRST MET,
U ARE *SPECIAL.*
"LONG AGO, IT WAS SAID THAT *YOU* WILL LEAD OTHERS TO A WORLD UNDREAMED OF.
"BUT STILL, AT THIS VERY MOMENT IN TIME HANGS THE DESTINY OF A FUTURE THAT *MAY*-- OR MAY *NOT*--BE.
"AND I AM THE CATALYST. MY HAND MAY CHANGE THE COURSE OF THIS WORLD FOR EONS TO COME. REST NOW AND RECOVER FROM MY MIND PROBE."

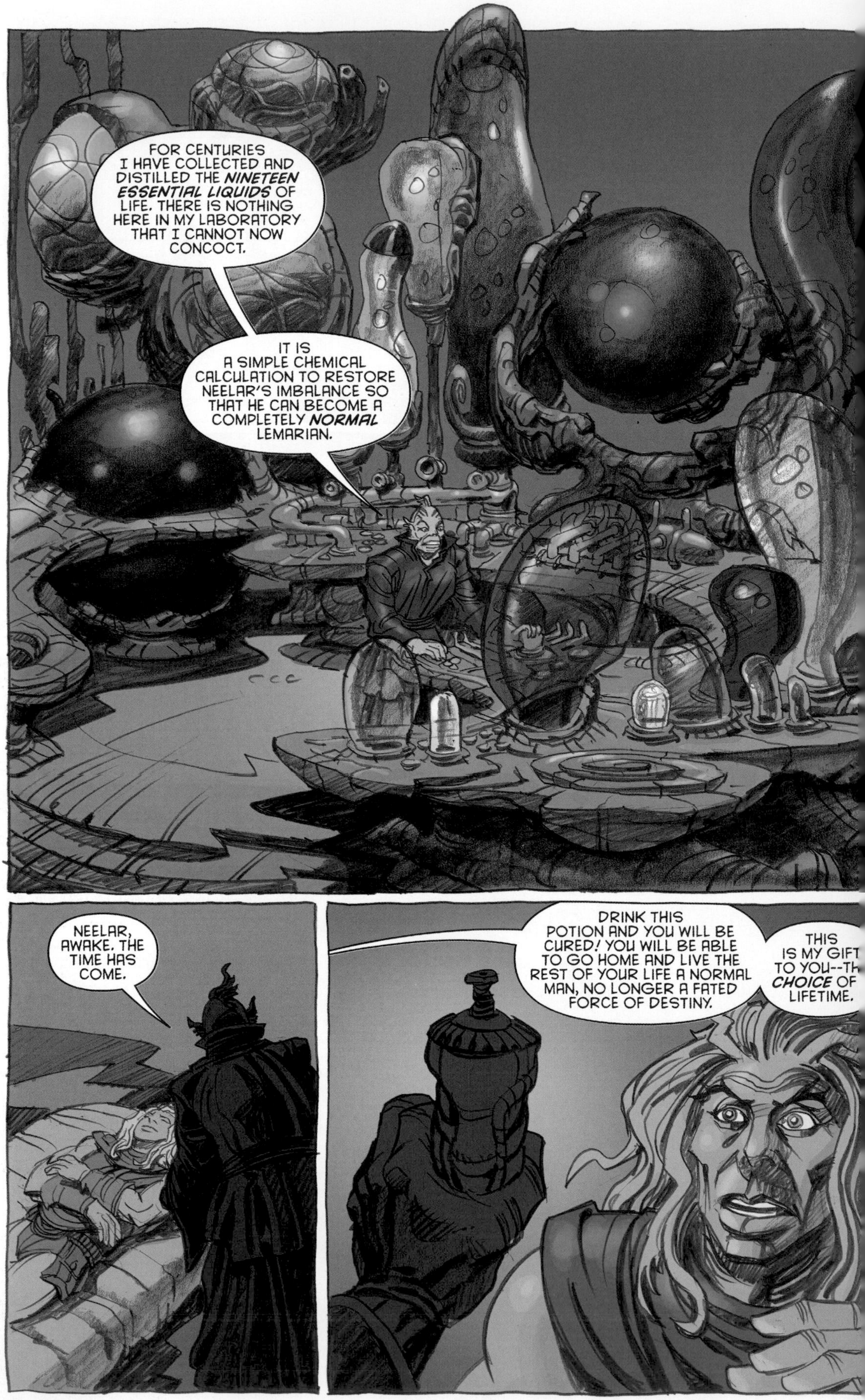
FOR CENTURIES I HAVE COLLECTED AND DISTILLED THE *NINETEEN ESSENTIAL LIQUIDS* OF LIFE. THERE IS NOTHING HERE IN MY LABORATORY THAT I CANNOT NOW CONCOCT.
IT IS A SIMPLE CHEMICAL CALCULATION TO RESTORE NEELAR'S IMBALANCE SO THAT HE CAN BECOME A COMPLETELY *NORMAL* LEMARIAN.
NEELAR, AWAKE. THE TIME HAS COME.
DRINK THIS POTION AND YOU WILL BE CURED! YOU WILL BE ABLE TO GO HOME AND LIVE THE REST OF YOUR LIFE A NORMAL MAN, NO LONGER A FATED FORCE OF DESTINY.
THIS IS MY GIFT TO YOU--TH *CHOICE* OF LIFETIME.

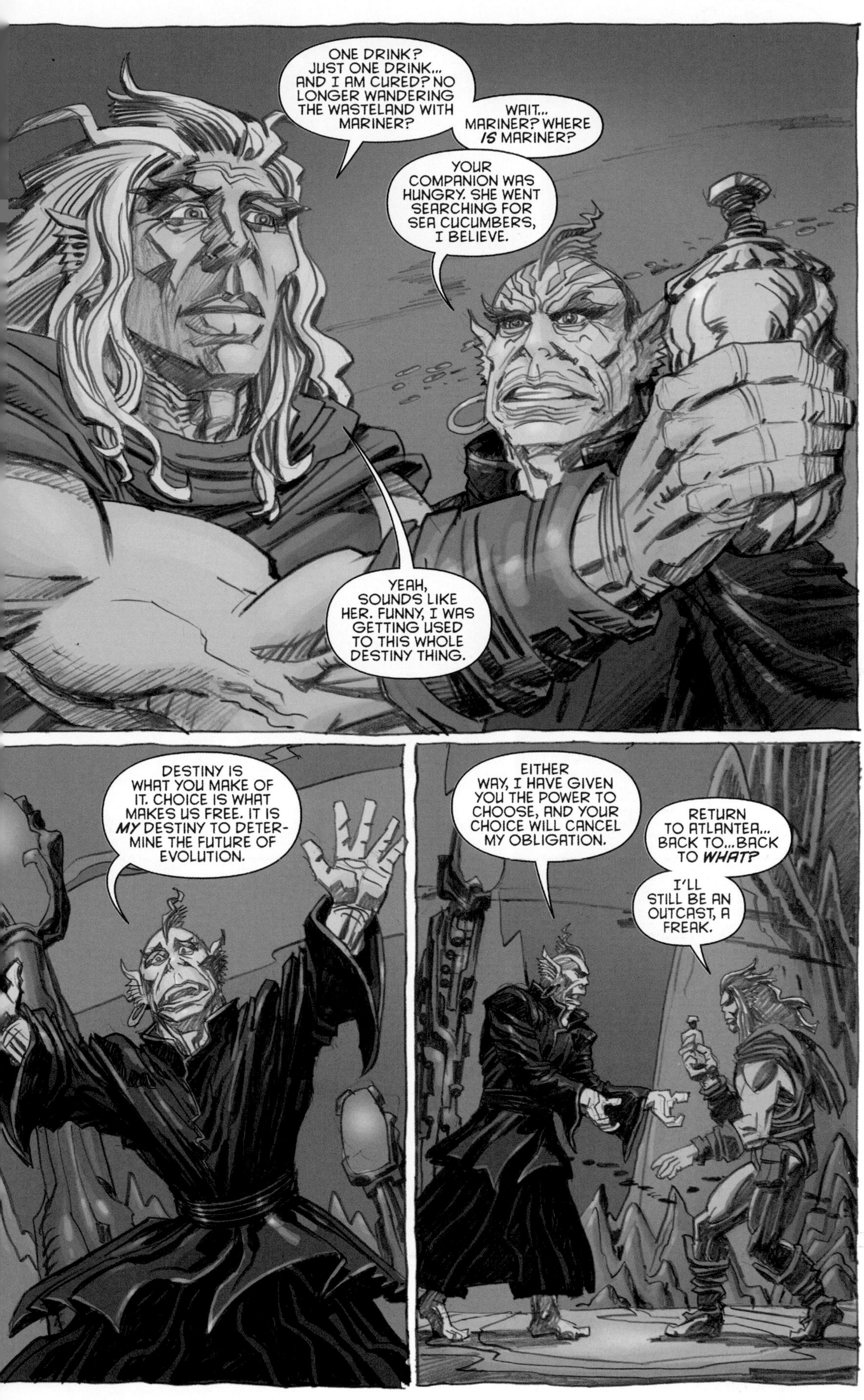
ONE DRINK? JUST ONE DRINK... AND I AM CURED? NO LONGER WANDERING THE WASTELAND WITH MARINER?
WAIT... MARINER? WHERE *IS* MARINER?
YOUR COMPANION WAS HUNGRY. SHE WENT SEARCHING FOR SEA CUCUMBERS, I BELIEVE.
YEAH, SOUNDS LIKE HER. FUNNY, I WAS GETTING USED TO THIS WHOLE DESTINY THING.
DESTINY IS WHAT YOU MAKE OF IT. CHOICE IS WHAT MAKES US FREE. IT IS ***MY*** DESTINY TO DETERMINE THE FUTURE OF EVOLUTION.
EITHER WAY, I HAVE GIVEN YOU THE POWER TO CHOOSE, AND YOUR CHOICE WILL CANCEL MY OBLIGATION.
RETURN TO ATLANTEA... BACK TO... BACK TO ***WHAT?***
I'LL STILL BE AN OUTCAST, A FREAK.

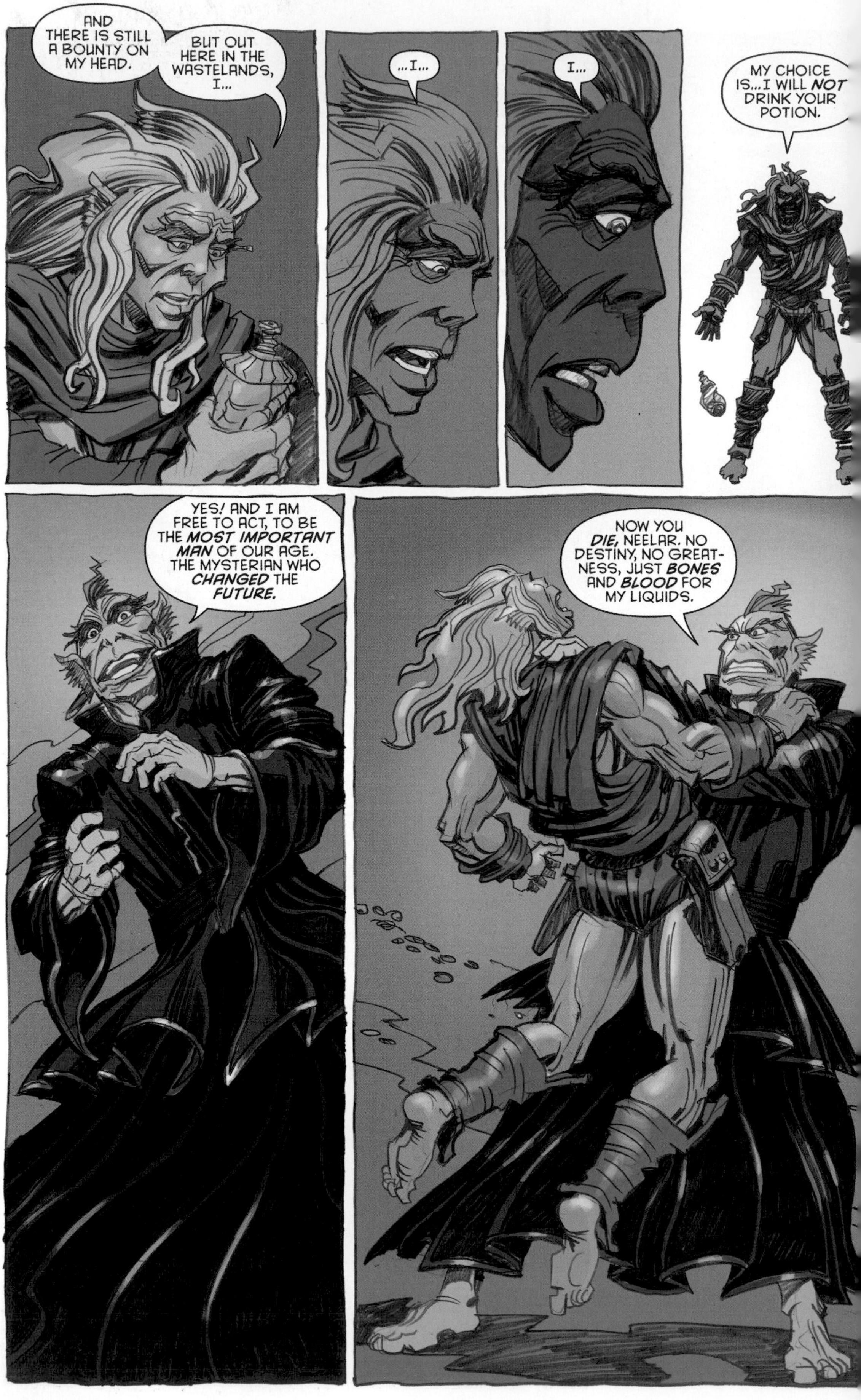
AND THERE IS STILL A BOUNTY ON MY HEAD.
BUT OUT HERE IN THE WASTELANDS, I...
...I...
I...
MY CHOICE IS...I WILL NOT DRINK YOUR POTION.
YES! AND I AM FREE TO ACT, TO BE THE MOST IMPORTANT MAN OF OUR AGE. THE MYSTERIAN WHO CHANGED THE FUTURE.
NOW YOU DIE, NEELAR. NO DESTINY, NO GREATNESS, JUST BONES AND BLOOD FOR MY LIQUIDS.

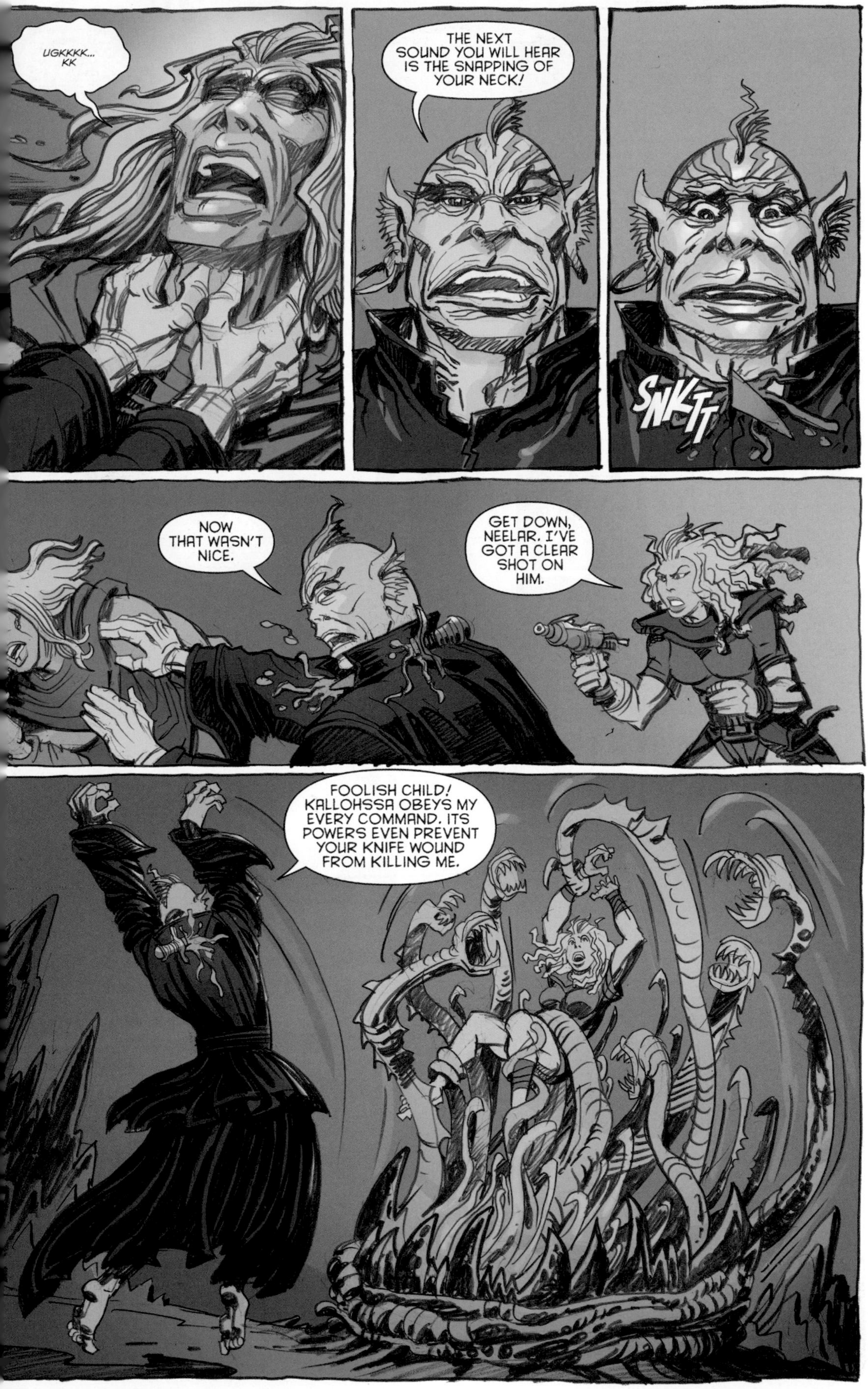
UGKKKK... KK
THE NEXT SOUND YOU WILL HEAR IS THE SNAPPING OF YOUR NECK!
SNKTT
NOW THAT WASN'T NICE.
GET DOWN, NEELAR. I'VE GOT A CLEAR SHOT ON HIM.
FOOLISH CHILD! KALLOHSSA OBEYS MY EVERY COMMAND. ITS POWERS EVEN PREVENT YOUR KNIFE WOUND FROM KILLING ME.

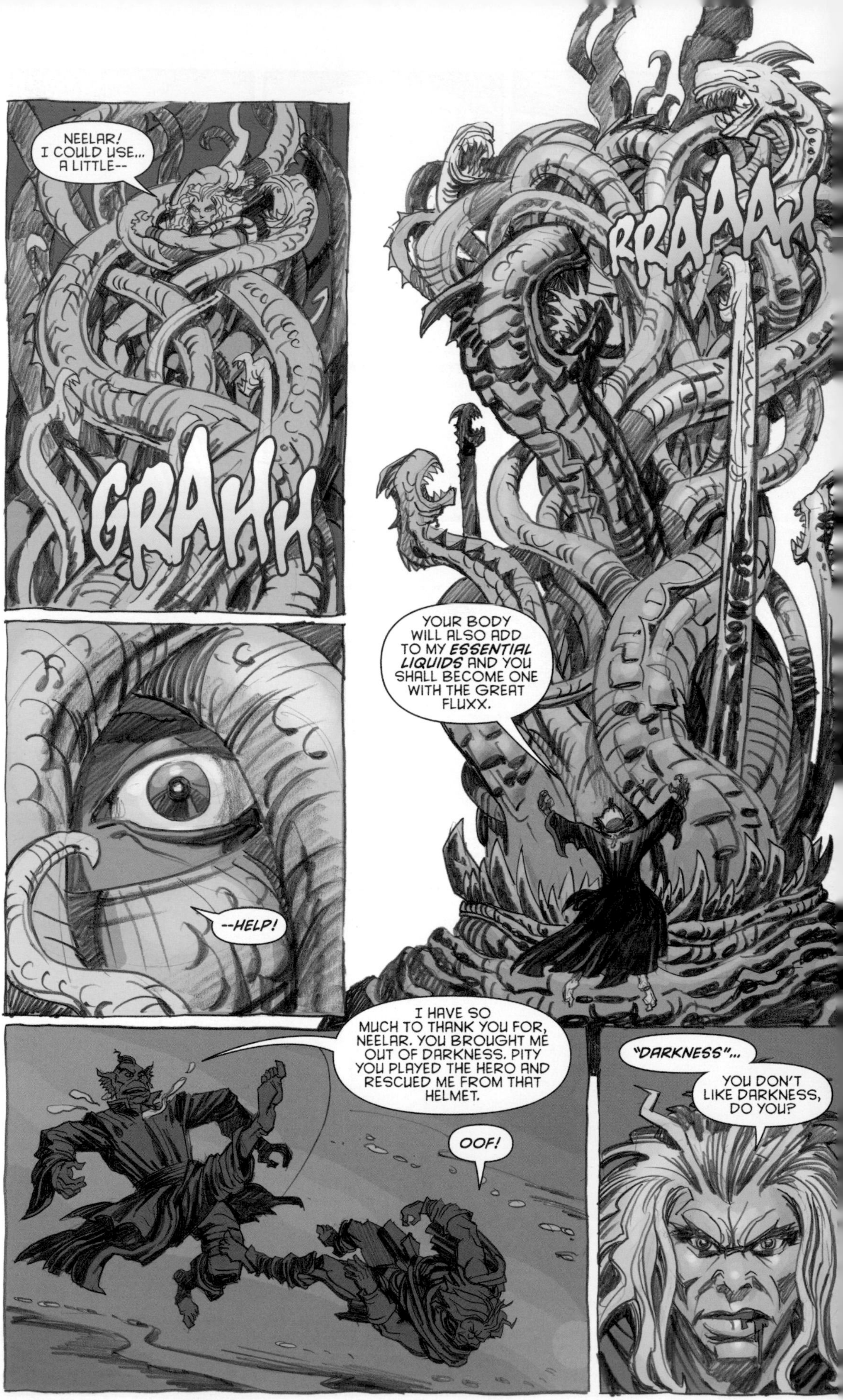
NEELAR! I COULD USE... A LITTLE--
GRAHH
--HELP!
RRAAAH
YOUR BODY WILL ALSO ADD TO MY ESSENTIAL LIQUIDS AND YOU SHALL BECOME ONE WITH THE GREAT FLUXX.
I HAVE SO MUCH TO THANK YOU FOR, NEELAR. YOU BROUGHT ME OUT OF DARKNESS. PITY YOU PLAYED THE HERO AND RESCUED ME FROM THAT HELMET.
OOF!
"DARKNESS"...
YOU DON'T LIKE DARKNESS, DO YOU?

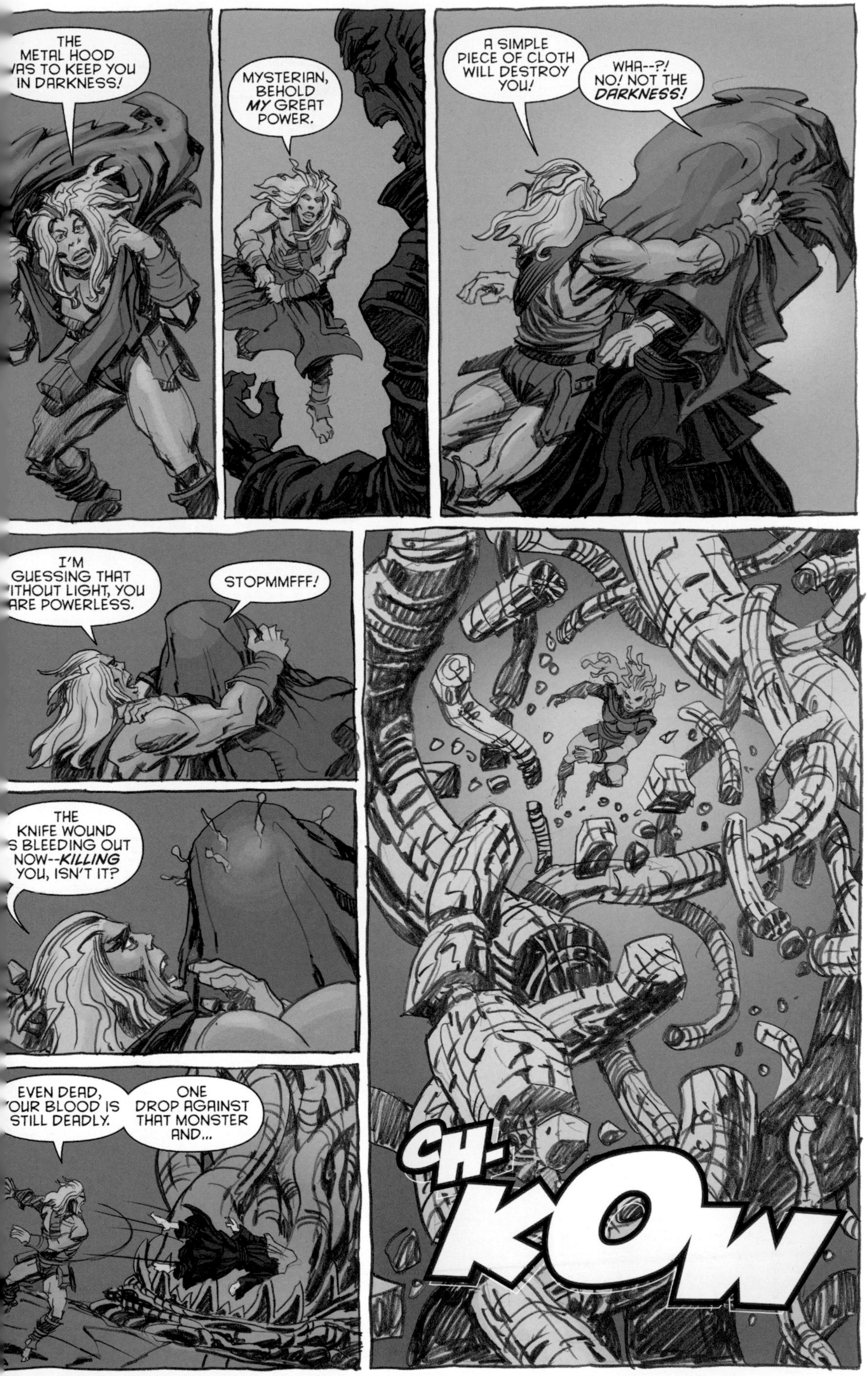
THE METAL HOOD WAS TO KEEP YOU IN DARKNESS!
MYSTERIAN, BEHOLD MY GREAT POWER.
A SIMPLE PIECE OF CLOTH WILL DESTROY YOU!
WHA--?! NO! NOT THE DARKNESS!
I'M GUESSING THAT WITHOUT LIGHT, YOU ARE POWERLESS.
STOPMMFFF!
THE KNIFE WOUND IS BLEEDING OUT NOW--KILLING YOU, ISN'T IT?
EVEN DEAD, YOUR BLOOD IS STILL DEADLY.
ONE DROP AGAINST THAT MONSTER AND...
CH-KOW

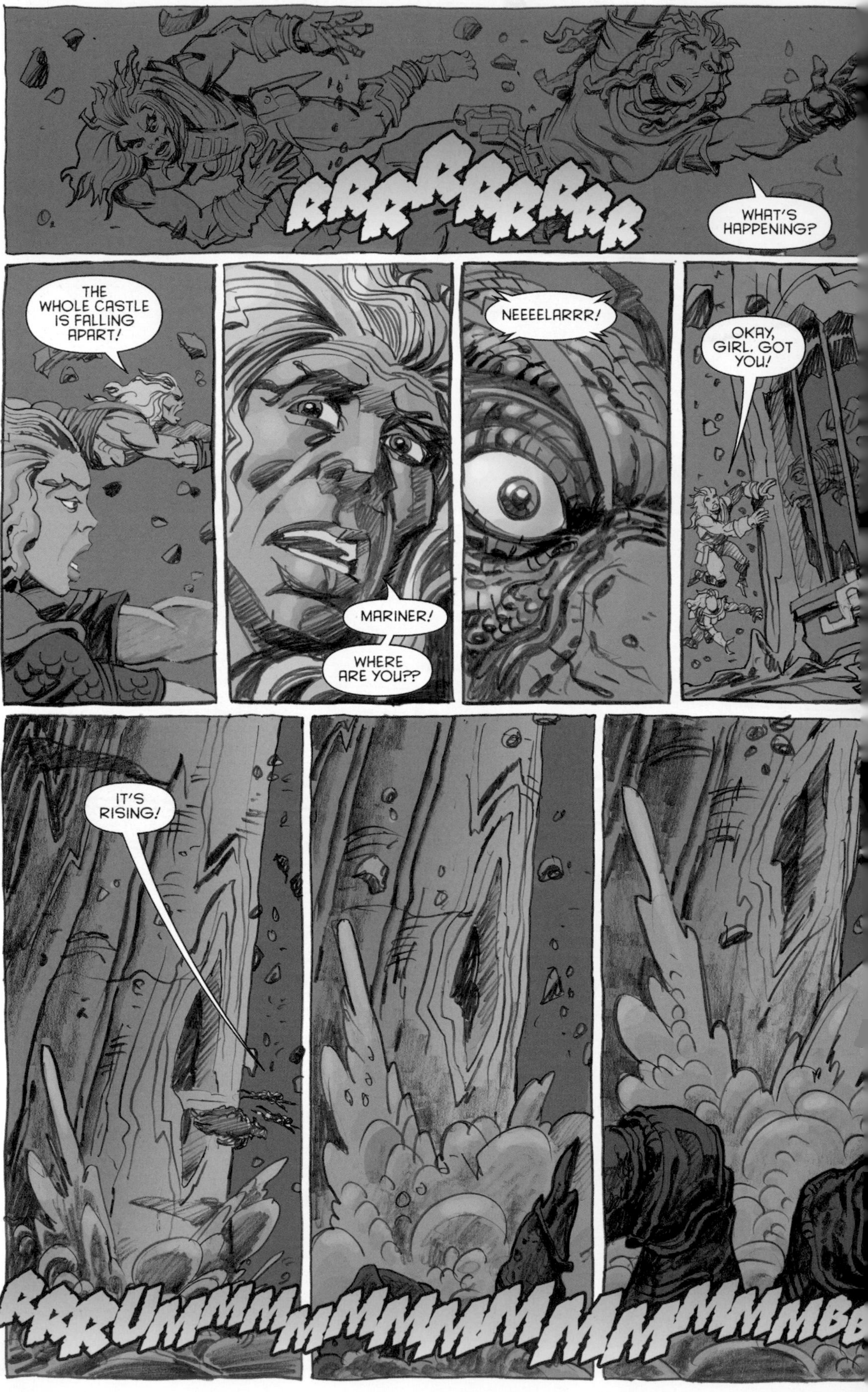
RRRRRRRRRRRR
WHAT'S HAPPENING?
THE WHOLE CASTLE IS FALLING APART!
MARINER!
WHERE ARE YOU??
NEEEELARRR!
OKAY, GIRL. GOT YOU!
IT'S RISING!
RRRUMMMMMMMMMMMMMMMMMMBE

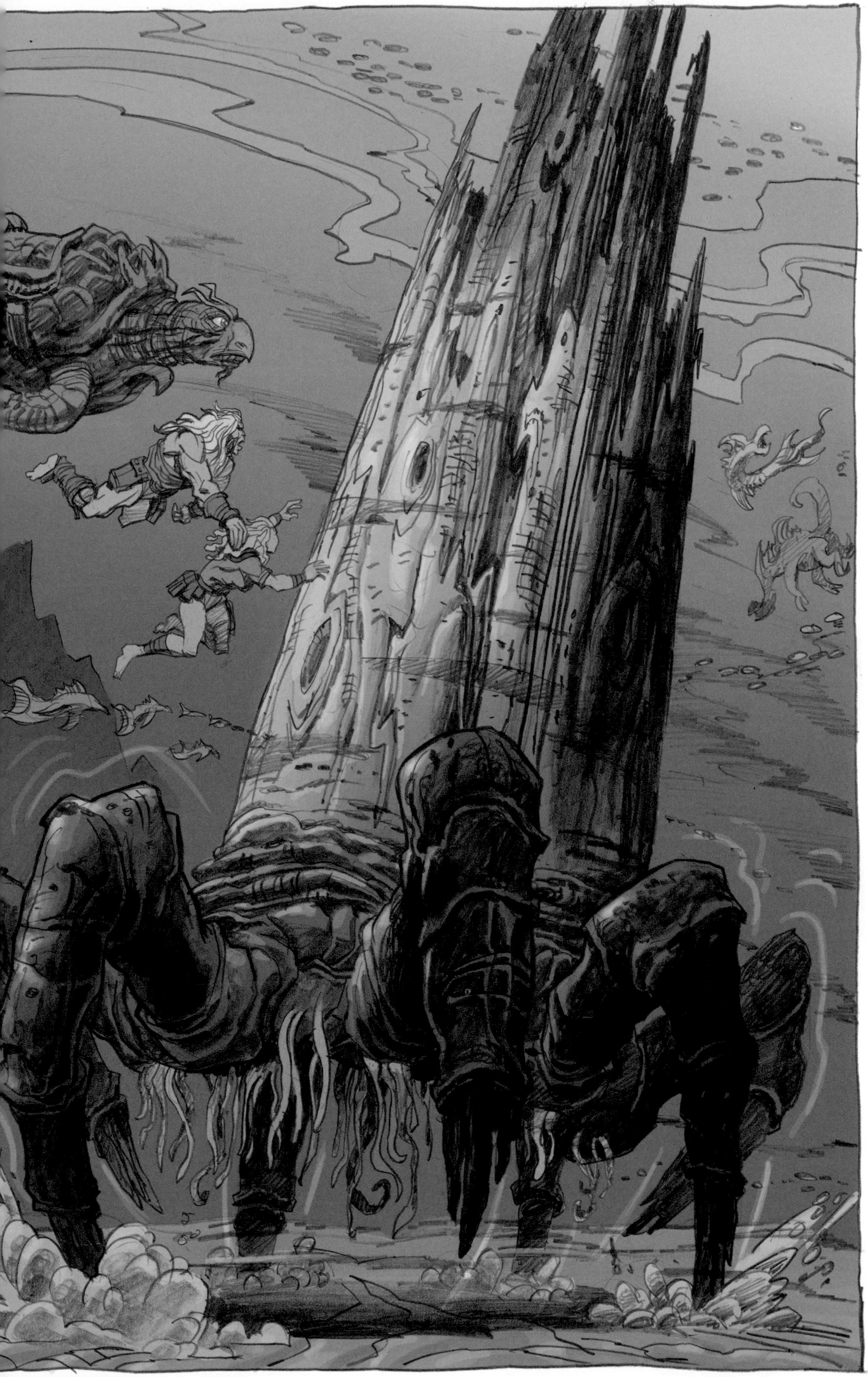

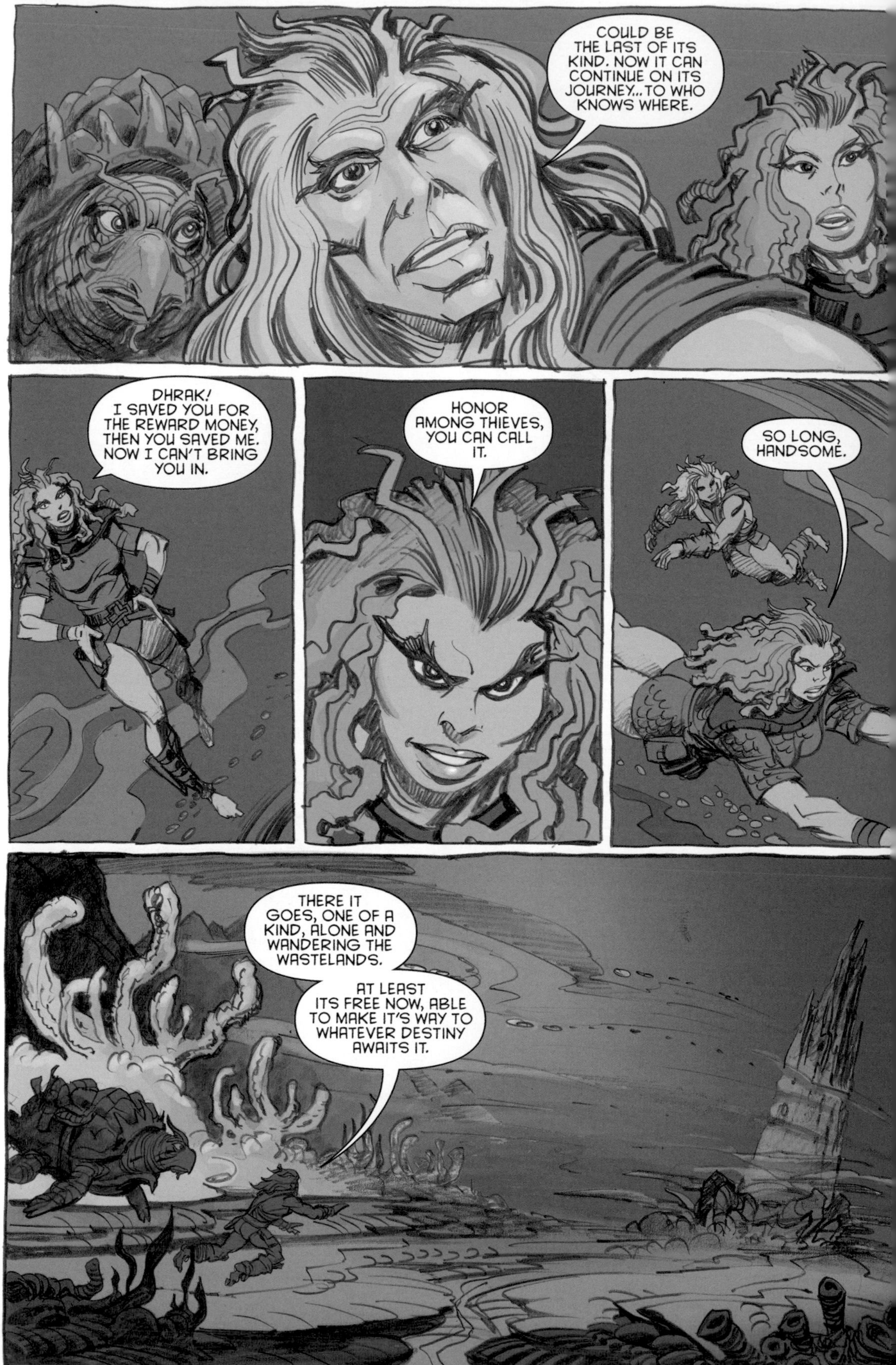
COULD BE THE LAST OF ITS KIND. NOW IT CAN CONTINUE ON ITS JOURNEY...TO WHO KNOWS WHERE.
DHRAK! I SAVED YOU FOR THE REWARD MONEY, THEN YOU SAVED ME. NOW I CAN'T BRING YOU IN.
HONOR AMONG THIEVES, YOU CAN CALL IT.
SO LONG, HANDSOME.
THERE IT GOES, ONE OF A KIND, ALONE AND WANDERING THE WASTELANDS.
AT LEAST ITS FREE NOW, ABLE TO MAKE IT'S WAY TO WHATEVER DESTINY AWAITS IT.

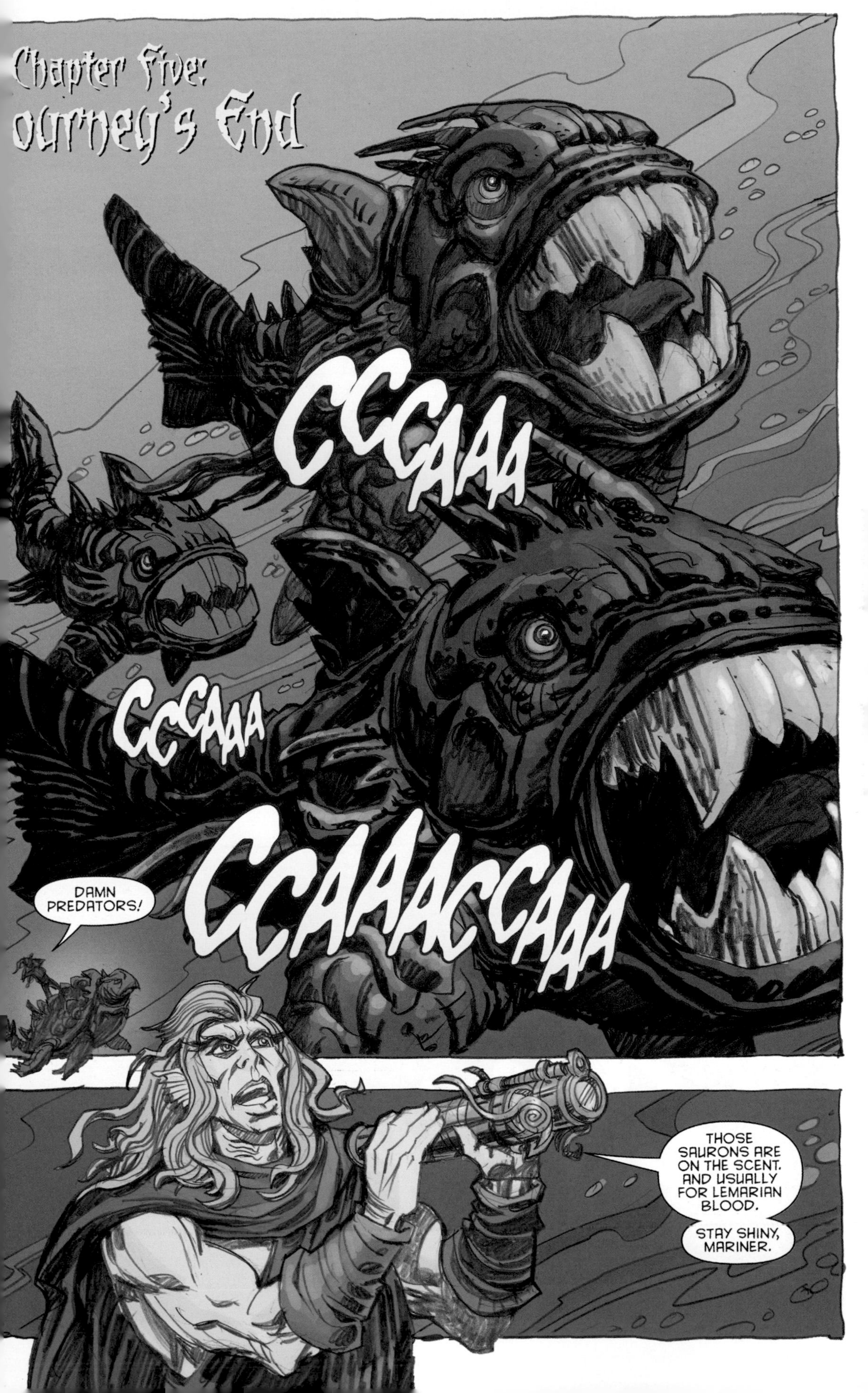

Chapter Five:
ourney's End
CCCAAA
CCCAAA
CCAAACCAAA
DAMN PREDATORS!
THOSE SAURONS ARE ON THE SCENT. AND USUALLY FOR LEMARIAN BLOOD.
STAY SHINY, MARINER.

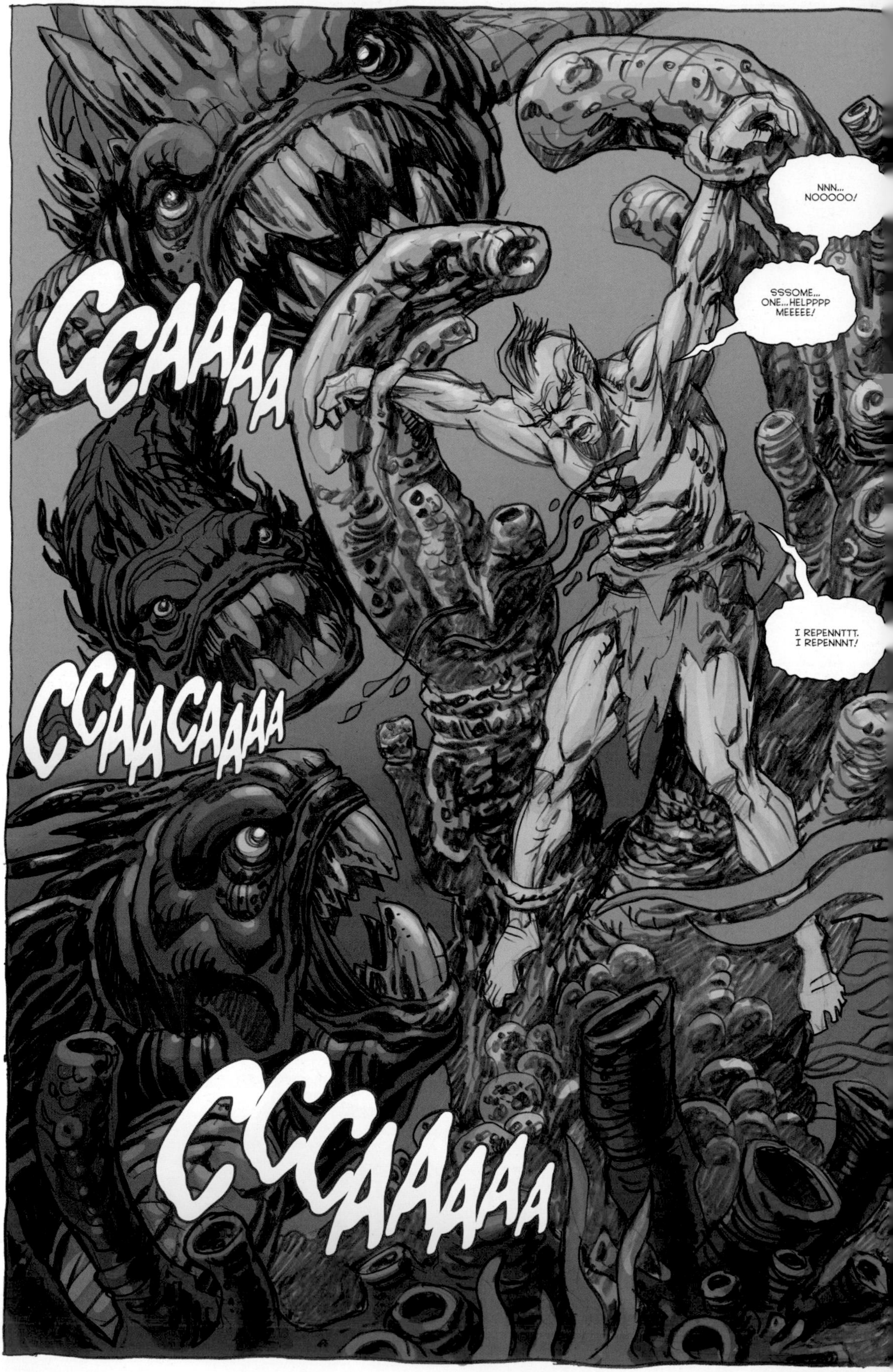
NNN... NOOOOO!
SSSOME... ONE...HELPPPP MEEEEE!
I REPENNTTT. I REPENNNT!
CCAAAAA
CCAACAAAA
CCCAAAAA

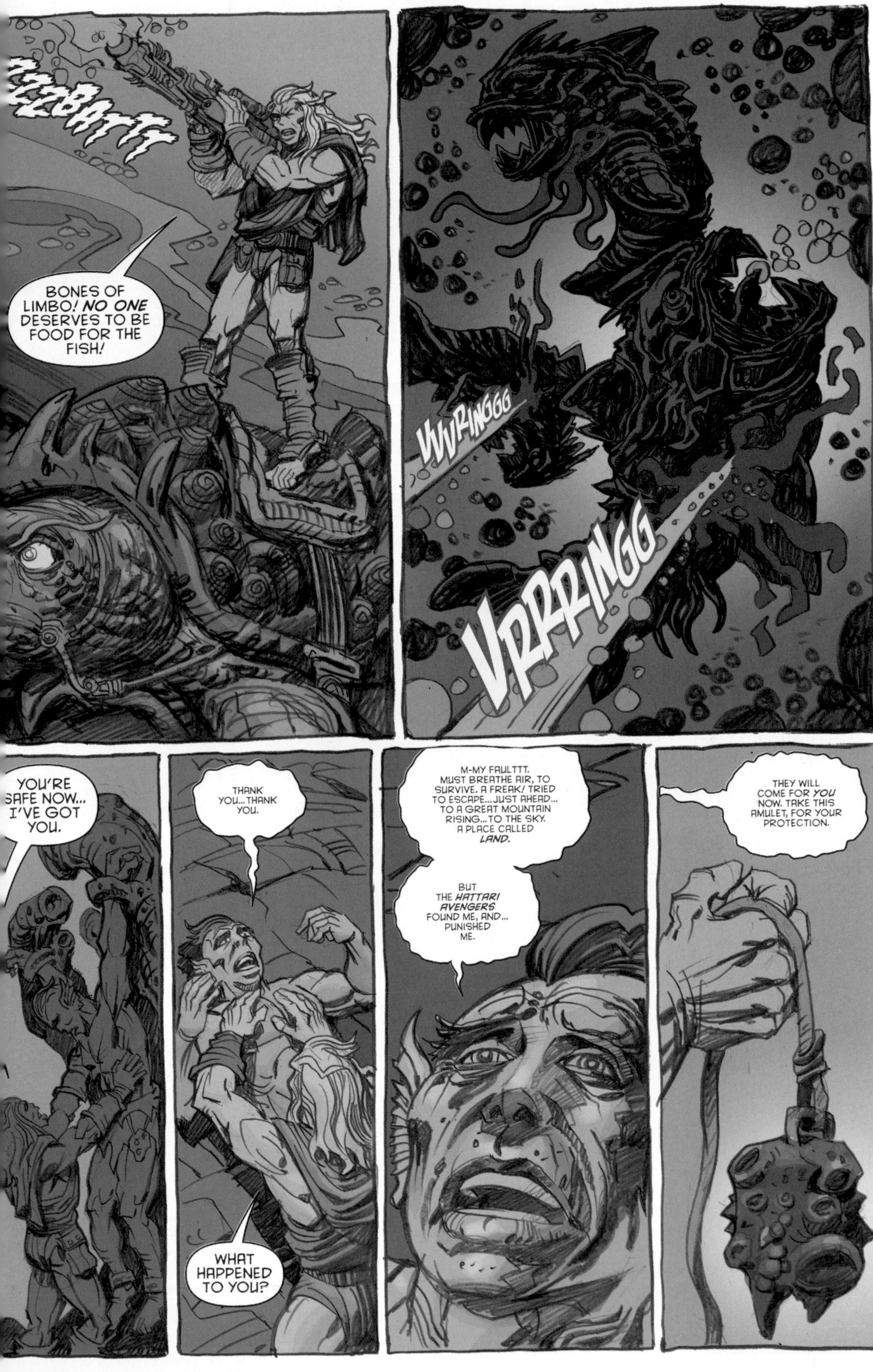
ZZZBATTT
BONES OF LIMBO! NO ONE DESERVES TO BE FOOD FOR THE FISH!
VVVRINGGG
VRRRINGG
YOU'RE SAFE NOW... I'VE GOT YOU.
THANK YOU... THANK YOU.
WHAT HAPPENED TO YOU?
M-MY FAULTTT. MUST BREATHE AIR, TO SURVIVE. A FREAK! TRIED TO ESCAPE... JUST AHEAD... TO A GREAT MOUNTAIN RISING... TO THE SKY. A PLACE CALLED LAND.
BUT THE HATTARI AVENGERS FOUND ME, AND... PUNISHED ME.
THEY WILL COME FOR YOU NOW. TAKE THIS AMULET, FOR YOUR PROTECTION.

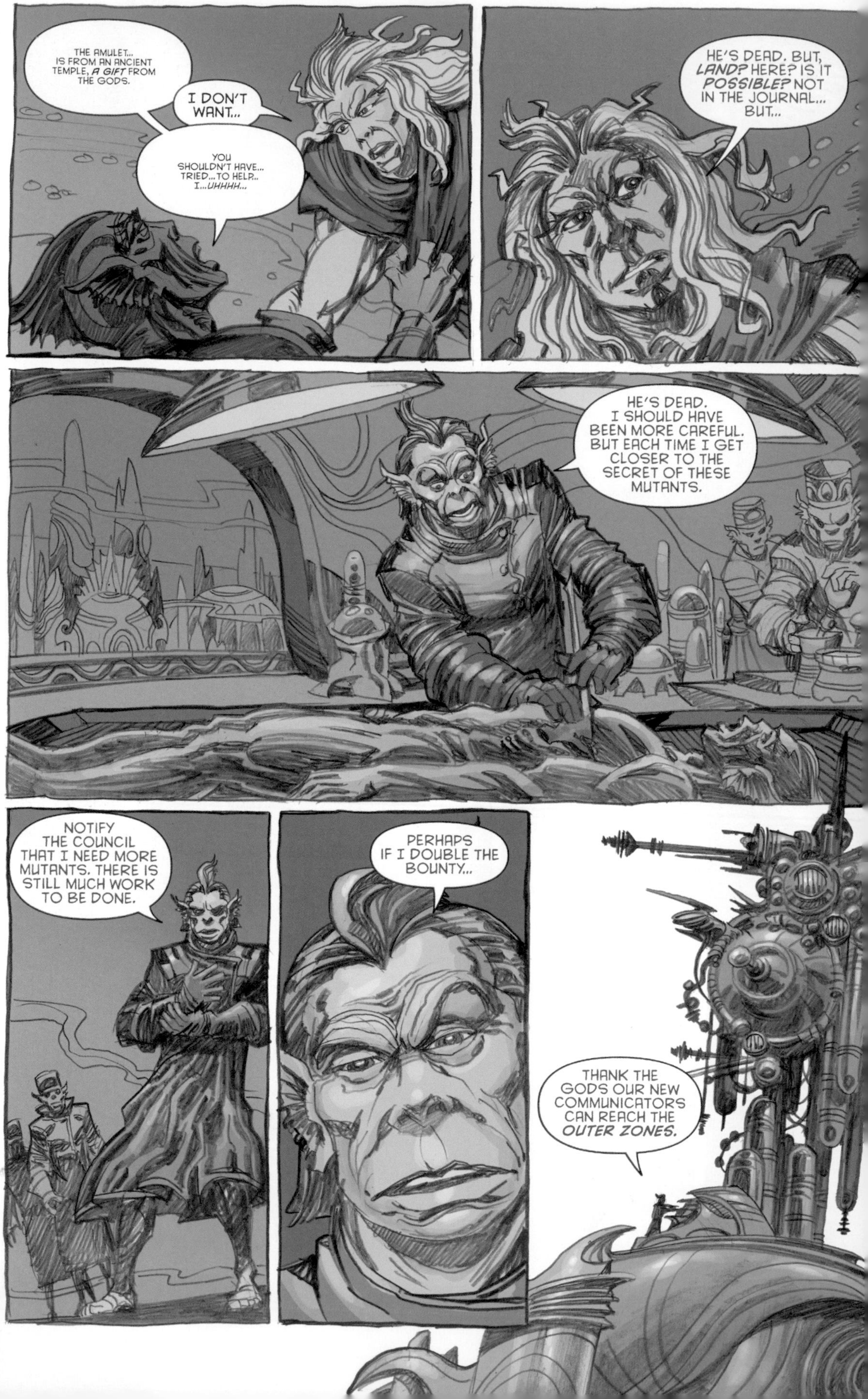
THE AMULET... IS FROM AN ANCIENT TEMPLE, A GIFT FROM THE GODS.
I DON'T WANT...
YOU SHOULDN'T HAVE... TRIED... TO HELP... I...UHHHH...
HE'S DEAD. BUT, LAND? HERE? IS IT POSSIBLE? NOT IN THE JOURNAL... BUT...
HE'S DEAD. I SHOULD HAVE BEEN MORE CAREFUL. BUT EACH TIME I GET CLOSER TO THE SECRET OF THESE MUTANTS.
NOTIFY THE COUNCIL THAT I NEED MORE MUTANTS. THERE IS STILL MUCH WORK TO BE DONE.
PERHAPS IF I DOUBLE THE BOUNTY...
THANK THE GODS OUR NEW COMMUNICATORS CAN REACH THE OUTER ZONES.

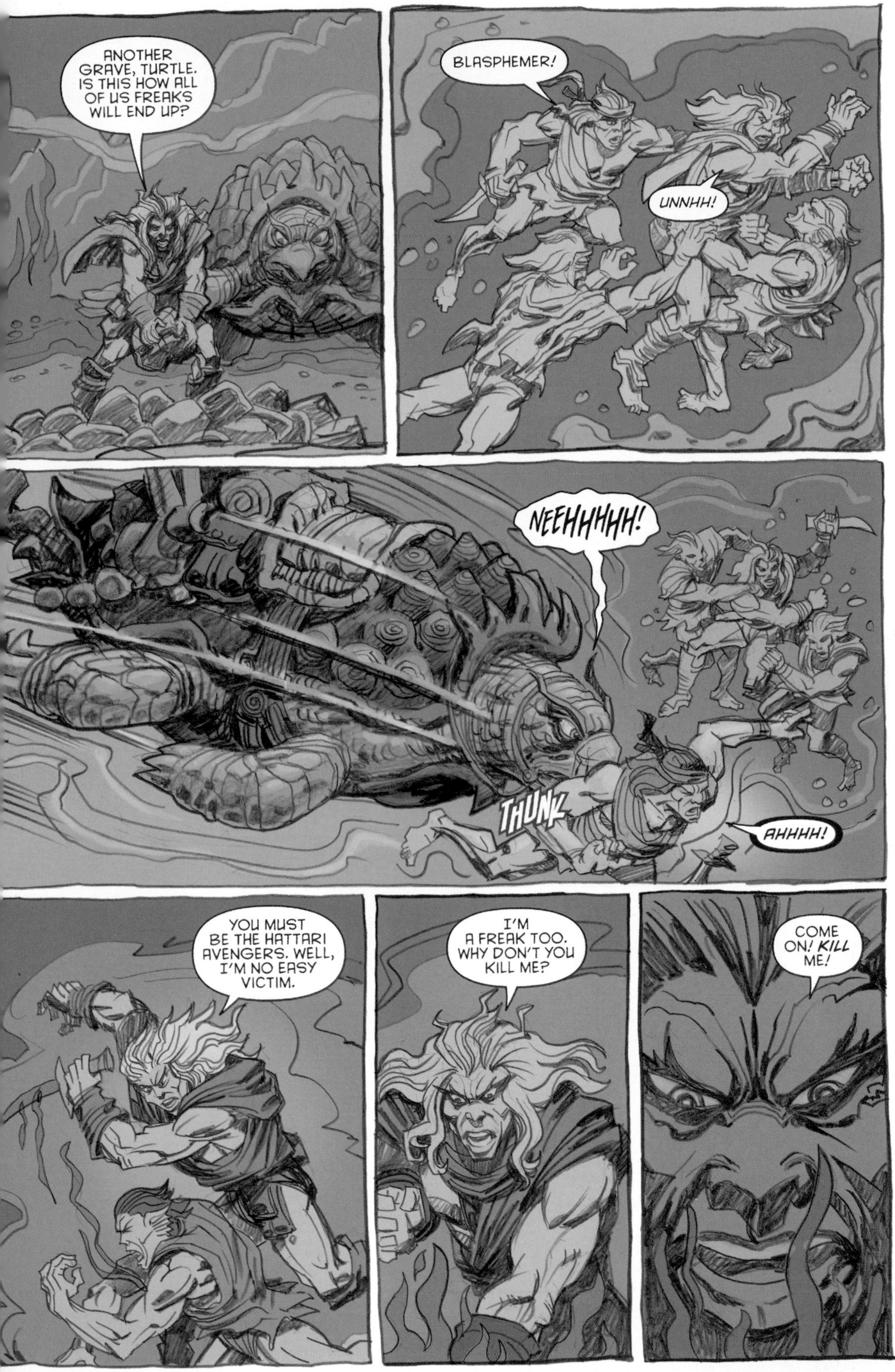
ANOTHER GRAVE, TURTLE. IS THIS HOW ALL OF US FREAKS WILL END UP?
BLASPHEMER!
UNNHH!
NEEHHHHH!
THUNK
AHHHH!
YOU MUST BE THE HATTARI AVENGERS. WELL, I'M NO EASY VICTIM.
I'M A FREAK TOO. WHY DON'T YOU KILL ME?
COME ON! KILL ME!

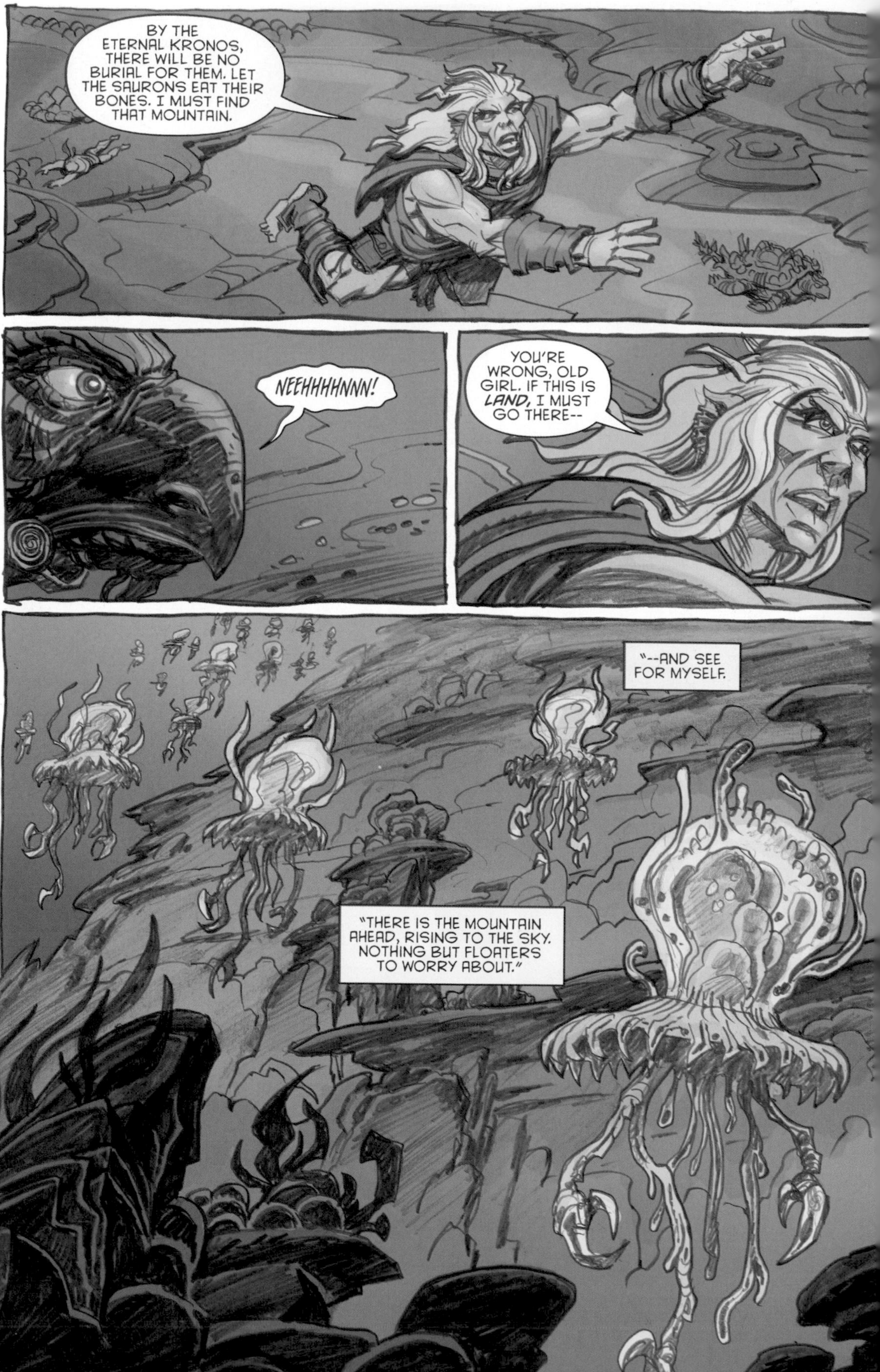
BY THE ETERNAL KRONOS, THERE WILL BE NO BURIAL FOR THEM. LET THE SAURONS EAT THEIR BONES. I MUST FIND THAT MOUNTAIN.
NEEHHHHNNN!
YOU'RE WRONG, OLD GIRL. IF THIS IS LAND, I MUST GO THERE--
"--AND SEE FOR MYSELF.
"THERE IS THE MOUNTAIN AHEAD, RISING TO THE SKY. NOTHING BUT FLOATERS TO WORRY ABOUT."

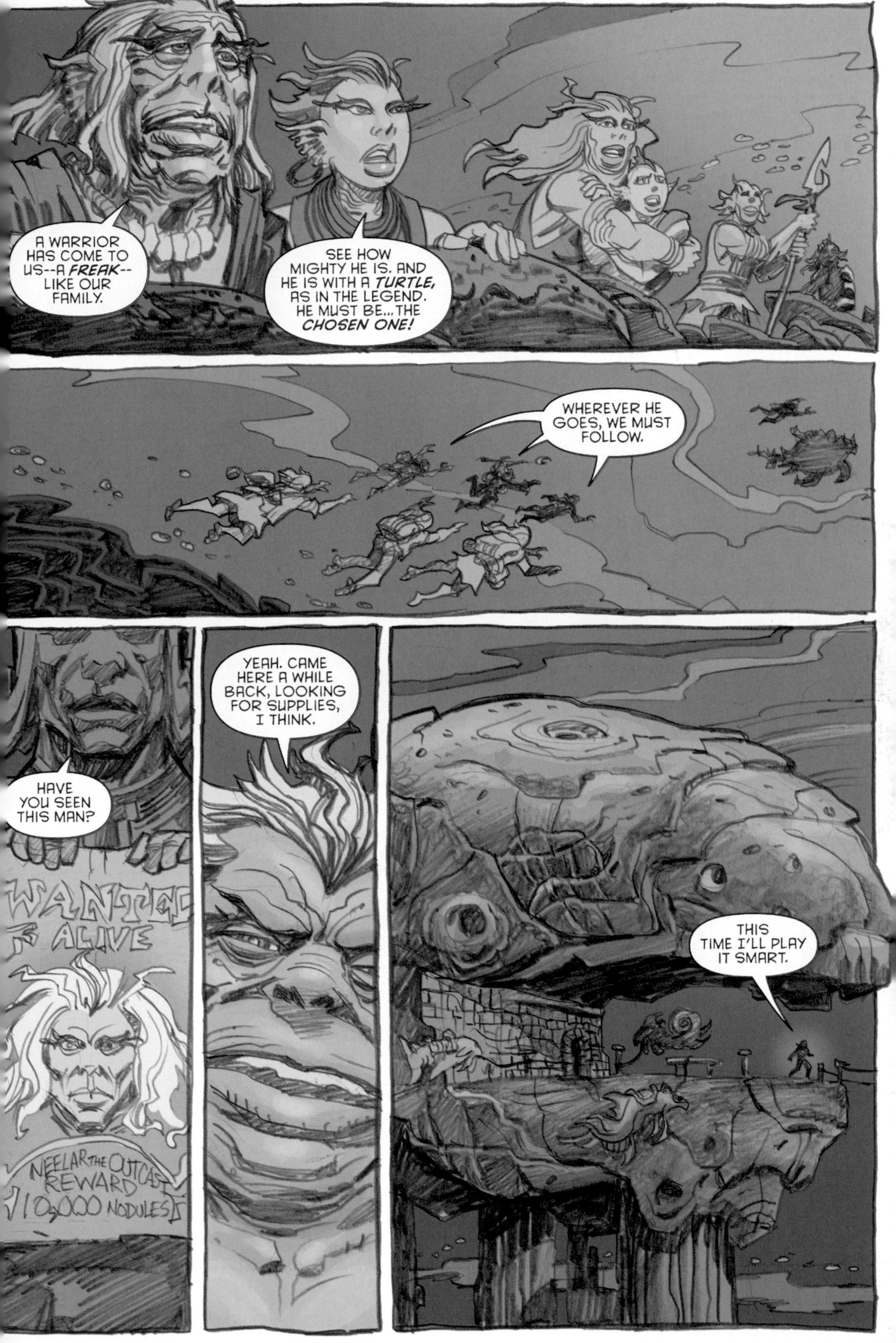
A WARRIOR HAS COME TO US--A *FREAK*--LIKE OUR FAMILY.
SEE HOW MIGHTY HE IS. AND HE IS WITH A *TURTLE,* AS IN THE LEGEND. HE MUST BE...THE *CHOSEN ONE!*
WHEREVER HE GOES, WE MUST FOLLOW.
HAVE YOU SEEN THIS MAN?
WANTED ALIVE
NEELAR THE OUTCAST
REWARD
10,000 NODULES
YEAH. CAME HERE A WHILE BACK, LOOKING FOR SUPPLIES, I THINK.
THIS TIME I'LL PLAY IT SMART.

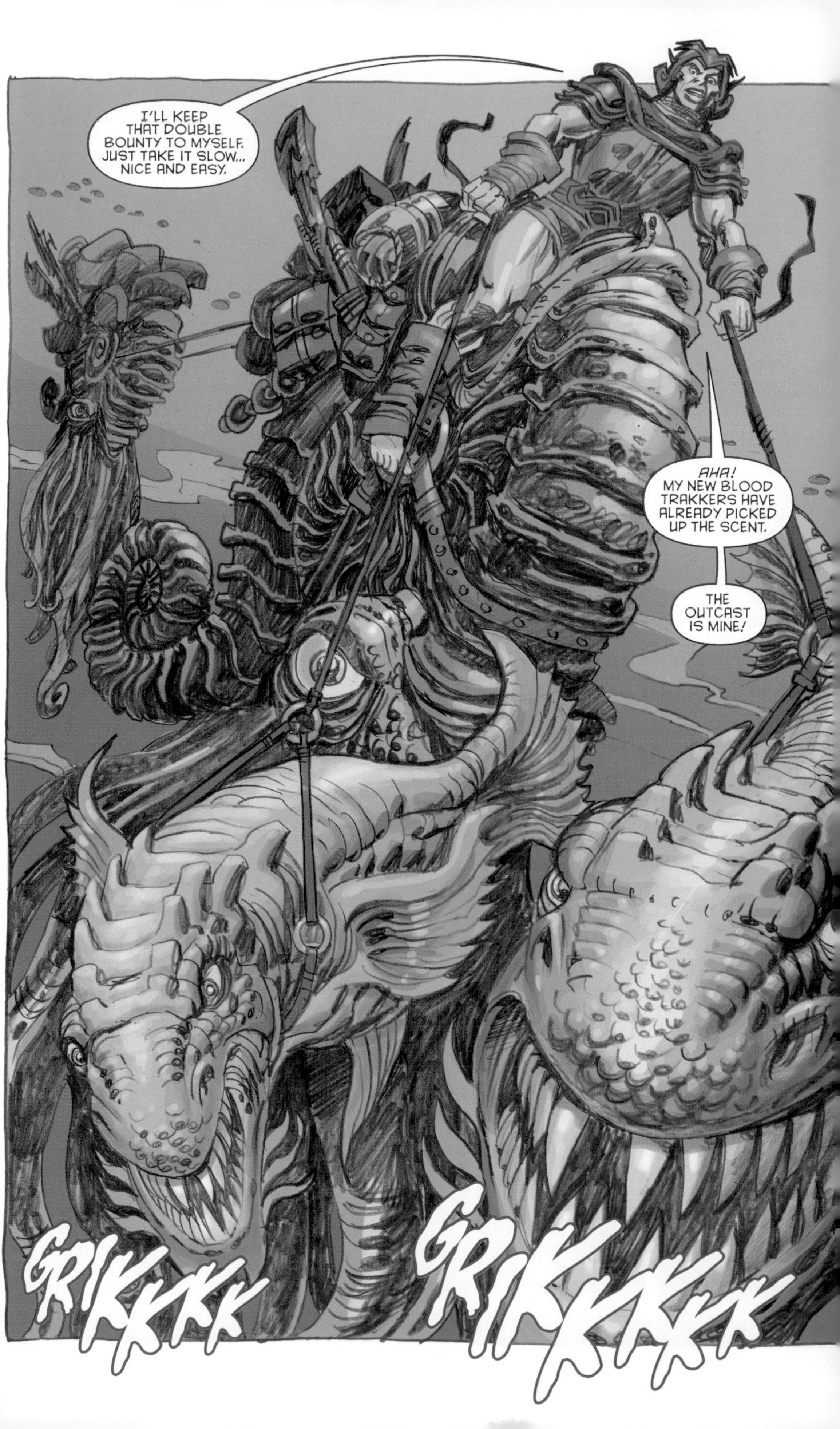
I'LL KEEP THAT DOUBLE BOUNTY TO MYSELF. JUST TAKE IT SLOW... NICE AND EASY.
AHA! MY NEW BLOOD TRAKKERS HAVE ALREADY PICKED UP THE SCENT.
THE OUTCAST IS MINE!
GRIKKKK
GRIKKKKKK

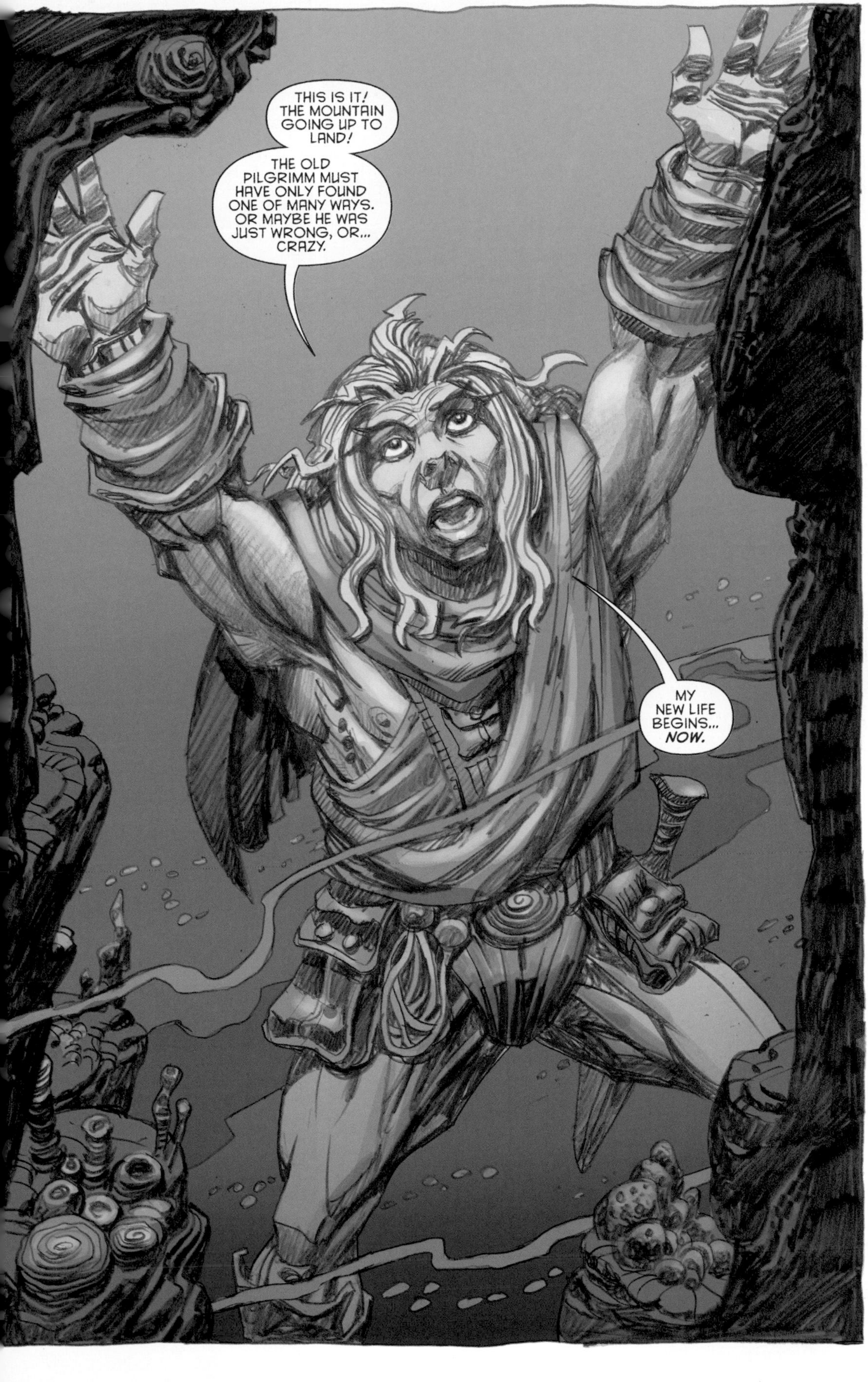
THIS IS IT! THE MOUNTAIN GOING UP TO LAND!
THE OLD PILGRIMM MUST HAVE ONLY FOUND ONE OF MANY WAYS. OR MAYBE HE WAS JUST WRONG, OR... CRAZY.
MY NEW LIFE BEGINS... *NOW.*

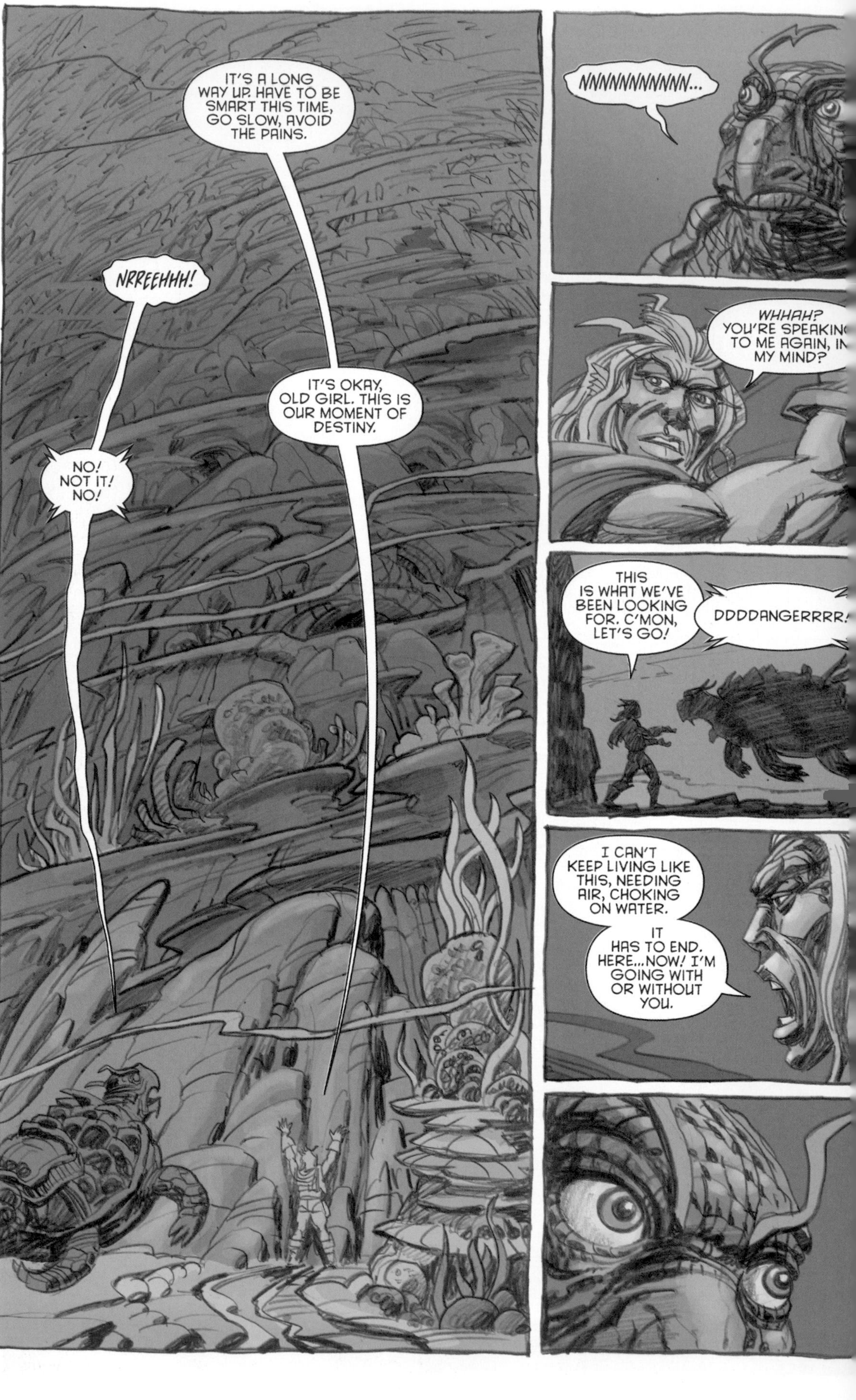
IT'S A LONG WAY UP. HAVE TO BE SMART THIS TIME, GO SLOW, AVOID THE PAINS.
NRREEHHH!
IT'S OKAY, OLD GIRL. THIS IS OUR MOMENT OF DESTINY.
NO! NOT IT! NO!
NNNNNNNNNNN...
WHHAH? YOU'RE SPEAKIN TO ME AGAIN, IN MY MIND?
THIS IS WHAT WE'VE BEEN LOOKING FOR. C'MON, LET'S GO!
DDDDANGERRRR
I CAN'T KEEP LIVING LIKE THIS, NEEDING AIR, CHOKING ON WATER.
IT HAS TO END. HERE...NOW! I'M GOING WITH OR WITHOUT YOU.

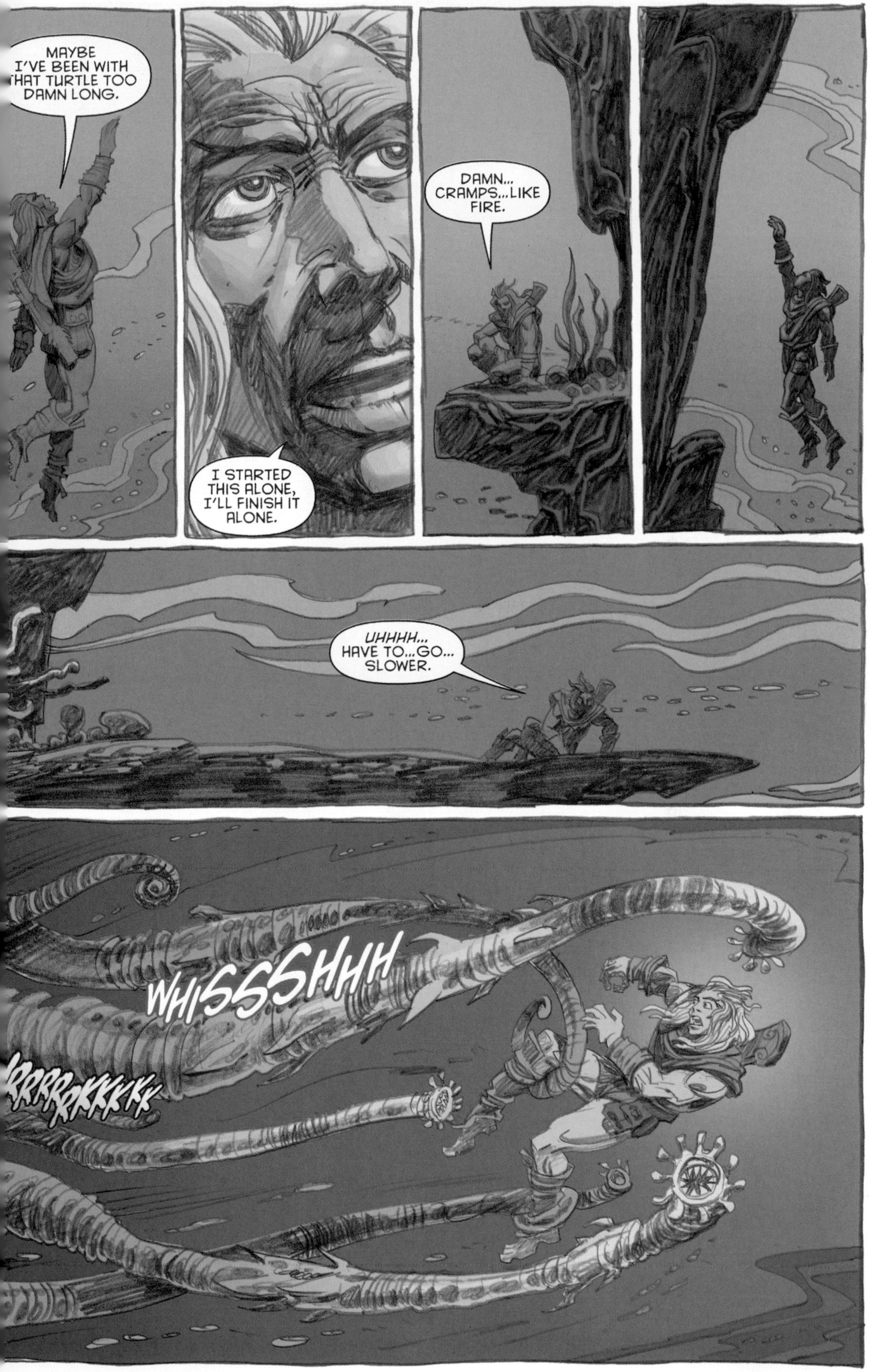
MAYBE I'VE BEEN WITH THAT TURTLE TOO DAMN LONG.
I STARTED THIS ALONE, I'LL FINISH IT ALONE.
DAMN... CRAMPS...LIKE FIRE.
UHHHH... HAVE TO...GO... SLOWER.
WHISSSHHH
RRRRRKKKKKk

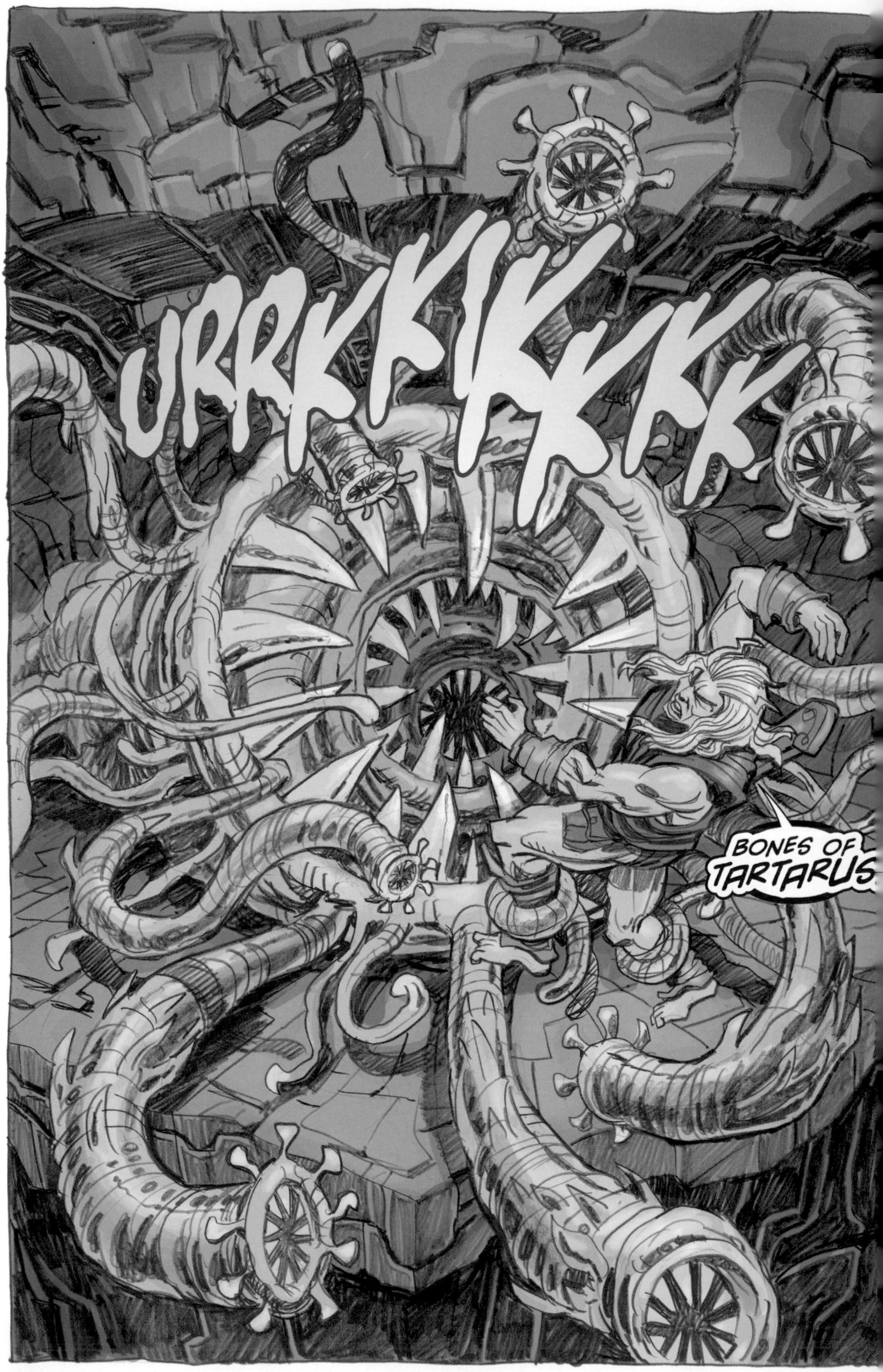
URRKKKKKK
BONES OF TARTARUS

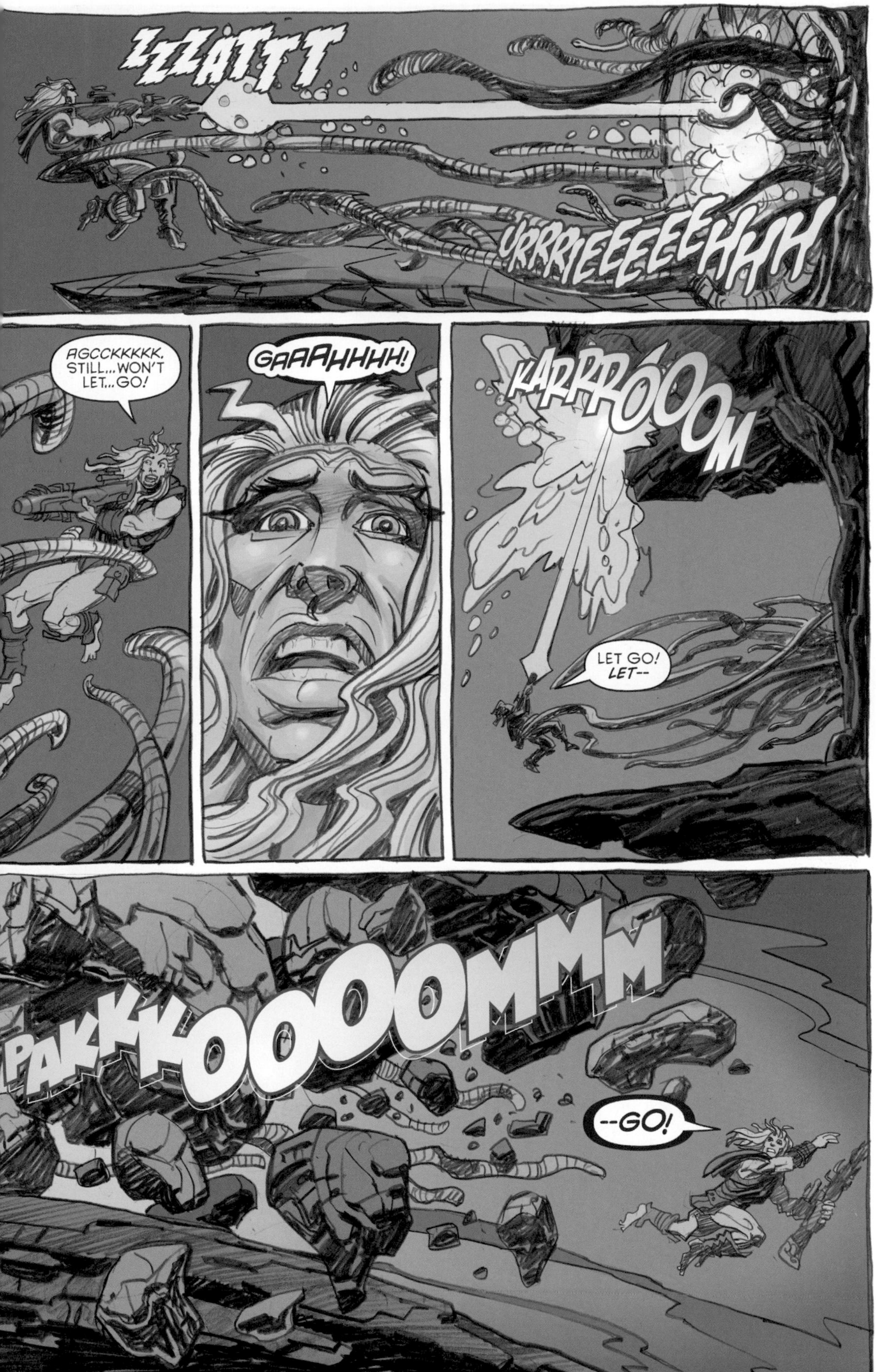
ZZZATTT
URRRIEEEEEEHHHH
AGCCKKKKK. STILL... WON'T LET... GO!
GAAAHHHH!
KARRROOOOM
LET GO! LET--
PAKKOOOOOMMM
--GO!

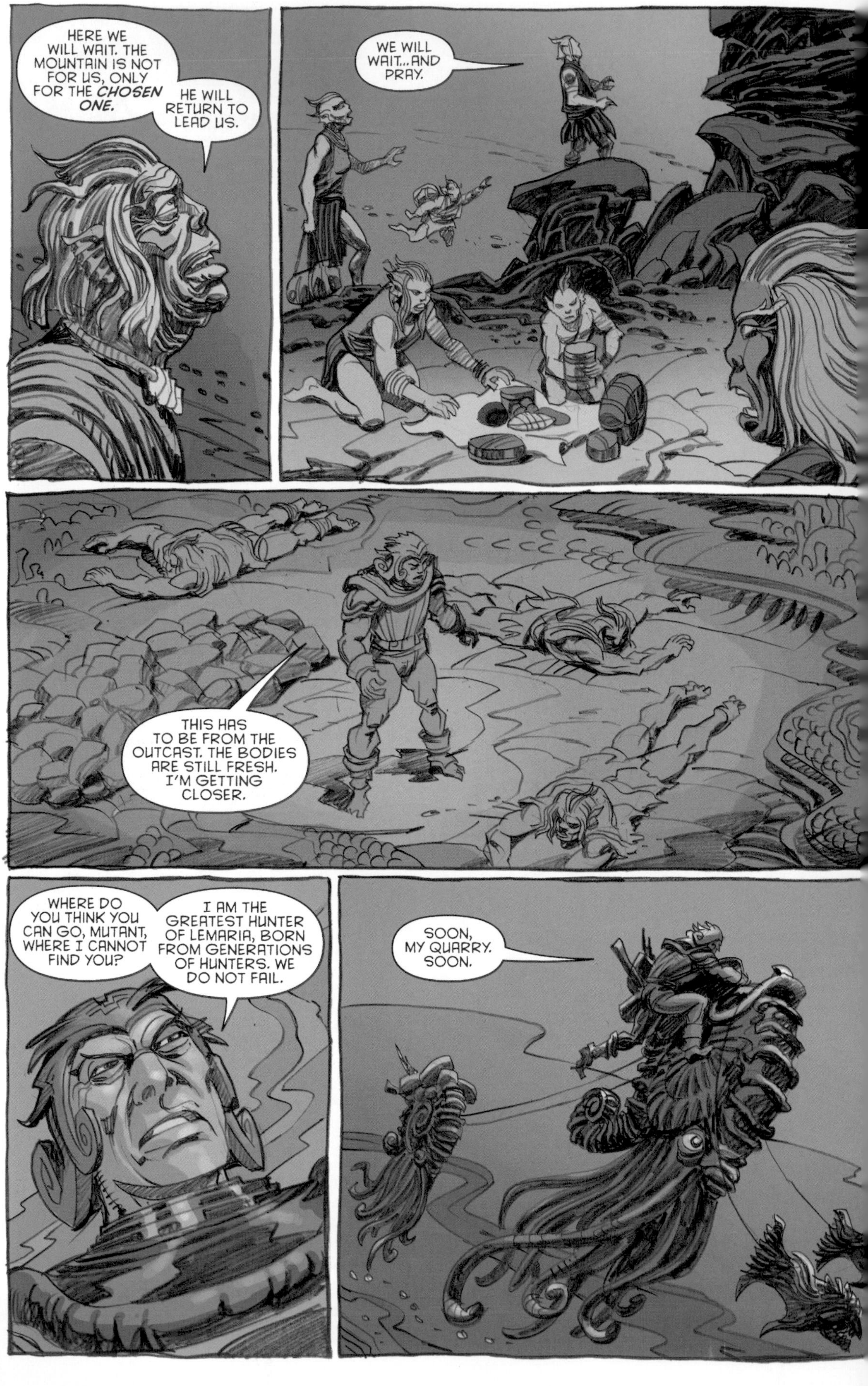
HERE WE WILL WAIT. THE MOUNTAIN IS NOT FOR US, ONLY FOR THE *CHOSEN ONE.*
HE WILL RETURN TO LEAD US.
WE WILL WAIT...AND PRAY.
THIS HAS TO BE FROM THE OUTCAST. THE BODIES ARE STILL FRESH. I'M GETTING CLOSER.
WHERE DO YOU THINK YOU CAN GO, MUTANT, WHERE I CANNOT FIND YOU?
I AM THE GREATEST HUNTER OF LEMARIA, BORN FROM GENERATIONS OF HUNTERS. WE DO NOT FAIL.
SOON, MY QUARRY. SOON.

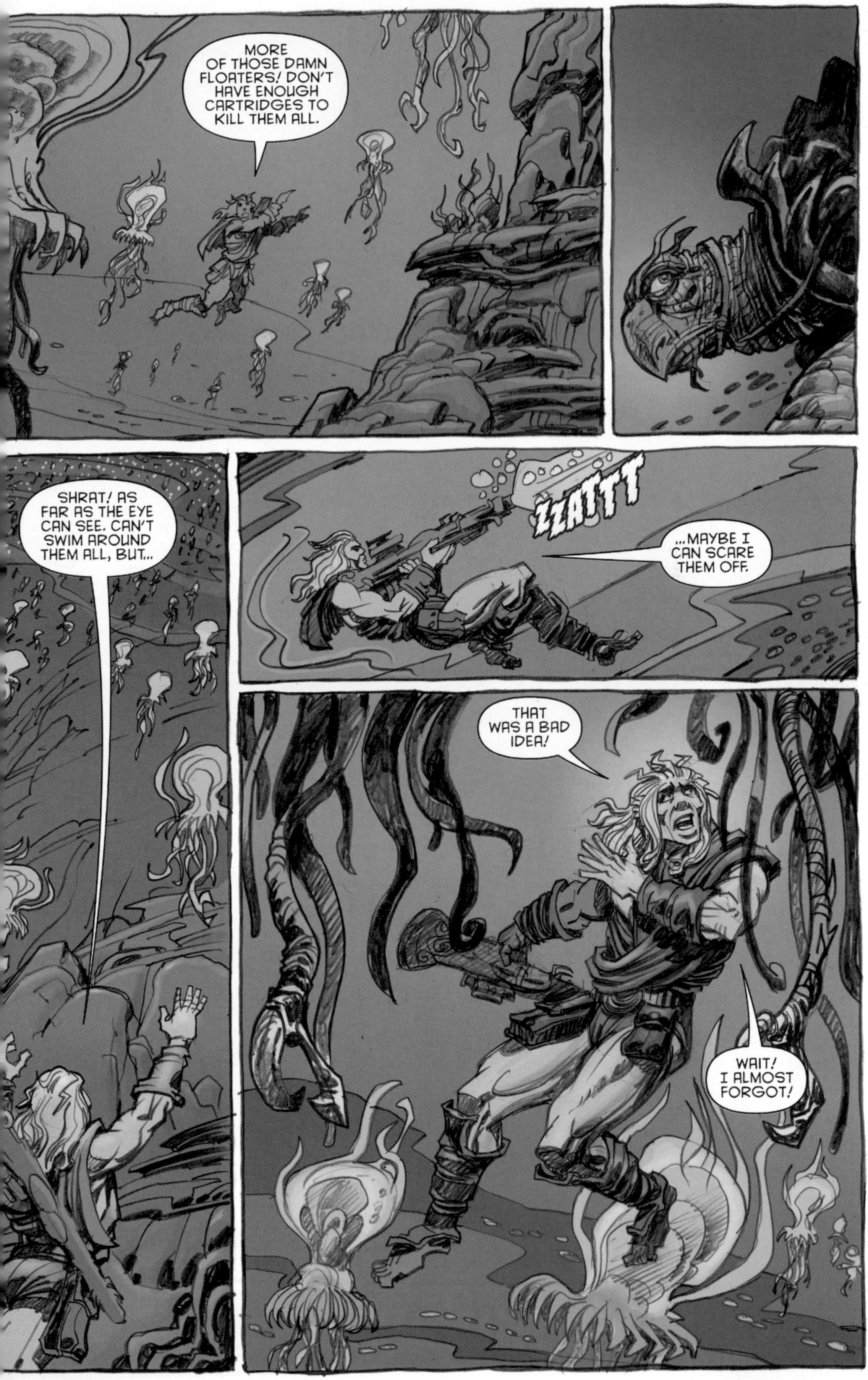
MORE OF THOSE DAMN FLOATERS! DON'T HAVE ENOUGH CARTRIDGES TO KILL THEM ALL.
SHRAT! AS FAR AS THE EYE CAN SEE. CAN'T SWIM AROUND THEM ALL, BUT...
ZZATTT
...MAYBE I CAN SCARE THEM OFF.
THAT WAS A BAD IDEA!
WAIT! I ALMOST FORGOT!

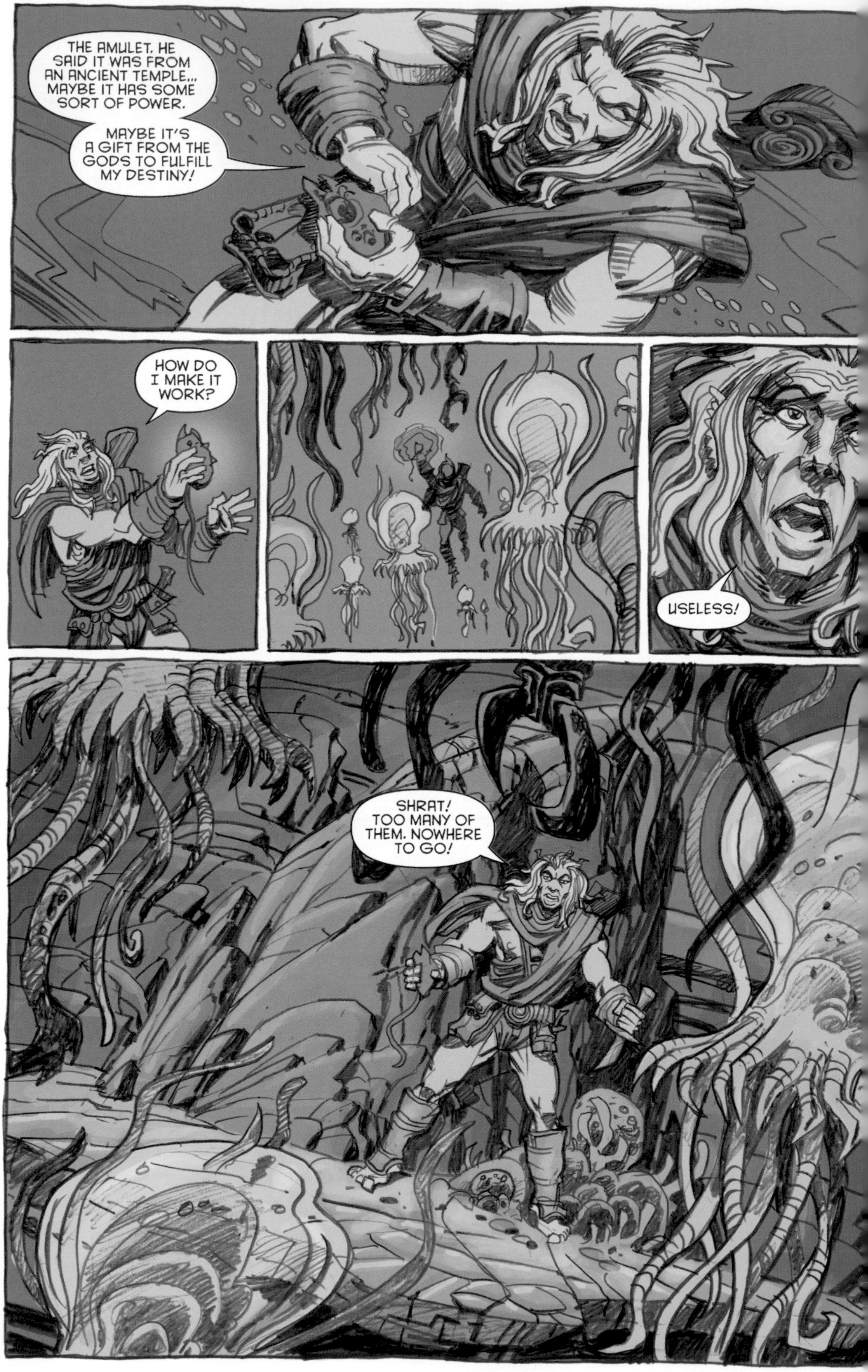
THE AMULET. HE SAID IT WAS FROM AN ANCIENT TEMPLE... MAYBE IT HAS SOME SORT OF POWER.
MAYBE IT'S A GIFT FROM THE GODS TO FULFILL MY DESTINY!
HOW DO I MAKE IT WORK?
USELESS!
SHRAT! TOO MANY OF THEM. NOWHERE TO GO!

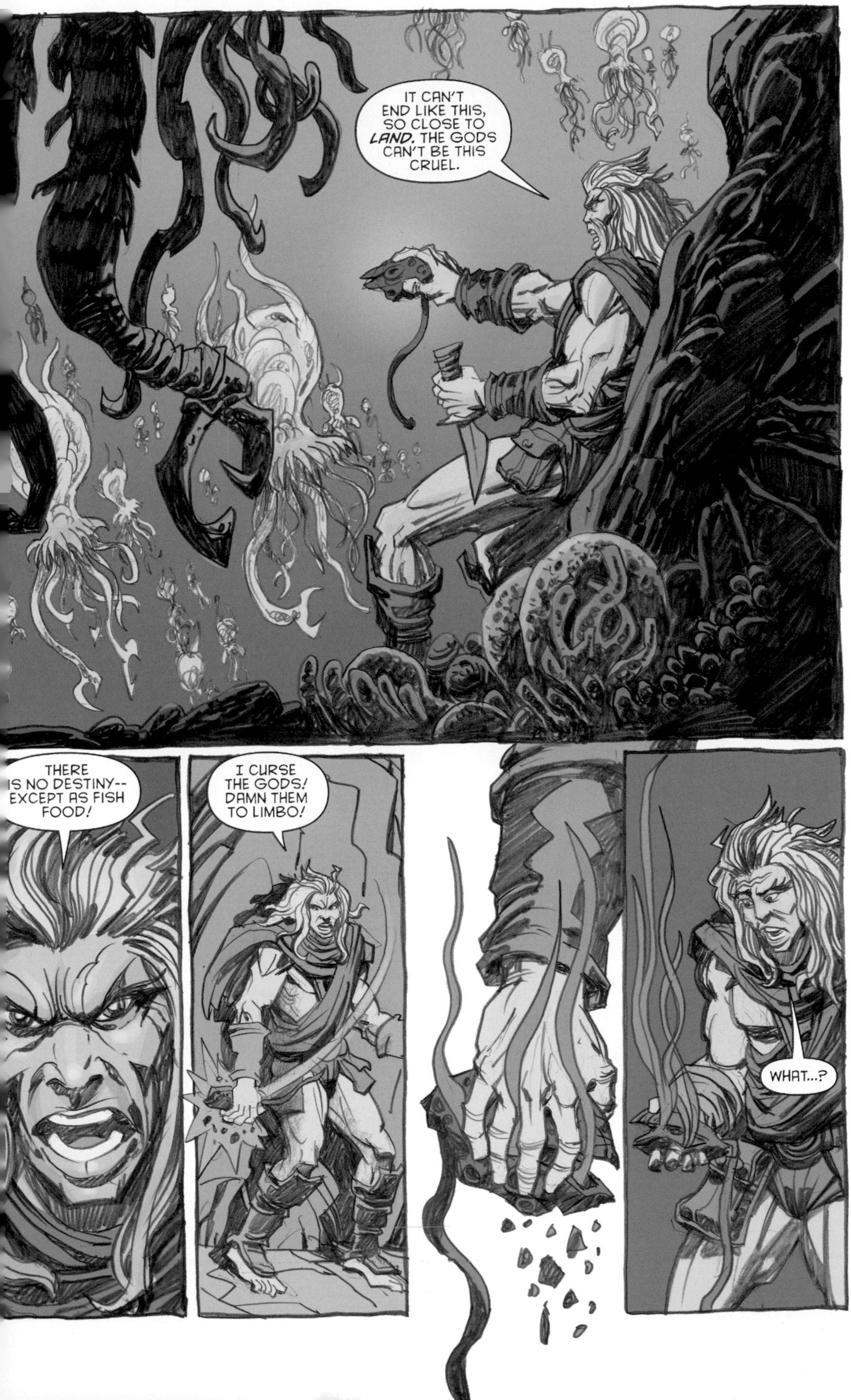
IT CAN'T END LIKE THIS, SO CLOSE TO *LAND.* THE GODS CAN'T BE THIS CRUEL.
THERE IS NO DESTINY-- EXCEPT AS FISH FOOD!
I CURSE THE GODS! DAMN THEM TO LIMBO!
WHAT...?

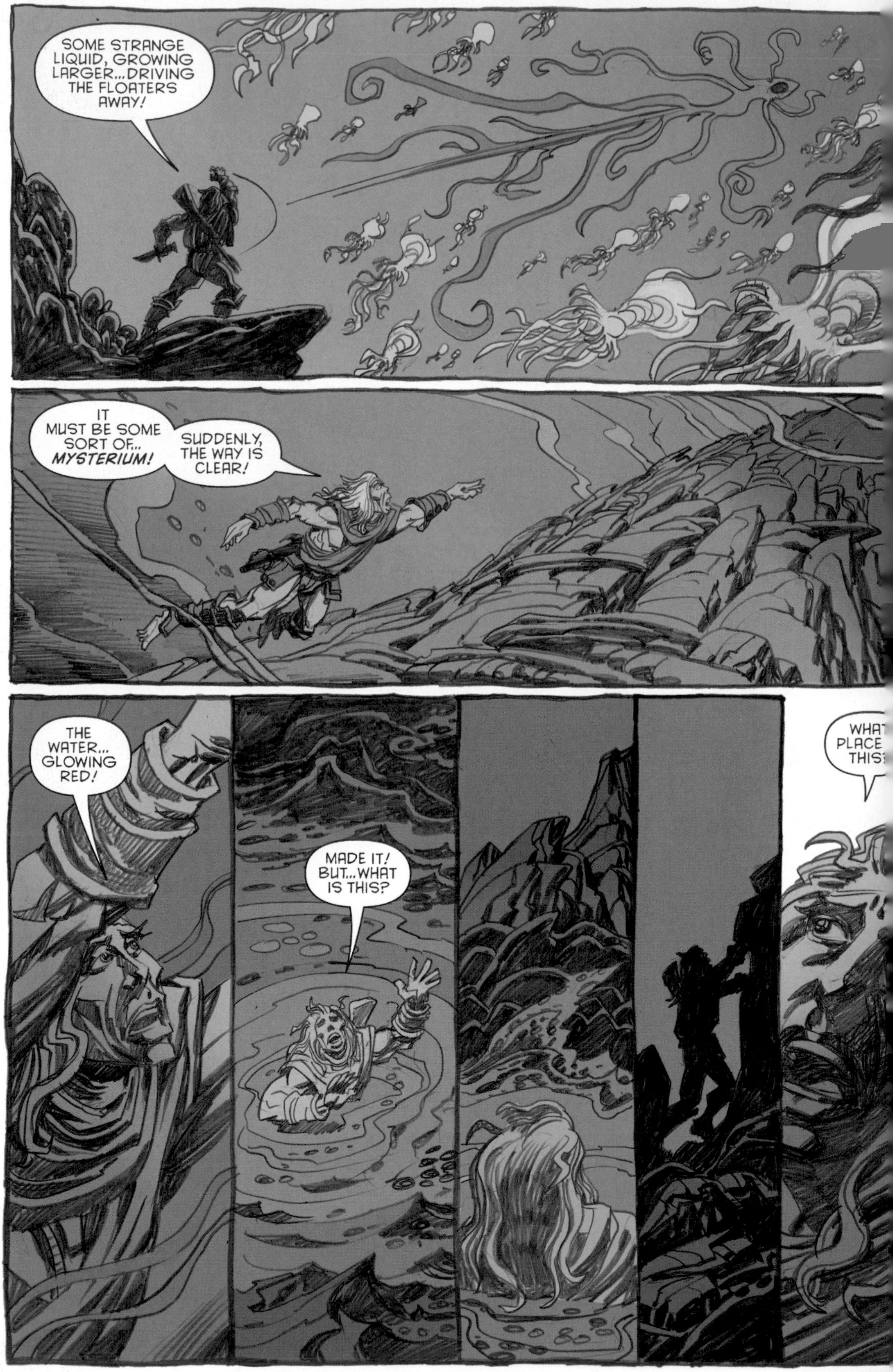
SOME STRANGE LIQUID, GROWING LARGER...DRIVING THE FLOATERS AWAY!
IT MUST BE SOME SORT OF... *MYSTERIUM!*
SUDDENLY, THE WAY IS CLEAR!
THE WATER... GLOWING RED!
MADE IT! BUT...WHAT IS THIS?
WHAT PLACE THIS

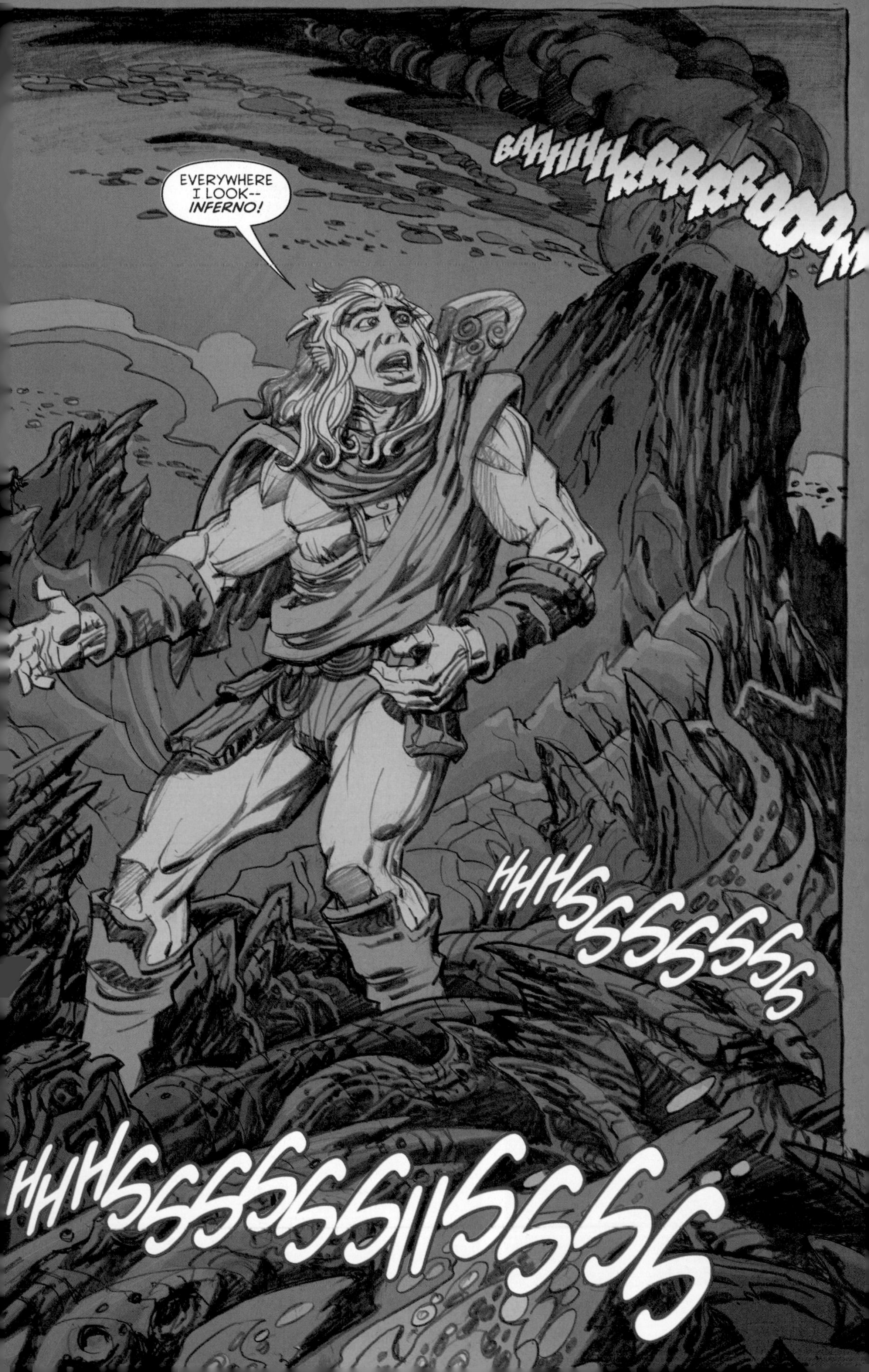
EVERYWHERE I LOOK-- INFERNO!
BAAHHHRRRRROOOM
HHHSSSSSSSS
HHHSSSSSSSIISSSSS

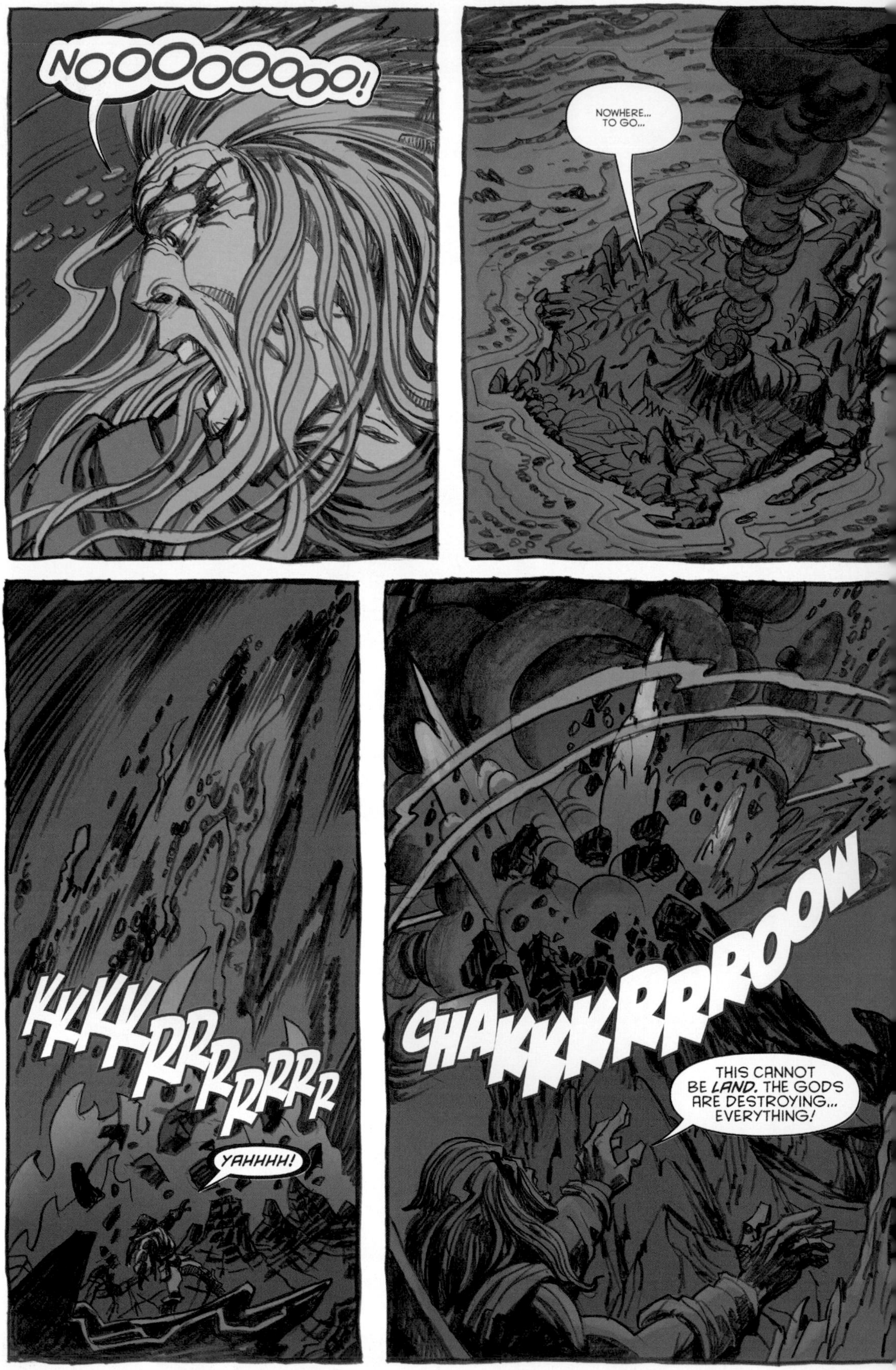
NOOOOOOOO!
NOWHERE... TO GO...
KKKKRRRRRRRR
YAHHHH!
CHAKKKKRRRROOW
THIS CANNOT BE LAND. THE GODS ARE DESTROYING... EVERYTHING!

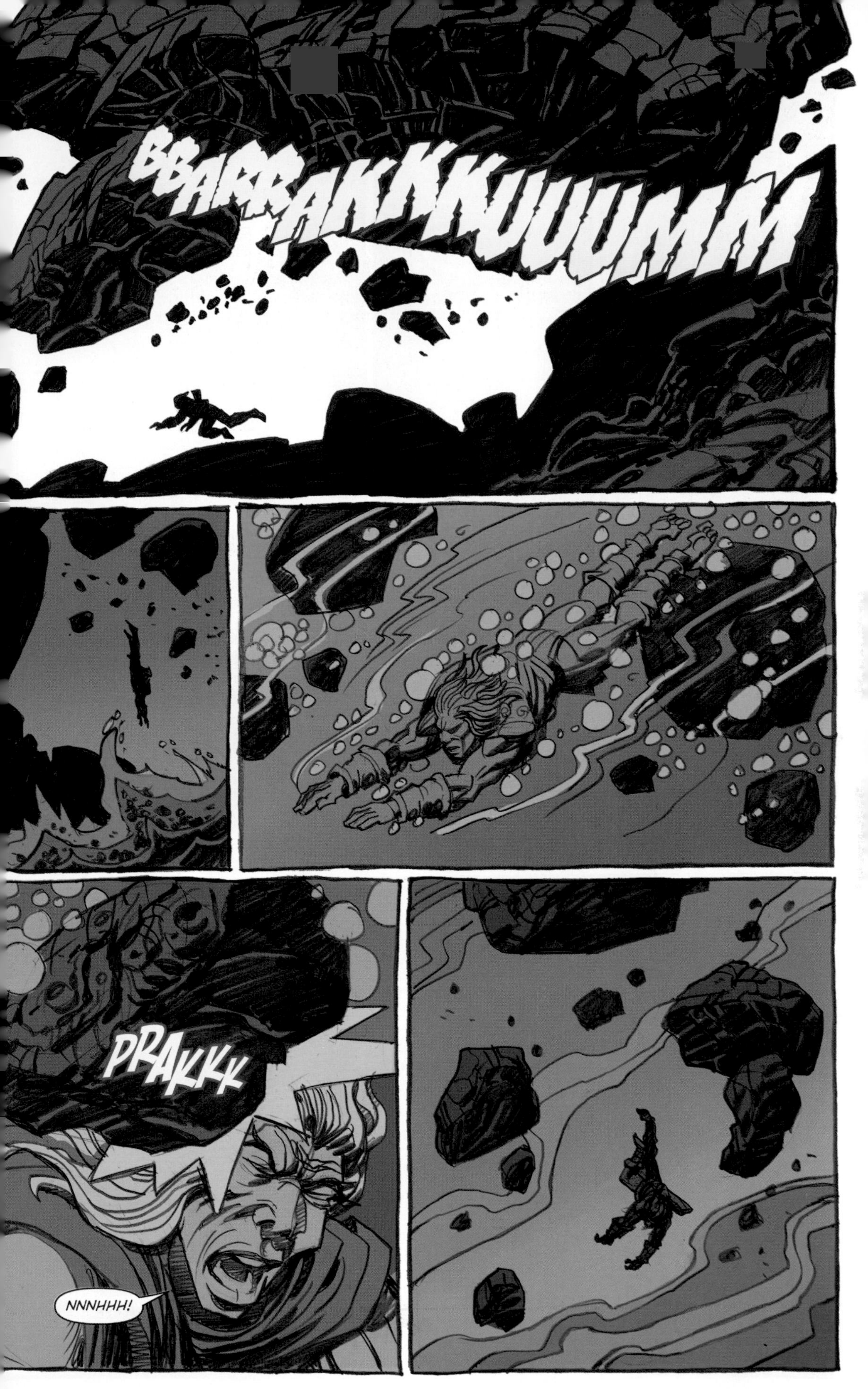
BBARRAKKKUUUMM
PRAKKK
NNNHHH!

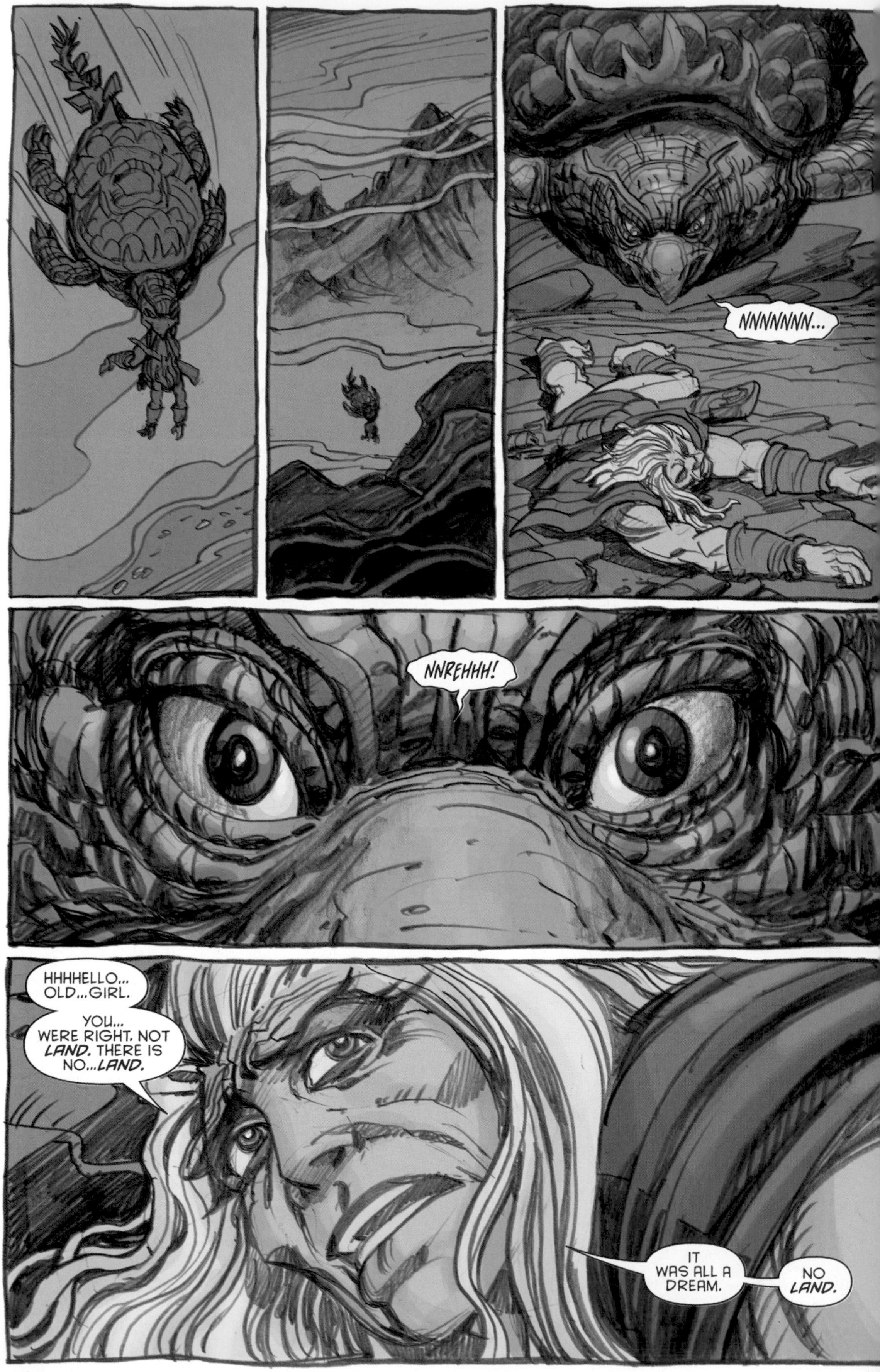
NNNNNNN...
NNREHHH!
HHHHELLO... OLD...GIRL.
YOU... WERE RIGHT. NOT LAND. THERE IS NO...LAND.
IT WAS ALL A DREAM.
NO LAND.

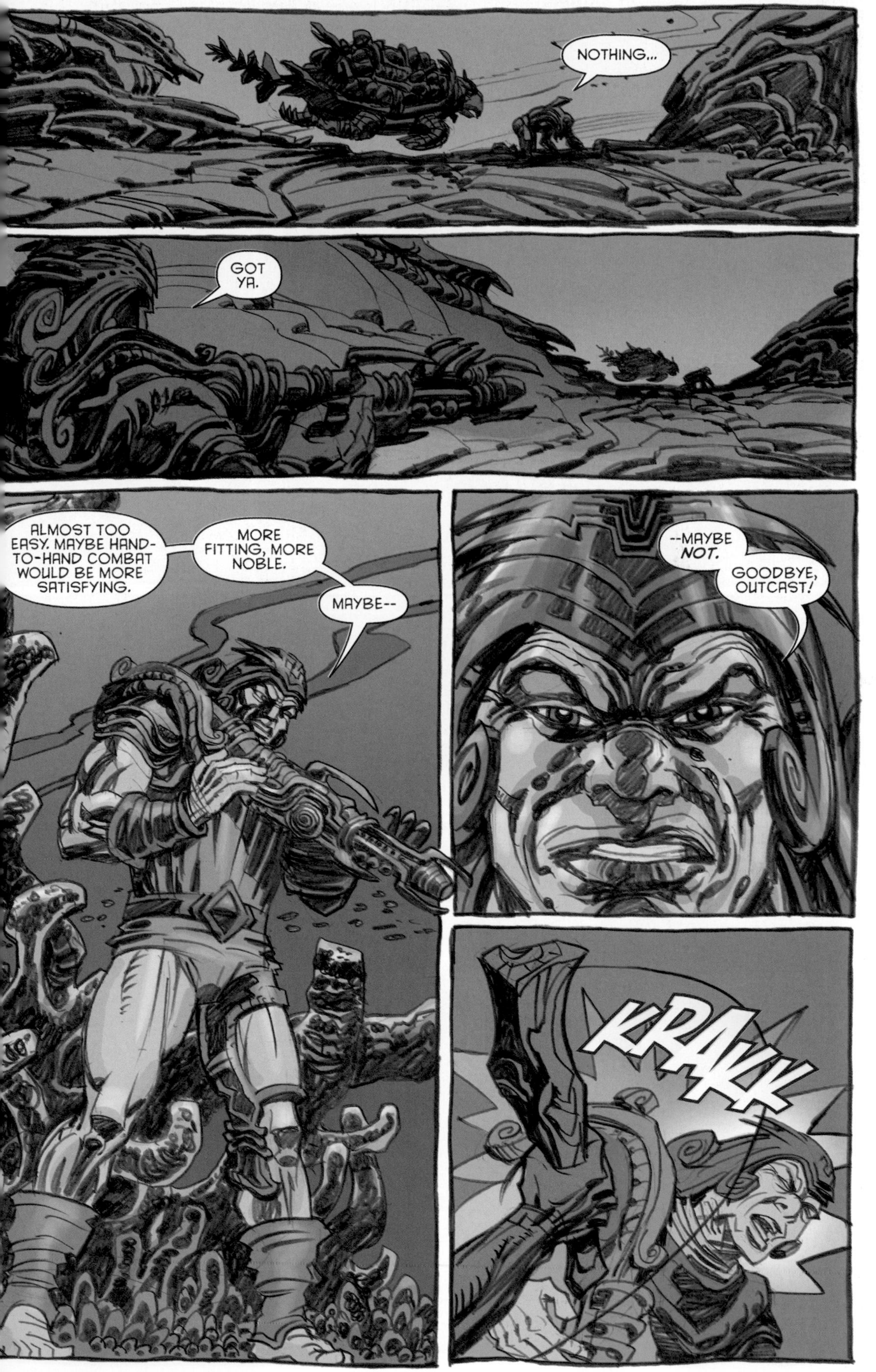

NOTHING...
GOT YA.
ALMOST TOO EASY. MAYBE HAND-TO-HAND COMBAT WOULD BE MORE SATISFYING.
MORE FITTING, MORE NOBLE.
MAYBE--
--MAYBE NOT.
GOODBYE, OUTCAST!
KRAKK

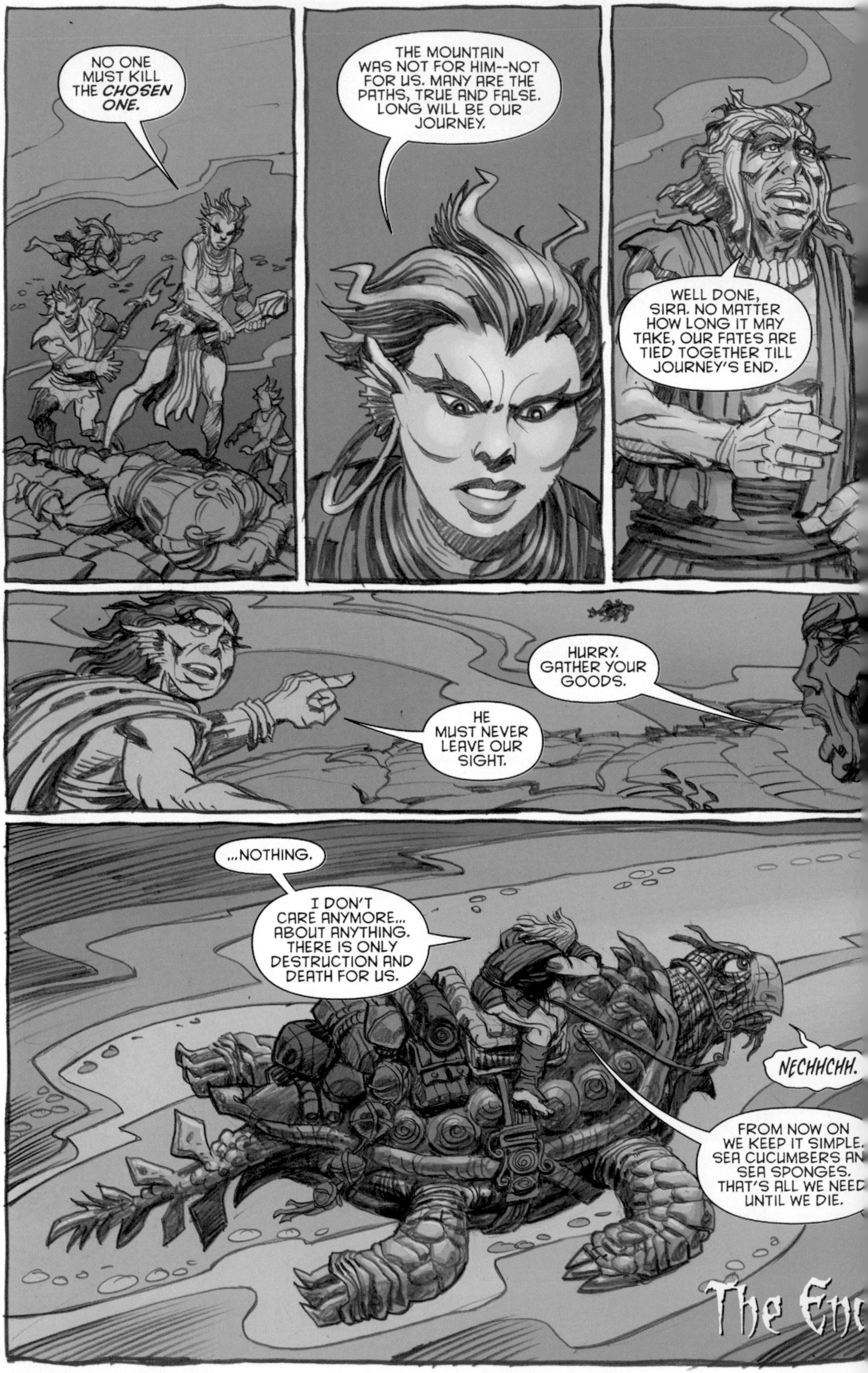
NO ONE MUST KILL THE *CHOSEN ONE.*
THE MOUNTAIN WAS NOT FOR HIM--NOT FOR US. MANY ARE THE PATHS, TRUE AND FALSE. LONG WILL BE OUR JOURNEY.
WELL DONE, SIRA. NO MATTER HOW LONG IT MAY TAKE, OUR FATES ARE TIED TOGETHER TILL JOURNEY'S END.
HURRY. GATHER YOUR GOODS.
HE MUST NEVER LEAVE OUR SIGHT.
...NOTHING.
I DON'T CARE ANYMORE... ABOUT ANYTHING. THERE IS ONLY DESTRUCTION AND DEATH FOR US.
NECHHCHH.
FROM NOW ON WE KEEP IT SIMPLE. SEA CUCUMBERS AN SEA SPONGES. THAT'S ALL WE NEED UNTIL WE DIE.
The En

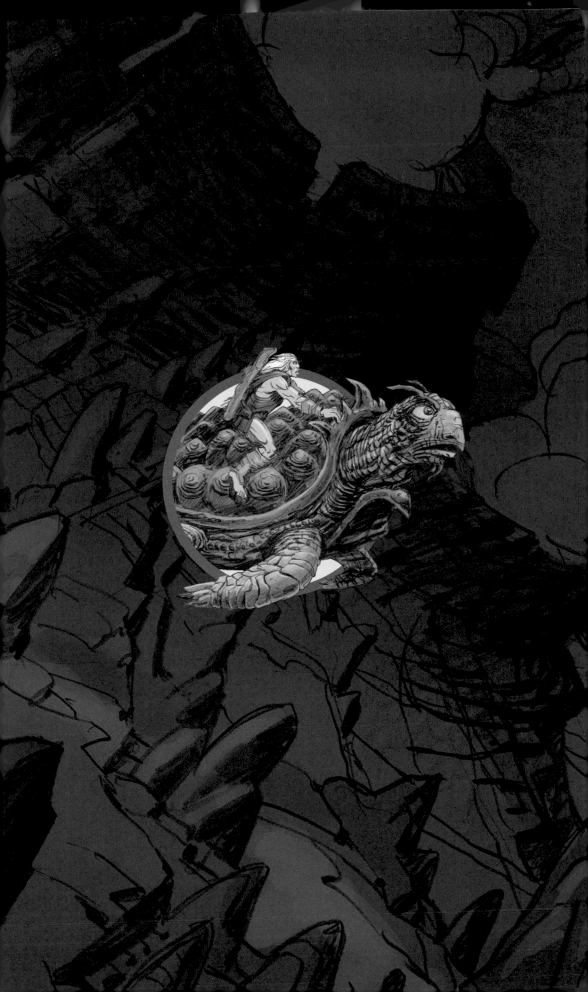